MORPHERS, MONSTERS & MAYHEM

MORPHERS, MONSTERS & MAYHEM

MY TRAVELS THROUGH THE POWER RANGERS GALAXY

DOUGLAS J. SLOAN

Copyright © 2025 by Douglas J. Sloan

All rights reserved.

No part of this publication may be reproduced, distributed, or transmitted in any form or by any means, including photocopying, recording, or other electronic or mechanical methods, without the prior written permission of the publisher, except as permitted by U.S. copyright law including the use of brief quotations in a book review.

This memoir reflects the author's personal experiences and memories. Some names and identifying details have been changed to protect the privacy of individuals. Events and conversations described have been recounted to the best of the author's memory, though some details may have been altered or condensed for narrative purposes. The views and opinions expressed are solely those of the author and are not intended to harm or defame any person, living or dead.

Fast Lane Custom Publishing

Cover Illustration by Héctor Castrillón

Cover Design by Xiomara Nieves

Editor: Dave Pasquantonio

ISBN hardcover: 979-8-9996329-0-6

ISBN paperback: 979-8-9996329-1-3

ISBN ebook: 979-8-9996329-2-0

ISBN audiobook: 979-8-9996329-3-7

This book is dedicated to those in my Ranger circle who are no longer with us. I miss every one of you and thank you from the bottom of my heart for the time we had together:

Erik Frank, Jason David Frank, Richard Genelle, William Immerman, Pua Magasiva, Scott Page-Pagter, Winston Richard, and Thuy Trang.

CONTENTS

Preface	ix
Introduction	xv
1. El Santo! El Santo!	1
2. New York, NY	7
3. Back to the Coast, Y&R, and Miss USA 1970	18
4. Have You Ever Had a Colonic?	25
5. Music by Shuki Levy and Kussa Mahchi	30
6. Shuki Wants To Meet You	32
7. "Where Are You Going?"	43
8. First Day of School	50
9. First Impressions	55
10. A Pig Surprise	63
11. Mutants and Sharks and Fleas, Oh My!	68
12. I Just Want To Do Cybertron!	77
13. Seriously Dude, I Just Want To Do Cybertron!	83
14. Introducing BZ and Little BZ	89
15. How About a Peace Conference?!	93
16. Trooper Transform!	101
17. We Are VR!!!	108
18. Doug, Rita Must Be Up To Something!	116
19. Perspective	119
20. You're Gonna Direct Today	122
21. You Need It When?	127
22. The White Light Shines Bright	132
23. The Rise of Dr. Poindexter	136
24. Fiddler On The Loose	141
25. Rise of the Red Python	145
26. Well, This is Freaking Awkward	152
27. Touchdown On The Dark Planet	158
28. Our Savior Arrives (Heavens Open, Angels Sing)	162
29. Tommy With a Side of Korn	165
30. Mighty Morphin Power Rangers: The Movie	173
31. BZ Backs Up	180
32. R.I.P. Season Two	185

33. Bad, Bad Boy	189
34. Love You, Buddy	192
35. What A Strange, Strange Year It Was	198
36. Ann and I Get Our Wings!	206
37. The Elevator Goes Up, The Elevator Goes Down	210
38. The Slow Boat to Mayhem	218
39. Hello Kitty!	230
40. Winding Down MMPR	236
41. The Alien Rangers of Aquitar	240
42. Sakamoto-San and the Battle Grid	246
43. Stronger Than Before: Power Rangers Zeo	252
44. "Am I Crazy?"	256
45. Snowblinded	259
46. Bit by Bit, Putting It Together	270
47. Guy Rides Up On A Horse	273
48. BZ Loses His Voice—Creatively	279
49. Zeo Kept a Rollin' All Night Long	282
50. Late Night Atta Boy	290
51. "It's a Little Long, No?"	294
52. The Truth About Turbo (AKA The Catastrophe That Was Carranger)	299
53. Freaking Turbo	302
54. How It All Came To Be—The Reader's Digest Version	317
55. My Wonderful Wacky Week with Shell	323
56. Little BZ Bids Farewell…Sort Of	329
57. Turbo—It Is Alive!	331
58. Where Oh Where Has Our BZ Gone?	339
59. A Development In The Divatox Department	345
60. "You Are Stealing Food Out of My Children's Mouths!"	352
61. Countdown to Crash Landing	365
62. I Help The BZ's Push It Across the Goal Line	377
Acknowledgments	391
Special Thanks	393
About the Author	395

PREFACE

At 11 a.m. on February 21, 1994, a line of stopped traffic stretched for more than five miles up the 101 Freeway in Los Angeles, ending at the entrance to the Universal Studios Theme Park. Overhead, helicopters circled the massive entanglement of outraged motorists, all pushing toward the same destination an inch at a time. Los Angelenos are used to sitting in traffic. It's an everyday thing, as predictable as the pleasant weather.

However, this was not just another rush hour. This was 20,000 screaming kids and their parents descending on Universal Studios, not to experience a newly opened ride, see a popular musical act, or even watch the premiere of a new Jurassic Park film. This was the birth of a pop culture phenomenon that would remain successful, generating billions of dollars, airing in hundreds of countries around the world, for the next 30 years.

These poor families, stuck in their cars on the 101, honking in vain, were there with their kids to see the one and only *Mighty Morphin Power Rangers*, defenders of the galaxy, heroes to boys and girls of all ages, backgrounds, and economic strata. This crayon box of brightly colored spandex, leather boots and plastic weapons were what kids thought about from the moment they woke up and flipped on the morning showing on Fox to the time they drifted off for a nap after a full helping of Tommy, Kimberly, Trini, Jason, Billy, and Zack in the afternoon block known as FOX KIDS.

The live *Power Rangers* show had been scheduled to take place in a small theatre as a side attraction for the day; a filler, something extra for little ones to keep them engaged long enough so that Mom and Dad could peacefully empty their pockets for the full Universal Experience of food, toys, T-shirts, the works. What no one over the age of eleven seemed to realize was that *Mighty Morphin Power Rangers* was only getting started, and it would be years before it would reach terminal velocity. This low-budget, mishmash of a TV series that had been on in Japan for decades was being chopped up and combined with footage of teenage American actors and was reaching levels of fan engagement that had never been seen before. *Power Rangers* was completely, utterly, and inexplicably a smash hit, the biggest thing ever in kids TV. The show was routinely getting Nielsen ratings (the dominant system by which a show's popularity was measured at the time) equal to primetime shows that cost 20 times the *Power Rangers* budget of $235,000 per episode.

Mighty Morphin Power Rangers was the brainchild of Haim Saban, at the time a 50-year-old producer from Alexandria, Egypt, who had immigrated to Israel at a young age and was (and still is) an unstoppable force of nature. He and his partner, Shuki Levy, made their initial fortune in the cartoon music business, then with animated shows of their own, and were ready to take the next step with a property that Haim and a scant few Saban employees considered a sure thing, but that everyone else considered impossible to even watch.

At the time, I was a 32-year-old struggling actor, managing an apartment building in Hollywood for free rent and helping fellow thespians with their audition pieces for a few bucks here and there. It was on a bright spring day shortly after the Universal insanity that there was a knock on my door. I opened it, and there he was, a young man, no more than 19, perfect skin, bright smile, the longest eyelashes I'd ever seen on a man or a woman—the whole future star "vibe" cranked up past "11." He was wearing a shirt and tie and had a very earnest and serious look on his face.

He spoke after a moment. "Mr. Sloan?"

"Just Doug," I answered.

He laughed. "Sorry. I'm Jason. Shuki sent me to learn acting." And in he walked.

This was where my odyssey began. This was the moment I blasted off into the Power Ranger Universe—a trip that would last more than 20 years and take me from Valencia, California to New Zealand, Canada, Australia, and beyond. To this day, I am convinced that when I die, there will be a picture of a Power Ranger on my tombstone with a caption that reads, "Here lies Douglas Sloan. He made kids smile. And he pissed off their parents."

In the pages that follow, I will give you a glimpse behind the curtain of the most successful kids' show ever. My pledge to you, right here and now, is that I have been 100% true to my memories of my time there. I have based this account on my personal experience. These memories are mine, and I now share them with all of you.

Here's what you can expect from the read (or listen): Sometimes funny (hopefully), sometimes sad, sometimes tragic moments involving the Rangers with whom I had the pleasure (or misfortune) of working. A look behind the curtain of the most successful kids TV series ever. A bit of my comparatively boring life story, only to give context to what I was thinking and doing while at Saban and why I was doing it. (If you ever write your own book, you'll see why it's necessary.) And I will share some moments never before available for public consumption. These are the stories that directly involved me. I will offer my opinion in certain situations as to what was REALLY happening behind the well-guarded curtain, but it will be my opinion and reflect what I feel is the most logical explanation to what happened. What you won't get is a scandalous gossip report based on rumors and innuendo, heard through the Ranger grapevine that didn't involve me in any way.

As for my adversaries, I will be reporting on their behavior—I just won't be naming names for the purpose of revenge or cattiness. I will try to keep my potty mouth in check, although I have come to accept over the years that this is literally impossible. I hope you'll find that what I've written is a recounting of my experiences in which I am as hard on myself as I am on anyone. I was a relatively young, inexperienced guy with a lot of unresolved crap knocking around inside me. I did the best I could, but some of it isn't pretty.

Most of you who were there and are a part of the story will be perfectly happy with how you are portrayed in this book. Some of you won't care. A few of you will be angry, indignant, or feel you've been mis-characterized. Allow me to speak to that very quickly. All of this took place twenty to thirty years ago. I don't know about any of you, but I'm not the same person I was back then (thank God). I've grown up a ton, found the right mixture of medications to regulate my moods, and now look back on my time on *Power Rangers* as one of the best in my life. If you believe I've not been truthful about you in this book, I encourage you to really think back and look at the situation in question and be open to the possibility that maybe you remembered it in a way that would protect your feelings or the way others see you even to this day. And I totally get it. It's nearly impossible to put ourselves in a place of having to accept that we hurt someone's feelings or contributed to their emotional pain. For me, that's what this book is all about, and I'm going to throw myself on the fire when it's appropriate, in an effort to "clean up my side of the street," as my former partner and friend Art Brown likes to say.

I will not make myself out to be the victim and everyone else the a-hole, unless of course I was the victim and you were the a-hole, in which case you probably shouldn't have been an a-hole, and you wouldn't be reading about what an a-hole you were back then (a valuable life lesson, and glad I could help!). Try not to take what I say too seriously. I've come a long way, but for the most part

I'm still just a big dope who is learning every day how to exist in this insane world without pissing people off.

So that's it. Grab your morpher, pull that little bit of creeping spandex out of your butt, pull those Mega Zord belts tight, and I'll see you on the grid. This should be fun as hell.

INTRODUCTION

It's early 1995, and I'm sitting in my office in Valencia, rewriting the script for the two-part epic saga, "Storybook Rangers," which had several of the *Power Rangers* being teleported into an actual fairytale world and having to find/fight their way out, then rescue Angel Grove from a 60-foot-tall elf with a propensity for stepping on buildings. The script was a co-write with Cheryl Saban (Haim Saban's wife), who had come up with the original idea and needed help getting it across the finish line. Cheryl is a brilliant woman and a great writer of books, but she was still getting her bearings as it related to writing 22-minute scripts. As that was my job, I was only too happy to jump in and give a fresh perspective. In fact, she and I had forged what I thought was a nice friendship during this collaboration. (I would later find out that the warm fuzzies were mostly on my side. But more on that later.)

I had just been made the "Supervising Producer" of *Power Rangers*, leaving my post at *VR Troopers*, a move which at the time I considered to be both fortuitous and disastrous. *Rangers* had been in turmoil with the exit of half of the original cast, and the replacement actors were still trying to get up to speed, with varying degrees of success. I was safe and invisible at *VR Troopers*, and I kind of liked it that way. I was making great money (for me at the time) and had no desire to take the reins of the behemoth that *Mighty Morphin Power Rangers* had become. But, after some excellent advice from Bob Hughes, my boss at *VR Troopers*, I decided, "Screw it." What's the worst that can happen? As it turns out, I couldn't even imagine what crazy things would be hurtling at me through the PR Galaxy. But that's what this book is about. So, in the end, I made use of many of those moments.

On this day, I was deep into Cheryl's script, trying to make sense of a story that we had very little Japanese footage to support, when my assistant Jackie told me that Ronnie Hadar was looking for me. My heart immediately jumped into my throat.

Shit.

Ronnie Freaking Hadar.

Ronnie Hadar was one of the producers on *Mighty Morphin Power Rangers* (although we rarely saw him) and was generally considered to be someone you did NOT mess with. Haim's right-hand man, Ronnie had been a member of a secret branch of the Israeli Army, specializing in counterterrorism and diplomat protection, which I think helped Haim sleep soundly at night.

NOT SO FUN FACT: Ronnie had witnessed, firsthand, the terrorist attack on the 1972 Olympic village in Munich, having been there as a guest of the Israeli wrestling delegation. Apparently, he was lucky to have survived. That was insane to me back then and still is to this day. END OF NOT SO FUN FACT.

When I first met him on *Rangers*, Ronnie seemed like most other overworked producers, except for two things.

First, Ronnie never went anywhere without his massive German Shepherd. This dog looked like it could swallow a full-size human, or at least one of the Olsen Twins, whole, at the flick of Ronnie's wrist or some other secret death signal. Ronnie spoke to the dog in a language I couldn't understand, but I assumed it was a specialized training thing they did so attack dogs would never misread everyday conversation as an order to kill.

Second, Ronnie was ALWAYS armed and was NOT particularly

concerned about hiding that fact. I was told that because *Rangers* was a non-union production, we constantly faced the wrath of the Teamsters Union of truck drivers anytime we went on location and were exposed in public. Ronnie, the dog who only listened to Ronnie, and Ronnie's pistol were always there to make sure things didn't go too sideways, according to Ronnie. In truth, I always felt that this combination was the exact recipe that would make things go VERY sideways. But what did I know? The guy had survived a terrorist attack when he was a teenager. All I ever did at that age was smoke weed and argue with my parents about the fact that I was smoking weed.

On this day, Ronnie had driven up from the Saban offices in Burbank specifically to see me. I asked my crack assistant, Jackie, if she knew anything about why. She did not and had a look on her face that told me she was just glad he wasn't looking for her. It was generally accepted in the world of *Power Rangers* production that if Ronnie was looking for you, it probably meant that Haim Saban was attempting to pass a message along, one that he himself would not care to deliver personally. This was a concern. I thought back to my brief time on Rangers. I couldn't recall anything in particular that I'd done wrong. I thought Cheryl's draft of the script was not so great, but I hadn't said it out loud. So, what the "F" was Ronnie Hadar doing here? Seriously—what the "F"?

I looked up to see that a menacing figure appeared in the doorway. It was the German Shepherd. He just stood there for a long moment, staring me down. All I could think to do was wave at the dog and hope that it wasn't mistakenly an attack command. The dog clearly didn't give a crap as he just stood there, unmoved by my attempt to greet him. To this day, I would swear he even rolled his eyes at me in disgust.

Moments later, Ronnie appeared and motioned for me to follow him without saying a word. Quickly glancing at the VERY nervous Jackie, I left my office to follow Ronnie and the dog to parts unknown.

Ronnie walked down the production office hall, checking each room for an empty place where we could "talk" or do whatever it was we were going to do. Finally, we came upon a broom closet. Ronnie opened the door, slipped into the darkness with me and the dog following close behind, and closed the door. This allowed only a sliver of the fluorescent light from the offices to stream through, just enough to see one another. At this point, my head was spinning. What had I done to end up in a broom closet with Ronnie Hadar? The smell of Pine-Sol and dirty mops, combined with the Drakkar Noir he was wearing, was becoming overpowering. I prayed to myself that he would just get it over with, whatever "it" was. At that moment, he reached into his jacket pocket. Was that the side where he kept the gun? I had forgotten. Shit. Was this how I was going to go out?

Clearly, it was not, as I am here writing this book. But from what I understand, these kinds of books need a bit of setup, just like any good story. And my time in the broom closet is one of my favorites. Before I tell you what happened, I need to rewind a little and "Reader's Digest" my path to the show for you. How I got the job on *Rangers* is both ridiculous and, as I look back, completely normal for this insane business. I hope you will appreciate some of the crazy things that happened to me (and that I caused) along the way. My family doesn't even know half of what I'm telling you, and my poor father is so nervous about what I might say, he pleaded with me to edit out anything that could be considered scandalous. Sorry, Dad! One thing I've learned is that you've got to call yourself out before you can turn the focus on anyone else. You and Mom did your best. I'm lucky to have such loving parents. The crap in this book is all mine to own.

That said, if you're only here for the *Power Rangers* stories, and my path to the galaxy isn't of interest, go ahead and skip to the last few pages of Chapter Three. I won't be insulted, I promise. And for the hardcore fans, this book covers my first gig at Saban Entertainment through my unceremonious ousting during *Power Rangers Turbo*.

To everyone: please accept my apologies in advance for any

holes or errors in my timeline. This all happened thirty years ago, and I never, in a million years, could have predicted I'd be writing this book. If I had, I would have kept a diary.

Finally, in putting this together, I had to decide who to name and who not to. I did my best to protect the kind, innocent, and talented—or at least tell what I witnessed honestly and respectfully, as I remember it. I omitted or changed a few names when asked. When it comes to the very real (and despicable) players I've dubbed BZ, Little BZ, Jabba, and to a lesser extent, Jabba Jr., I chose to use these "nicknames" because of the unflattering way they are portrayed here based on how they treated me and my staff. Every single memory is exactly as I recall, and I stand behind my recounting. If you're just here for what is, hopefully, a good story punctuated with entertaining anecdotes, the substitute names should do fine. If you want to know their true identities, they are easy to figure out with a few quick Google searches.

Okay, let's do this!

CHAPTER 1
EL SANTO! EL SANTO!

I entered this world on June 16, 1961 in New York Hospital at 4:17 a.m. Three years later, I was joined by my sister, Julia, and my memories start to become clear around the time we moved to Watertown, Massachusetts so that my father could get his PhD at MIT in Cambridge. I should also mention that my mother has a degree from Brown University and attended Rhode Island School of Design simultaneously, which sounds impressive. And let's face it, that is impressive. Here I was, three years old, and already the idea of living up to Mom and Dad's educational achievements was off the table. I was screwed from the get-go. And, I still had to survive the upcoming year in Lima, Peru, South America, our next family destination.

My father had decided that his thesis for MIT would be a study of the current political system in Peru and, over the course of a year, observing and reporting on how that system fared. Great idea, were it 2025 and he could have done most of the work from the comfort of the MIT library or our Watertown home via Zoom and typing his 300-page thesis in Microsoft Word instead of having my mother type it on a typewriter after we returned from a year on the ground in freaking Lima, Peru.

Now, please don't misunderstand. I'm sure it was quite the cultural bonanza down there. I'm told we traveled to Machu Picchu, Lake Titicaca, and assorted Incan ruins that were nothing short of mind-blowing. But those aren't MY memories.

Here's what I recall: the nuns at my Catholic school tying me to a tree for drawing a seagull incorrectly. I guess I was supposed to just do the wavy line thing, whereas I drew the entire bird from "beak to butt," the result of which had me super stoked. The sisters, on the other hand, were far less stoked, as they had determined that a four-year-old must have had help from Satan or some other dark forces to draw this diabolical creature that appeared half-Toucan Sam, half-pterodactyl.

Then there were the swimming lessons. The swimming instructor had a unique method of discipline where he would force you to stand with another kid supporting a heavy surfboard on your heads, punishment for something neither of us ever figured out (maybe he had heard about the Satanic pterodactyl). All the while I was trying to prevent a giant crap I had in the chamber from exploding into my speedo-sized swim trunks and ruining any chance I had of making friends in this new shiny swim school.

Finally, there was the bullet. Yes, the bullet that flew through the front window of the house we were renting, landing on the carpet as the cleaning lady Mabel screamed, "El Santo! El Santo!" (the 1970s British TV series, *The Saint*, starring Roger Moore, was on the TV, and she was convinced he had tried to shoot her through the screen).

THAT was MY Peru. At that time, I had just turned four, so I'm going to give myself a break for remembering the traumatic experiences as opposed to the museums and national monuments. And I can't really blame Mom and Dad, as they were just trying to do what they thought was the best thing at the time for the future of our little family.

Where I actually have the fondest memories of my early childhood was Scarsdale, New York. We lived at 31 Claremont Road in a house my parents purchased for the exorbitant sum, at the time, of $17,000. Scarsdale was a sleepy little hamlet outside of New York City in Westchester County and a great place to grow up. You could walk or bike safely anywhere you wanted. The houses on the street all had kids racing in and out of them, regardless of whether they lived in said houses. You played baseball in the summer, football in the winter, and got an education at maybe the best school system in the country. (I often wonder where I would have ended up if we had stayed in New York and I had taken full advantage of those top-notch institutions.) As it happened, I only made it to fourth grade in Scarsdale before moving to California. But I still have clear memories of walking home from Greenacres Elementary School with my best friend Aaron Sorkin, hanging out at his house (which was usually empty because his parents both worked), and listening to him explain to me that no, The Partridge Family did not actually play their instruments, they were a bunch of kid actors, not a band. Crushing news at the time, as I was basing my entire plan to become a rock star on the idea that if Danny and Chris Partridge could play like that, what was stopping me? Under normal circumstances, if we were two normal kids sitting around talking casually about music, I would have called bullshit and just went on convincing myself that Aaron was full of crap and life would have gone on like normal.

But we weren't two regular kids. Aaron Sorkin, I believed, knew what he was talking about. Why? Because at age ten, in the 4th grade, he was in an actual, real rock band called The Electric Sun. These guys seemed like they were all in high school except for Aaron, and they played real songs through big amplifiers and a huge drum kit and sang harmonies. In my memory, they were amazing. They put on a concert after school one day and the auditorium was packed with other 4th and 5th graders all screaming and cheering. Many of you are probably saying, "So what? Everyone has a band. There's a little girl in Japan who can play Eruption, the Van Halen solo, note for note." But this was the late

60s, remember. To see and hear real live music being played by what was essentially a bunch of kids was unheard of, and my friend Aaron was a part of that. It gave him a serious advantage in any discussion pertaining to music. So, I could NOT deny the soul-crushing truth about The Partridge Family. Aaron Sorkin, at age 10, was already basically an adult and, incidentally, went on the become a very successful writer/producer/director. But I still had a dream, and so what if those kids in Hollywood didn't really play their instruments? That had no bearing on my path to rock-god status. The only thing I was lacking was the tool to make it all happen.

So, I spent that entire summer selling packets of seeds door-to-door to earn the prize of the brand-new guitar that would catapult me to rock superstardom. The guitar took six weeks to arrive. When it did, that cheap nylon-string acoustic that refused to stay in tune became the most important thing in the world to me. That guitar began a part of my life that gave me so many gifts: being in a popular local rock band in high school; later playing the Whisky a Go Go, The Roxy, the Troubadour, and the Starwood (all moderately famous Los Angeles rock clubs) as the guitarist for The Robbie Rist Band (who, in a strange twist of events had played TV's Cousin Oliver on *The Brady Bunch*); and studying with the late Randy Rhoads, perhaps one of the most influential people in my life even to this day, which is odd as Randy died in a plane crash in 1982. The guitar was my salvation from what would have otherwise been an emotionally non-survivable childhood.

I'm convinced, as is my analyst, that South America really messed me up. That, coupled with what would today be diagnosed with severe ADD and hyperactivity disorder, made growing up a serious pain in the ass. We moved to California so that my dad could continue his career in the entertainment industry, and my temper was uncontrollable by that time. I was so completely miserable, and I had no idea why. It just seemed that I needed something, wanted everything, and there was always someone there telling me I couldn't have it.

As I grew up, only physical objects gave me any sense of calm: a new part for my bike, a remote-controlled car, a new amp, a new guitar. I had to have "things," lots of "things," and I did whatever I needed to do to get them, as they were the only form of calm and joy that I could count on. When you're a kid and you have no money to acquire these "things," it's hard to get yourself into too much trouble. Sure, you may get caught trying to stuff something in your pocket at the local music store or incur your parents' wrath for nagging them incessantly about a new talk box like the one Peter Frampton used on "Show Me the Way." But at the end of the day, no harm done.

However, as an adult, shit can get real in a hurry when you fixate on the acquisition of "things," because the "things" you are now fixated on cost way more that the "things" you were previously fixated on. When you DO have money and great credit to go along with it, the cars you are buying become real ones that cost hundreds of thousands of dollars you don't have. The hobbies you obsess over that you were forbidden from participating in as a child end up being the first ones you reach for when you grow up. For me, it was dirt bike racing. I spent thousands of dollars on the equipment to participate in what was "just a hobby," to the point that I had three motorcycles, a truck, and a trailer to carry them, along with countless helmets, goggles, pants, gloves, and jerseys. It was insane, literally insane.

The other danger area a young dude with more money than he needs can get swallowed up in is the L.A. dating scene. It's remarkable how quickly you can rack up credit card debt trying to keep up with a Playboy Playmate's last boyfriend, who was making NBA money.

To this day I struggle with that part of my psyche. It's a constant battle, one that has led me down a very dark path many times. Most of you are probably thinking, "WAAAAA!!! Poor Mr. Sloan! He's had a great career, hung out with Playmates, produced hit TV shows, and acted on a successful daytime drama. BOO FREAKING HOO!!!" And you're right. I would never look for sympathy, as I have had an incredibly blessed life. I merely wanted to establish the issues at play deep in my psyche that entered my relationships on *Mighty Morphin Power Rangers*, *VR Troopers*, and in my own little world I called my life.

CHAPTER 2
NEW YORK, NY

After receiving a bachelor's degree in business from Whittier College, I quickly realized that I wasn't ready to hit the job trail, as I didn't want anything to do with the business of business but wanted everything to do with the business of show. So, I took Dad up on his kind offer to pay for me to attend graduate film school. I had worked summers for him as a P.A. and even an assistant film editor. Yes, nepotism was alive and well in the Sloan camp. And thank God it was, as that was the only way I was going to get into any respectable graduate film school. I needed a strong letter of recommendation from a serious heavy hitter to even be considered.

USC and UCLA film schools couldn't get the rejection notices out fast enough. It felt like by the time I had gotten home from mailing the applications, the denial form letters were already on the kitchen counter. I figured NYU's letter would be there in a few days, only delayed by the distance it had to travel to get to me. However, to my surprise, Dad had come to know a successful Hollywood producer (with serious name value) well enough to ask him to meet me and perhaps send out a letter of recommendation, provided he didn't think I was a complete tool when I went to see him.

Steve Tisch produced the film *Risky Business*. He was also from a family that was worth well into the billions, a family that had donated enough money to NYU to warrant the University naming the film and TV department the "Tisch School of the Arts." I met with Steve at his office on Sunset Blvd. one insanely hot day in 1983. He sat with me for an hour, telling stories, giving me advice, just being the cool dude he is to this day. (I've met with him several times since then, and Steve is still one of the nicest guys you'd want to meet in any business, let alone the movie business.) Needless to say, a few weeks later, I received a heavy packet from the Tisch School of the Arts with an invitation to join the fall class in the Master's Film Program.

The Island of Manhattan in 1983 was completely insane. The pace, the number of people, the noise—it all takes a while to get used to. Back then, it was not the gentrified playground of the wealthy that it is today. It was dangerous. There was still a lot you had to watch out for, places you shouldn't go, hours you shouldn't go to those places. It was, to say the least, an eye-opening experience.

Fortunately, again through Dad, I snagged a studio sublet apartment in what was a nice part of Greenwich Village. The tiny apartment on Bedford Street was $450 a month, a total rip-off back in the day. But who had any choice? That same place goes for $3500 today. Still a rip-off. But it's all about perspective. The good news was that it was cozy and nicely located in terms of my proximity to the school and was in a safe area of New York City. At least that was my impression at the time.

On the third day I was in New York, my cozy little apartment got broken into and cleaned out by an idiot who cut his hand on the window he smashed to get in. The genius then proceeded to spray blood all over my walls and floor before he helped himself to the stereo and TV I had just bought from Crazy Eddie's (a ritual at the time for young people moving to New York). And the cops who came after it happened basically told me I needed better gates on my windows or this would keep happening.

I took their advice and got massive security gates for all the windows. I then went about painting the apartment to cover up the splashes of blood that were still on the walls. With everything back to normal, I figured I was good. My little fortress cocoon was all safe and sound.

A few days later, I awoke to the sound of water spraying from the actual light fixture in the bathroom. It was also coming down the walls at an alarming rate, the new paint peeling off and forming a disgusting soupy muck on the floor of the one-room apartment. As it turns out, my elderly upstairs neighbor had been washing her rugs in the bathtub at three in the morning, slipped and fell in, where she eventually drowned with the water still running—down into my apartment. This all happened before I had even stepped foot onto the NYU campus or film school.

Screw it. Moving on!

It was the first day of classes, and I was convinced this would do wonders to erase the creeping feeling of regret I was experiencing. Strangely, the highly regarded, super-expensive Graduate Film school was located in a grungy, damp basement between Second and First Avenues, only a few blocks from the famous CBGB's nightclub and a few doors down from the coffee shop made famous by John Belushi on *Saturday Night Live*. I don't know what I was expecting, but this wasn't it. We were in a pocket of New York City that was surrounded by some seriously bad areas. Long before the renovation of NYC, if you happened to walk a few blocks in the wrong direction, get off at the wrong subway stop, or encountered the wrong people, you were completely screwed. Too far south or too far east, or too far north or west, it didn't matter. Alphabet City was three blocks from my school's front door, a place so jacked up that they made a movie about how jacked up it really was. In a bizarre twist, years later, my sister Alix opened a high-end art gallery close to Avenue B where there was once a different kind of gallery—a shooting gallery. (For those unfamiliar with illicit drug culture, "shooting galleries" are old burned-out buildings where junkies go to inject themselves and enjoy their ride undisturbed.)

There were many nights when editing would require us to remain at school until 11 p.m. or later, which, back then, was not an ideal time to be walking through the East Village. But we all did it, dodging the piles of human feces that littered the sidewalk. Fortunately, no one in my class ever got stabbed or robbed in the time I was there, probably a combination of luck and the fact that we usually moved through the streets in packs like frightened dogs, putting our lives in the hands of the "strength in numbers" survival tactic.

The professors all seemed like bitter hacks who had, at one time, worked on perhaps a movie or two, but whose careers never really took off. The equipment we needed to make movies was almost non-existent, save for a few old wartime Arri silent cameras and a couple of Moviola editing machines. Where the "F" did all the Tisch money go? Where was the state-of-the-art sound studio? Where was the state-of-the-art anything? I wondered if Steve knew where his family's money had ended up, because it sure wasn't here.

Regardless, I went about the business of making short films on the streets of New York. Eventually I made a few friends who became my core group. We were the only students who realized what pretentious assholes we all were, and we thought it was hilarious. When I needed to feel some family love, I hung out at jazz clubs with my uncle Marty (Dad's brother), a teacher in Manhattan at the time. Marty always seemed to have great weed or blow and insisted on driving everywhere in the city, cramming his tiny VW Bug into spots that I could never have imagined would fit a motorcycle, no less an actual car. He wrestled with leukemia on and off for twenty years, not allowing it to take a single moment of joy from his busy life. He finally passed away a couple of years ago. Marty was one of a kind, truly. I loved that guy.

Overall, things had improved. But not enough to keep my momentum moving forward. As we neared the end of year one, my best friend there, Les Firestein, who later went on to write for *The*

Drew Carey Show, announced that he was transferring to Columbia to study under Milos Forman and work with real film equipment. Ian Greenstein, who later became a successful agent, was leaving, or at least I think he was. Not sure. The fact was that as the days passed, fueled by my vicious ADD and my desire for something that would make me feel excited and alive again, I decided to flip the script (so to speak) and dedicate my life to a sexy new pursuit—acting.

This was completely absurd, as I had never acted before and had no idea what it entailed. When I revealed my plans to my father, I offered the excuse that it would help my filmmaking if I knew what actors go through. This idea was supported by an old friend of my father's, Clifford David, a well-respected acting teacher in New York, and the person I would study with for the next few years. Clifford was a legend. He had starred in some of the greatest Broadway productions in the history of modern theatre and was one of the most magnetic people I had met in my twenty-four years. He was also a gifted teacher and a great friend to me. (He recently passed away, and it remains a great regret of mine that we lost touch.)

So, I bid adieu to NYU to focus on acting, something I had never done before, and which I was giving up the thing for which my father had used up a valuable favor, and potentially, depending on how he reacted, burned his relationship with Steve Tisch. Dad wasn't crazy about the idea, as you can imagine, but supported it anyway. Even though he hated actors with a passion, having to deal with them all day when producing his own TV movies and series, he generously helped me get my SAG card by putting me in a TV movie starring Anthony Geary of *General Hospital*, and then another one opposite Kelly McGillis, who was playing a sex addict trying to pick me, a young New York businessman, up at a bus stop. This was before her breakout movie *Witness* had come out, but you kind of got the feeling she was going to be big news.

All I remember about her is that for someone playing a sex addict, she didn't have much sexual energy, at least towards me, which I later, idiotically, attributed it to her being gay. OF COURSE that's what I attributed it to. What a typical guy rationalization. As I grew older, I realized that it probably had a lot more to do with the fact that I was a schlub actor who had a couple of lines, wasn't very good, and made the whole idea of being sexually hungry for a stranger way harder to pull off than it needed to be. I mean, she was in *Witness* with Harrison Ford, and they seemed pretty connected in those scenes. Then with Tom Cruise in *Top Gun*. She managed to make *that* look steamy. Let's just say I probably wasn't the stud muffin I thought I was and leave it at that.

As I continued my studies, I started to wonder if this was the place for me to begin my journey as a working actor. Even I had the self-awareness to know that I was completely inexperienced and was not going to be taken seriously enough to get a Broadway, off-Broadway, or even an off-off-Broadway show any time soon. That being said, I did have the chance to audition for a replacement role in *Biloxi Blues* in front of Gene Saks, the director. (At least I think it was him, as I was on the stage where the show was currently running and all I could see out in the audience was a dark haze, eclipsed by the stage lights that were turned to maximum brightness. Not important.) Clearly, theatre in New York was, at that time, beyond my ability and experience. I should have realized this, as the best actor I personally knew in New York, a guy named Holt Wilson (later Holt McCallany), had been studying for years, doing off-off Broadway plays constantly and finally landed an understudy role on Broadway for a show in which he never once appeared. Holt was/is a brilliant actor, and his job consisted of showing up at the theatre an hour before curtain, seeing if anyone was sick or couldn't do the show, waiting for the curtain to go up, and for the parts he was covering to make their entrance. Once this was handled, and he knew he wouldn't be needed that night, it was off to the local bars to hang with a bunch of other theatre folks and see if anyone had heard when the next production was to begin casting. This was what it was to be a young actor in New York, trying to break into one of the most prestigious theatre scenes on the planet. I always wondered if Holt was conflicted when it came to that job. On the one hand, it was a paycheck he would collect as long as the show was running. In New York, that was a pretty great set up. Getting paid to be on call to act on a Broadway stage. No waiting tables or delivering packages or working in the theatre bookshop. No wonder Holt always had a smile on his face when he was at the theatre. On the other hand, he was a gifted actor who wanted to be on the stage, not at the stage door. I wonder if he would have traded the prestige of understudying in a Neil Simon production for a role in less important production doing eight shows a week.

Woody Harrelson was the other understudy in that show, and like Holt, Woody hadn't gotten a chance to perform his role. Rumor was that Woody was glad about this, as he hadn't quite learned all of Mr. Simon's lines to perfection. The feeling was that Woody was 100% sure he was going to book a big Hollywood movie and be off for parts unknown before he ever had to take the stage. So, why stress? That sounds a lot like the position a young Woody Harrelson would take. As it turns out, Woody was right. He booked a big studio movie with Goldie Hawn called *Wildcats* and was off to shoot it before most of the cast even knew he had left. It's one of the ironies of Broadway. The understudy waits for their chance to give just one performance, while the lead actor feels sorry for them a little, right up until the moment the understudy books a big movie or a TV series and leaves the show without so much as a wave.

When the original cast started to move on from *Biloxi Blues* and head out to Hollywood to try their luck in films and TV, the part of Wykowski, the big dumb Polish bigot, opened up, and that was the role I auditioned for. Of course, I was green as can be and up against hundreds of real New York actors. In the end, the show hired a much better actor fresh out of the Carnegie Mellon theatre program, who was amazing in the role. At the end of the day, I guess I can say I have performed Neil Simon on a Broadway stage, just not in front of a paying audience. But it was cool nonetheless. I lost track of Holt a little while later. I'm hoping maybe he'll read this and reach out on social media or something. He was one of the good ones.

The takeaway from my failed audition was that I had a lot of catching up to do, and this meant studying. I had to get on a stage whenever I could if this was going to work. So I did. I continued to grow through my scene study class, working with much better actors, learning from them. I also got a job working for the company that supplies wireless headphones to folks who need them to hear whatever Broadway show they are attending. I was assigned a different theatre each night and became friendly with a lot of the people who worked on the shows in various capacities.

Broadway was on a tear at the time, with some amazing work going on. And, because I was affiliated with this sound company, I had the privilege of walking into any theatre I wanted to on any night to watch the show. And, what a collection of shows: Judd Hirsch and Cleavon Little in *I'm Not Rappaport*, Jason Robards in *The Iceman Cometh*, Derek Jacobi in the Royal Shakespeare Company's New York residency, Matthew Broderick in *Biloxi Blues*, William Hurt in *Hurly Burly*, Betty Buckley in *Cats*. I didn't realize at the time how special this was. But I look back on it now and can see that this was the blessing of all blessings for a young acting student. I could never have afforded to see even one of these shows, let alone all of them. I was flat broke at the time—I mean *seriously* broke.

Little did I know that I would soon be presented with an opportunity that could solve all of my money problems.

I was working at the theatre where *La Cage Aux Folles* was running. For those of you who don't remember that show, it was a musical about an older gay couple who own a dance hall and must deal with the kooky show girls (drag performers) while trying to raise their straight son who is in love and wants to be married. I had gotten to know the stage manager, an energetic and fascinating guy called Roger, who, along with his normal duties, was assigned to keep an eye on the show's leading man, Van Johnson. Johnson was a star at MGM during the Golden Age of movies and a man enjoying the latter stages of his life, out and proud of his sexual orientation, which was kind of fascinating and really awesome.

One night, the stage manager, Roger, approached me with an offer, a financial windfall of sorts. These were the exact words he uttered: "Mr. Van Johnson, star of *La Cage Aux Folles*, would like to offer you $3000 to accompany him to his home with his partner. You will not be touched, but you will be asked to pleasure yourself in front of them to completion. When you're done, you will be paid in cash, and a car will drive you to your front door. What do you say?"

Wow. This was not how I figured my night was going to end up. I will not lie and say that I didn't, at least for a millisecond, think about taking Mr. Van Johnson up on his very generous offer. That was a lot of money, and my shoes were literally worn through the soles. But, in the end, I apologetically told Roger, "No thanks." He didn't seem to be too bummed, as I'm sure I was one of many young men who would receive an invitation that night. One of them would surely say yes. They always did, according to Roger.

As summer started to set in, the heat and humidity were beyond stifling. I was getting auditions but wasn't getting too far. Rarely did I get a call back. Again, New York was where the real actors were. My first film audition was for *Weird Science*, where I was paired up with a young Robert Downey Jr. I was to read for Chet, the role made famous by the brilliant Bill Paxton. Downey was reading for one of the leads, and as I remember, he was incredibly gracious. I could feel that he was probably a bit disappointed that he had drawn the short straw in terms of partners, but he never let that get in the way. God bless him, we soldiered on, and it was beyond obvious that he was trying to draw a performance out of me that would rise to the level of his own. It didn't. But I've always had a great affection for him because of that one encounter. In the end, he did get a supporting role in the film. I was pleased that I hadn't totally ruined it for him. I did not get any kind of role and was headed back to class to continue my training.

At that point, I had begun dating a Swedish model and actress, my only actual relationship the entire time I was in New York. Carrie Nygren was beyond stunning, blonde curls cascading down her back, lips permanently pursed, huge eyes. She was everything you would imagine a big-time fashion model to be. Never having been around one myself, it was a bit startling to be sitting behind one in my acting class, which is where we first met. Carrie was as successful as you could be without achieving "Supermodel" status, which was fine by her. She hated the industry that had made her a millionaire several times over. Her image was everywhere—on the sides of buses, on billboards in Times Square, and on a ton of commercials. The night we met was her first night attending Clifford's class, and the wolves were circling. (There were more than a few guys in the group who fancied themselves irresistible to the ladies.)

Over the next couple of weeks, all the Romeos in our class gave it their best shot. But it was clear that Carrie was there to learn—to become a real actor. One would think that with her looks—and what I soon learned was a truly hilarious, self-effacing personality—she would be a superstar. And she was already a very solid actor. There was only one thing holding her back. She had a very thick Swedish accent, and in the 80s, that wasn't anything that was selling in the good old U.S.A. Her commercials were all ones in which she didn't speak, I learned. And of course, magazine covers and billboards didn't care what you sounded like. It was a great waste of talent, I remember thinking. She refused to correct the accent, which I guess I understood at the time. If it were today, I'm sure that would have been the first thing she did, considering the number of foreign-born actors who appear in U.S. movies and TV series and speak with perfect American accents.

Carrie and I were put together by Clifford to work on a scene. I suppose there was something attractive about the fact that I was the only guy in class who didn't hit on her, because it wasn't long before we were together as more than scene partners. I was literally stunned every day that I woke up and realized she was my girlfriend, but I rolled with it.

Carrie's world was insanely opulent. All her friends were models or musicians. Things went well for a while. We had a lot of fun, laughed our asses off, and kept it quiet in class. It was awesome, except for the fact that I knew it would eventually come to an end. No way was this thing going to last. Not from my side, mind you. And I was right. After a while, she became tired of toting around a broke actor who was five years her junior, paying the check every time, and no doubt embarrassed in front of her friends.

Quickly, it became clear that our relationship was starting to implode. And I was not looking forward to a whole breakup scenario where I would have to see my ex in class. I lucked out, however, and by some act of God, she got a part in a Broadway show revival (*Night of the Iguana*) that was opening out of town. When she left, I felt like that was my cue to make a change. Carrie's show was in Baltimore for a brief preview run. Fall was turning into winter, and it was time. New York was not where I was supposed to be, I told myself. Too hard. Too cold. Too humid. Too much talent for too few parts. I needed to be in a place where I wouldn't be the worst actor in the room every time. I needed to be where idiots like me, with ridiculous dreams of stardom, were sometimes given acting jobs regardless of experience or talent.

I knew what I had to do.

CHAPTER 3
BACK TO THE COAST, Y&R, AND MISS USA 1970

Upon my arrival back in L.A., I rented an apartment near the Guitar Center on Sunset and began studying with legendary acting teacher Howard Fine. In fact, I was in the very first day of the very first class he taught in L.A., him having just moved out from New York as well. Howard is a funny, quirky, brilliant guy. He's a bit guarded, kind of shy, but boy, is he passionate. And he knows his craft. I had somehow lucked into getting in on the ground floor of what would become the only place in L.A. to study if you were serious about becoming a legitimate working actor. Other students of Howard's included Christopher Meloni, Lori Loughlin, John Corbett, Heather Locklear, and Will Smith, and the list continues endlessly.

Howard's classes ranged from basic technique, where you learn the foundations "method" to scene study, where you chose a partner, chose a scene, and presented it in class after working on it all week. I always found this incredibly stressful, as I really wanted to please Howard and impress my classmates. But Howard was no pushover, and he did NOT mince words. If he didn't like what he was seeing, he would stop the scene. And, he could be a real a-hole, calling you out for not understanding the material, for not rehearsing enough, for missing basic character stuff that you were supposed to have learned in the technique class. One thing that really put him over the edge was when you didn't take risks in your performance. Funny enough, I was supremely gifted at not taking risks. It seemed so natural to me to say the lines, do the blocking, and stop there. It was as far as I was willing to go. I was painfully insecure, terrified to put myself out there, afraid of what the other actors would think, unwilling to do the one thing an actor MUST always do: share their "inner life" with the audience.

For those future thespians out there who are pursuing a life on stage or in front of the camera, hopefully you will end up in an acting class at some point on your journey. The most important thing you need to remember is that everyone in that class is scared about getting up there and opening themselves up to ridicule. It's a fact. Every single student in that audience is thinking the same thing when you're on stage getting reamed out: "Glad it's not me!" And the more famous you were, the worse it was. Your classmates expected brilliance, and when you were the lead on a series and couldn't get through a scene from *The Odd Couple*, it had to be a mind-numbing experience.

I would get torched in class by Howard at least once every couple of months, in front of all my buddies and whatever new crop of "the most beautiful women on the planet" were auditing the class that night. It seemed like subjecting myself to this was getting me nowhere and it might be time to come up with a new plan, which I did. As I was formulating this "new plan," something completely crazy happened. I landed myself a job. A real legitimate acting job!

Come to find out, the only thing more powerful than my stomach-churning self-doubt was my propensity to obsess on things I really wanted. And at this point in my life, for some strange reason, I wanted a regular role on a soap opera. WHAT THE…? Yes, it's true. I guess I figured I was never going to make it big in movies or nighttime TV, and there seemed to be A LOT of parts that came up for young guys like me in the daytime drama arena. After all, at the peak, when I was trying to get work, there were seventeen soaps on the air. Seventeen! The money was great on a soap, and from what I could see, you could basically stay there forever if you so desired. This sounded perfect to me, and I was in it to win it. I wanted one of those parts. I was going to be on a soap, dammit!

Six months later, I was. My sheer obsessive will and blind determination landed me the part of young medical student and unsuspecting father Jeff on *The Young and the Restless*, a part that lasted about nine months and remains the best job I've ever had to this day. When I look back, there was no particular reason that I should have landed that role, as my psyche was still in full self-destruct mode. But the only thing more powerful than my lack of confidence was my propensity to obsess on "things" I want until I got them. I had made this a "thing," so I guess I approached it differently.

My path to Y&R came through my great friends, the late Jerry Douglas and his then-wife Kym. I met Jerry, who was a fixture on *The Young and the Restless* for years, through Kym, a scene partner from class. Through my relationship with them, I was introduced to a lot of the cast, became friends with a few, and started hanging out with them—hell, I even got invited to a bris, at which, after the Mohel did his thing, everyone shouted mazel tov and downed what must have been $1000 worth of El Pollo Loco chicken. You wouldn't think so, but this was perfect après bris dining.

It got to the point where I was even playing tennis on the weekends at the home of the *Y&R* creators William and Lee Bell and their daughter Laura Lee, who had also become a great friend. It was a fantastic time. I was super comfortable around these people who were so kind to me and, through Jerry and Kym, had brought me into their inner circle (or as close as you can be without working with them). When the time came to audition for *Y&R*, I sailed through to the screen test, only needing to beat out four other guys to land a coveted three-year contract role. I think I did pretty good at the test. They must have thought someone else did pretty "great," though, as one Saturday at tennis, Mr. Bell explained that it just wasn't the right part and that he would someday find the right one. True to his word, a year later, when another cast member left the show, I was called to audition for the part, and by that evening, I had the role.

Now, some of you will say that I got the part because of my relationships with the families and cast members. That's not quite true. I got the auditions through those friends and family, without a doubt. But you don't get a regular role on a TV show or an important part in a movie because you're pals with the boss. There's way too much money at stake, a brand to protect, etc. The actors on any show or in any movie are there because they are right for the role. Of course, this isn't the case 100% of the time. There are those rare exceptions, but friends get *opportunities* much more often than *jobs*. And as we continue with my story, you will see that this is almost always the way introductions are made. Anyway…

There's nothing better than walking into class as a working actor. It's like climbing down the stairs of the dugout after hitting a dinger over the left field fence for a walk-off win. Howard was genuinely pleased. And through this achievement, I experienced a valuable and profound awakening. Because I had been validated by getting that job, performing now became fun, easy, and stress-free. They say that work breeds work. You go into other auditions not giving a crap because you already have a job. Seeing this and feeling it, the casting directors and producers immediately want to give you another job—their job.

Looking back on the whole experience, I shouldn't have felt ANY sense of job security. The storyline was falling apart, as one of the actor's personal issues with cocaine had infested the workplace and become a serious issue. (Once cocaine enters your bloodstream, it's hard to hide the jitters, sweat, and whacked-out pupils that come with it. People knew what the deal was.)

Mr. Bell was no doubt growing frustrated with B.S. that could easily tarnish the name he and his wife spent years cultivating into the highest quality TV for the genre. The characters at the forefront of our storyline were not of any real import to the entirety of *The Young and the Restless* and could easily be written off.

So, nine months into my run on the show, a script arrived in my mailbox, and the last line spoken to me was, "Have a nice life, Jeff." And just like that, the dream was over. But again, it remains to this day the best job I've ever had. If I were ever given the chance to appear on another daytime drama, it would take me all of about five seconds to make that decision. I loved working there. At the same time, I have the greatest respect for the late Mr. and Mrs. Bell for making the decision to clean out the garbage and restore the set to a safer, more stable working environment for everyone. They were legends, truly missed, by anyone who worked with them or knew them personally. I feel blessed that I was able to spend time away from the job with them and just hang out.

After I left *Y&R*, I screen-tested for six other shows. Once you've done one soap, you have a leg up, as you supposedly know the deal with the hours, the pay, the memorization, etc. Apparently, that didn't pertain to me, as I landed exactly zero of these other roles and was back in Howard's class within a month.

I could always return to Howard. That was the great thing about our class. It was like a home. And even though I wasn't working again, being exposed to Howard's brilliant insights every week was not a bad consolation prize. In fact, it was in Howard's class that I learned much of what I use today in my work as a producer. He is one of two educators in my life whose teachings truly had a lasting effect on me and whose wisdom I refer to every single day.

The other was a guitar teacher I had in my late teens. A local legend and the guitar player for an early incarnation of the metal band Quiet Riot, he taught out of a tiny conservatory in North Hollywood and was the most inspirational artist of any kind that I've been around to this day. Like Howard, he also loved to teach. He cared deeply about his students and was able to see what it was going to take to awaken their inner Eric Clapton. Tragically, that virtuoso musician, Randy Rhoads, passed away in a horrific plane crash in 1982.

Howard and Randy were two completely different people. Yet

they had very similar teaching philosophies. Howard has this incredible connection to actors and the uncanny ability to pinpoint what is holding them back, then help them to release that emotion, allowing a more heartfelt and real performance. Randy, a posthumous member of the Rock and Roll Hall of Fame, was a groundbreaking musical genius who was serious about practicing for hours daily and making use of every second we were in our lesson. For Randy as well, feeling was a huge part of his technique. If you watch the videos of him on YouTube, you will see raw emotion with every note he plays.

Howard teaches you to learn the scene until you can recite it in your sleep. Then you can play with it, go wild, have fun. But the meaning of the script is always there. Randy would compose his guitar solos one note at a time after all the other instruments had been recorded. He would then play through it a bunch of times, framework in place, finding the magic, making little changes here and there. Finally, he would put it to tape, then double it, then triple it, making it sound bigger and bigger every time. But the foundation of the song and the music was always there. That's what he taught his students as well. Compose the solo, then find the magic. It seems so simple, but oftentimes the things that work the best ARE the most obvious.

> SIDE NOTE: I still think about Randy almost every day. It's impossible not to. When I started studying with him, he gave me a finger exercise to warm up my digits every time I sat down with my guitar. That exact exercise, note for note, later went on to become the opening riff for "Crazy Train" by Ozzy Osbourne. A day rarely goes by that I don't hear that song playing somewhere and think back to those days in the tiny conservatory, and how the music world lost one of the true greats. I'm glad Randy is finally getting the recognition he deserves. He was one of a kind. And I thank all of you for indulging me in something that has almost nothing to do with *Power Rangers*.

So, back to Howard, where my journey through the Power Ranger Universe really got started. Monday night class seemed pretty much like old times upon my return—a lot of the same faces, a few newbies. But, on this night, as the doors were about to close, in walked possibly the most stunning woman I had ever seen in person. She was in her late 30s to early 40s, with black hair that was so dark it was almost reflective, huge, beautiful eyes, a body that was just inconceivable, and her smile. JUST NOT FAIR. Yep, Deborah Dale Shelton (Mandy Winger on *Dallas* and Miss USA 1970) was in the building, and I quickly realized that the only empty seat in the place was next to me. My life was about to change forever.

CHAPTER 4
HAVE YOU EVER HAD A COLONIC?

The idea that I was ever going to have anything but a passing friendship with Deborah Shelton was not even a consideration at the time. The gargantuan diamond wedding ring on her finger was definitely a deterrent, which I later discovered was precisely the intention. You see, Deborah was indeed married. However, she and her husband, an Israeli musician named Shuki Levy, had separated, and Deborah wanted no part of a long line of actors trying to get with her when all she was trying to do was become a better actor.

We chatted that first night after class and decided that we would do a scene together. She invited me over to her magnificent, gated estate on Coldwater Canyon Avenue, where we read through a stack of plays to try to find the right one for both of us. It had to be a scene from which we could each grow. Anyone who has been in an acting class will tell you this is not easy and usually takes up the first two days of rehearsal. Fortunately, we made quick work of the task and started working on the scene. It was a perfectly pleasant evening where I also got to meet her 10-year-old daughter Tamara and their German Shepherd Tasha, who bit me hard, squarely on the ass, just to let me know there would be no funny business. For some reason, Tamara and Deborah thought it was hysterical.

We continued to work on the scene over the following weeks. It was not going well. I thought that maybe if we just spent some time together hanging out, it would help our characters gain some familiarity. The problem was that I could never get Deborah to spend any time with me outside of our scene work. I asked if she wanted to meet at a restaurant for lunch. She said that she did not. I asked about maybe a coffee at Starbucks, the new cool coffee place that had just opened on the top of Beverly Glen Drive. Nope. She was guarded, rightfully so, and wanted nothing we did to be misconstrued as a social engagement. We were scene partners, and that was it, which was fine with me. She was still mourning the loss of her marriage, a loss that had devastated her, a dream life crumbling at her feet, with nothing she could do to stop it. And who was this Shuki, who could walk away from a goddess like Deborah Shelton? What a dope!

One day, out of the blue, we were working on our scene, when Deborah looked up at me and asked, "Dougie, have you ever had a colonic?" I stared at her blankly. I had no clue what that was, but I was assuming with "colon" in the name, it was nothing enjoyable. Turns out I was right. During a colonic, a specially trained "colon therapist" uses a machine mounted on the wall to shoot water up your ass with a tube. The warm water then sits in your colon for a few minutes before it is released back out of your ass and down another tube. This dislodges waste from your colon that would otherwise remain there and floats it away, never to be seen again. I thought the whole thing sounded insane and unpleasant. That being said, I realized that this was my first and perhaps only opportunity to spend time with Deborah outside of rehearsing our scene that was dying on the vine. And she was so giddy with the idea that she could introduce someone new to the fabulous life one can have with a sparkling clean colon that she seemed to forget we would be hanging out without the protection of the scene book she clutched so hard in her hands whenever we rehearsed.

The colon therapist was in Santa Monica, which was a bit of a drive. That was okay, since I really wanted just to have the chance to talk to Deborah Shelton, the woman I was spending most days with but knew nothing about. I thought it would be like pulling teeth, but this could not have been further from the truth. Once we started chatting, we covered a variety of topics, none of which I had anticipated. I was thinking I would hear about *Dallas* and Miss USA and the other stuff she had done, as you would with most actresses. But not Deborah. She was on a road of self-discovery. She was doing whatever she could to mend the heart that had been broken by the mysterious Shuki Levy. Finally, there was that connection that had been missing in our scene this whole time. At the very least, this outing would perhaps rescue our class work provided my ass didn't explode in a horrible colonic mishap.

The colon therapist was a funny, sweet woman named Carolyn. She knew it was my first time, so she was very low-key and spoke quietly as she nudged me onto the table. She and Deborah chatted about new health foods and cleansing rituals as Carolyn lubed up a strange-looking device hooked up to two tubes with hoses coming from it and gently pulled my legs apart. Thankfully, the insertion was made much less traumatic by the fact that Deborah had taken my hand and was stroking it with her thumb. WTF? Where did this come from??? How much weirder was this going to get?

The water rushed into my body and, as the cavity inside me filled up, it became uncomfortable to the point that I pleaded for mercy. Carolyn relented, and after what seemed like an eternity, she turned a red knob, then out rushed the water that was supposed to contain the waste that had clung to my colon walls. Unfortunately, there was no waste. Carolyn commented that this often happened to first timers. She tried again. Nothing. Again. Nothing. Deborah refused to give up. She urged Carolyn to continue, but in the end (no pun intended), it was not to be. I was seriously jammed up, and we weren't going to be getting any sort of release at that moment.

Deborah, on the other hand, emptied half her insides on the first go. She followed it up with another three magnificent releases and hopped off the table as if she'd been having her eyes checked. As we were leaving, Carolyn said to me that I might have a "nice release" later, but not to worry. It would be a great relief. "Cool," I thought, then Deb and I left. As a reward for my having that tube up my ass for 45 minutes, Deborah offered to take me to lunch at the local mall in Century City. On the way over, I started to feel a little crampy in my gut. But it would come and go, so I wasn't too put out by it.

At the restaurant, we ordered, and as we awaited our food, things started to go south, quite literally, in a hurry. My entire intestines felt like they were going to explode out of my ass and drench anyone within ten feet of me. I clenched as hard as I could and finally told Deb, "I think I'm having that release." Her response was, "Oh, Dougie, that's fantastic!" I respectfully disagreed and leapt out of my chair in search of the bathroom. I found it. Unfortunately, there was a line. A FREAKING LINE!!!! I'd never done this before and have never done it since, but on this day, I boldly pushed to the front and proclaimed that it was a medical emergency and to get out of the way. The door opened after a few loud poundings from me. I entered the room and when I say barely made it…it was a photo finish. I'll spare you the details.

Once out of the restroom, I returned to Deborah, who was beaming. I told her about my release, and she hugged me so tightly I thought I was going to have another release. But she was just so happy for me that for a moment I forgot that I was being hugged and kissed on the cheek for executing the simple task of emptying thirty-one years' worth of unprocessed fecal matter into the porcelain bowl at the Century City Mall.

That night at Deborah's house, we began to act out the scene. For the first time, it felt real, it felt emotional, and there was an intimacy that had been missing. After a few times through, it happened. The first kiss. And what a first kiss. There was so much emotion tied up in it on both our parts. Me wanting desperately to find a deeper connection with this wacky, beautiful, amazing woman, and her just wanting to be shown romantic love, which I assume, like with any marriage that was over, had disappeared long ago for Deb and Shuki. I was more than happy to accommodate that desire.

And so that began the five-year odyssey that was our relationship. I will say it again: Deborah Shelton was and is an amazing human being. She's a unicorn. Magical, mysterious, and unlike anyone I'd ever met. The only other "unicorn" I've ever come across in my life is my wife, Mindy. I'm so freaking lucky.

Later, I'll tell you all about the one *Power Rangers* event Mindy attended and how bizarre it ended up being. I would tell it now, but there are a few things you need to know if you are to understand how truly bizarre it was. For now, let's get this thing cranked up and head over to the morphing grid.

CHAPTER 5
MUSIC BY SHUKI LEVY AND KUSSA MAHCHI

As Deb and I grew closer, the relationship grew complicated. She didn't want anyone to know about us in any real detail, including her daughter Tamara. So, we never publicly displayed affection, keeping up the ruse that we were just friends. She insisted to me that the reason it would never happen was our age gap, her being more than a decade older than me and feeling like she would be judged for dating such a youngster. I knew there was more to it than that. But I was willing to accept the terms and conditions that came along with being in her world. I was willing to hop the ten-foot wall of her Coldwater Canyon mansion in the middle of the night to see her after Tamara had gone to bed. I was willing to hide in the closet when Tamara had nightmares, came into the room where Deb and I had been cuddled up, and took my spot in her bed. I was willing to trail around her life as her "best friend," even though it was clear as day that we were far more than that.

And then there was Shuki Levy, Deborah's soon-to-be ex-husband. I had only seen photos of him, but he looked like a cross between Jesus Christ and a super-cool movie assassin. As it turned out, he was neither. He was merely a talented musician who had come to the U.S. with his partner Haim Saban to start a company and break into show business. As I mentioned earlier, they began as a music company, creating scores for animated kids TV series. Shuki and Haim became the guys for cartoon music. In fact, if you look at a lot of the older animated series, you will see "Music by Shuki Levy and Kussa Mahchi," which was Haim's nom de plume and translates to "Stuffed Zucchini" in Hebrew.

At the same time, they were providing musical scores for American shows like *Dallas* when they were re-dubbed for broadcast in other countries. In truth, Shuki was the one who wrote all the music. Later, that task was passed on to an entire floor of young, hungry composers who worked for $20 per hour to crank out music that Shuki and Kussa Mahchi could put their names on and claim the royalties. This was a theme in the world of Saban back then. Hire inexperienced kids who want a break, then pay them very little in exchange for the chance to work on real TV shows and movies. While most people thought it was criminal, and that is not a hard argument to back up, my feeling was that Saban Entertainment was the equivalent of paid film school. I learned more in my years with Saban than I did at NYU by a wide margin. The money was crap, but let's face it, I was young, and no one else was going to let me write, produce, direct, and act in a giant TV show.

CHAPTER 6
SHUKI WANTS TO MEET YOU

Anyone who has ever expressed any interest in *Mighty Morphin Power Rangers* knows the story of how the show came to be in the U.S. So, I will "Readers' Digest" it as quickly as I can.

Haim was in Japan on a business trip. The T.V. in his hotel room was playing a Japanese series called *Super Sentai*, which was the original *Power Rangers* made specifically for Japanese audiences. Haim was fascinated by it and figured he could, without a doubt, sell it in the States, with a bit of Americanization. So, he secured an agreement to pitch the show in the U.S. from the Japanese production company, Toei.

In Haim's mind, it was a no-brainer. How could the U.S. broadcasters not see what he saw? As it turned out, they did not. And for years, Haim peddled the idea of the show around town, trying everything to find a broadcaster to come on board and produce his vision for the series. It became clear that no one was going to get it unless there was some sort of proof of concept. So, Haim, with his infinite wisdom and giant brass balls, spent his own money to finance a pilot. The pilot that was produced was like the series we've grown to know and love, with a few minor differences. The

Yellow Ranger was later recast. Zordon was called Zoltair and kind of had a sense of humor, or at least attempted, I guess is the way to put it. Kimberly was the total valley girl, an airhead, and Bulk and Skull were more threatening and less comedic. So, Saban and his top brass went off to sell the show, with something in hand that would end up being the difference between us never hearing about *Power Rangers* and what we know today as the lasting evergreen property it is.

As they hit the pitch trail, there were the usual number of "no's" along the way. When they arrived at Fox Kids, Margaret Loesch, president of the newly formed "sub network" of Fox, didn't see how the show could succeed. She was aware of *Super Sentai*. But the Saban pilot was SO cheesy and SO awful. How could it possibly garner anything but ridicule? Fox Kids was the home of successful shows as *The Tick*, *Eek the Cat*, and *Bobby's World*. These animated series were well written, well produced, and generally considered to be quite clever and upper shelf for kids' programming. This was the brand Fox Kids was determined to maintain back in 1992. For some reason, however, they reluctantly agreed to set up a focus group to test Haim's pilot and see what actual kids thought of *Mighty Morphin Power Rangers*. After all, this wouldn't be the first time that parents didn't get a show that kids became obsessed with.

Focus groups consist of a small number of members of a specific demographic, who are paid to participate in the study of a product in order to collect data that will help inform the researchers as to the viability of said product. The study tries to root out the positives and negatives and eventually the likelihood that the members of the group would purchase the product. It basically comes down to engagement. How engaged are the group members with what they are being asked to check out? In the case of a TV series, researchers will often employ a "Dial Test." This is where the viewers are each given a box with a dial on it and asked to turn the dial to the right if they like something, to the left if they don't, and anywhere in the middle depending on their thoughts on a specific moment in the movie or show.

In the *Power Rangers* test, kids were given the dial boxes and, a few moments later, the pilot started to roll. Within maybe thirty seconds, the dials were all slammed all the way to the right and stayed pinned there for the entire duration of the show. The kids were completely mind-blown. This was unlike anything they had ever seen. It was a colorful symphony of robots, dinosaurs, teenagers, karate, gymnastics, and on and on. Every focus group that day had the same reaction—full "right dials" from start to finish. Margaret still had her doubts, but Haim offered Fox Kids a generous piece of the pie in terms of licensing and toy sales, which, if the show became a hit, could amount to a fortune. Also, there were the test results. It was becoming almost impossible to say no.

A normal order for a kids' series in those days was 60 episodes. This may seem like a lot, when compared to nighttime shows. You must remember, kids watched their favorite series every day without fail (or at least that was the hope). So, if you do the math, 60 episodes is a very small number to stretch out over the course of a year, even with repeats, special events, shifting time slots, etc. It required VERY smart and creative people in the programming department to give the illusion that the show was new and fresh every week, even if this was the fifth time the episodes had aired. So, 60 was not a huge number in the grand scheme of things. Not by a long shot.

However, for *Power Rangers*, 60 was too big a number for the network to stomach. Even at the measly license fee (what the network pays the producer to make the show) of around $225K per episode, they only ordered 40. One executive who was with Fox Kids at the time recalls that Margaret Loesch had done the math and told this person that all they had to do was keep it on the air for 40 episodes and they would break even. Anything beyond that was icing on the cake. Of course, we all know what eventually happened with the show and how they all eventually drowned in icing. But there were still a few hitches in the beginning that few people are aware of. The first hitch was the affiliates.

The OG TV networks are set up as, well, networks, meaning

that there is a central body, usually located in L.A. or New York or both, that creates content. The affiliate stations, independent entities not owned by the network, play that content on their channel in return for compensation, known as retransmission fees. Most stations are contractually bound to air what the network provides them. However, back in the day for Fox, that was not the case. And, when many of the affiliates saw the pilot for *Mighty Morphin Power Rangers*, they refused to air it, on the grounds that it was "off brand" and "utter crap," as one station owner put it. This was clearly going to be an issue. Fox Kids had to find a way to prove to this group of station owners that Rangers was viable and would be a money maker for them all (good luck with that!).

Another challenge was whether Saban would be able to produce the show for the meager amount they were getting from the network. It seemed impossible to complete a full half-hour TV show for what they were being given. And Haim was done reaching into his own pocket. What the number crunchers and naysayers at the time didn't understand was that they were only shooting 11 minutes of original footage per 22-minute episode. The other 11 minutes that would comprise the standard half hour was preexisting material from Japan, of which the cost was amortized over the course of the season. This ended up being around $25,000 per episode the first year. That was less than half the cost of a day of shooting, and they were getting 11 minutes out of it. Not only that, the decision was made to "block shoot" the series. This is a technique used by productions to work through all the shots that face one direction before turning the cameras and lights around, saving hours out of a day. Saban took block shooting a step further. They broke four scripts up based on where the scenes took place. So, on day one, they would shoot all the Command Center scenes for those episodes. On day two, all the Juice Bar scenes would be done, day three would be at the park, and on and on. This allowed the company to shoot four episodes in 10 days! That's 2.5 days per episode. So, coming in under the license fee was not going to be an issue. In fact, it was widely believed at the time that Haim was not returning the unused money but keeping it for other expenses related to the series, such as marketing and advertising. It wasn't enough for anyone to get cranky over, but it was just another example of what makes Haim so brilliant. If they had asked for it back, he most likely would have handed it over. They never asked, and he never offered.

The salaries of everyone on the crew and in the cast were as woefully low as the legends have maintained. But, as I said before, these were all people, me included, trying to break into the business, and it was non-union, which was a rarity in those days. This would be a regular job that would last months, then years, that did not require one to be in any of the performance unions. The Yellow Ranger from the pilot demanded that she be paid union wages, far more than what was in the contract she signed. This was the first indication anyone got that this type of demand would not be tolerated. The actress was fired, and Thuy Trang was brought in to take her place. So, the series was cast, the writing began, and pre-production started ramping up.

As all of this was going on, I was still spending most of my time with Deborah, going to self-help seminars, getting more colonics (successful ones, even!), attending Indian sweat huts; all that weird shit you hear about celebrities doing to dispose of the income they can't possibly spend. Acting class was becoming less of a joy and more of a chore, which was not a good sign for my future endeavors in front of the camera. I had reached a certain amount of success (although minuscule in the grand scheme of things), enjoyed the few times I was recognized in public while on the soap, and spent most of the money from it on Air Jordans and a new guitar (I hadn't touched one since Randy passed away, but I figured that would not have been what he wanted from any of his students). I was starting to think that maybe I had taken my acting talent as far as it could go.

Deborah was at the point in her career where the parts were becoming a bit scarcer and she was being sent out for roles that all seemed pretty much the same: the sexy woman who witnesses a crime and has to be protected by a guy she initially loathes but ultimately falls in love with as they endure hails of bullets and massive explosions. The latest of these auditions was for a movie called *Silk Degrees* (Boz Scaggs will be scarred for life if he ever sees this film). I read the script, and in my humble opinion, it kind of sucked. Deborah agreed but went to the audition at the urging of her manager. At the audition, they immediately wanted her for the role, of course. But she was concerned about the script. It was NOT great or even decent, and she felt like she needed to turn it down. However, in an unsurprising, selfless move that showed the depth of her kindness and desire for me to transition to adulthood by getting a real job, she agreed to do the film on the condition I was hired to rewrite it.

Wow. Who ever saw that coming? Certainly NOT her manager, a hyper-chatty human who only had one other client and was scrounging for any crumbs left by the actors who had already passed on the role. This woman was terrified that the production company was going to tell Deborah to go pound sand. And why wouldn't they? What had I ever written besides a couple of spec scripts for my dad and the two *Love Boat* scripts that got me into NYU film school? I certainly hadn't had any work produced. Looking back now her demand must have infuriated the producers. I'm sure they would have loved to move on to another actress. But there was no other option who would have brought the added value Deborah did in the foreign film market. So, kicking and screaming, the sleazy production company, headed by an arrogant jerk who looked like he was wearing a black Harpo Marx wig and spat when he talked, agreed to the conditions and hired me. They paid me a couple of thousand dollars, which at the time was money that saved my bacon. I was truly grateful. And I remain grateful to Deborah Shelton to this day, for that and many other moments of true selflessness and love.

Speaking of Deborah, as entrenched as we were in one another's lives, I still hadn't met Shuki, her soon-to-be ex. And she was determined to do anything to ensure that never happened. It was Deb's routine to lock me in the bedroom or the closet or whatever hiding place was closest when Shuki arrived every Friday to pick up Tamara for the weekend. I must admit, it was a bit degrading, crouching down in the dark waiting for the coast to be clear. But, when you're thirty-two and are sitting on top of the most sexual energy you will ever have in your life, you shrugged off a little shame if it meant sharing the bed of the most amazing woman you've met up to that point in your life.

On one particular Friday, I was in one of my normal hiding areas, the room that Marta, the live-in assistant/cleaning woman/nanny, occupied. We were watching a Spanish broadcast of *Speed Racer* or some other oldie but goodie on the Spanish station with Marta's 2-year-old son, when Deborah barged into the room, brimming with excitement, tears in her eyes, smile as wide as I'd ever seen it. She hugged me tightly and said nothing, leading me out of the room. Marta shook her head and rolled her eyes, which she did when Deborah behaved in a crazy way, which was more often than not.

As we sat in the kitchen and drank green tea, Deborah revealed why she was so over the moon. Apparently, Shuki, while waiting for Tamara to pack her things and make her way down the gigantic Tara-esque staircase, had picked up a script that was sitting on the coffee table in the living room. This script was for a movie entitled *Billy Two Toes Rainbow* and it was based on a book written by an Australian author about the opal trade in the outback and the deadly consequences of stirring up trouble in a dangerous mining town. My father had optioned this book for the company he was running at the time, but none of the writers they had hired had been able to crack the script, and the option was running out, which meant they would lose the right to continue developing the project or sell it to a network. On a lark, I volunteered to take a turn at writing a script. It was an arduous task, and I'm not sure if my draft was any better than the others. But my father seemed to think it wasn't bad and congratulated me on a good effort. Unfortunately, the movie didn't sell. But this was the script that Shuki started to read that day while waiting for his daughter.

Apparently, he had been able to make it through the first act before Tamara arrived, and he had to put it down. And apparently, he loved it! He was impressed with the writing and wanted to know who the author was. Deborah told me she had blurted out that it was "a friend from her acting class." This was her attempt to keep the real nature of our relationship, which she was determined to protect, a secret. I think she had completely blocked out the idea that pretty much everyone else knew what was going on and really could not have given a crap, including her 12-year-old daughter, who might just have been the smartest pre-teen on the planet who wasn't studying thermal dynamics at Cal Tech. In fact, Shuki, I later learned, was overjoyed that she had found someone to keep her occupied in the hopes that the obsession she still had for him and for bringing their family back together would somehow subside. (It never did, as far as I know.)

The point of this was that Shuki thought my work had promise. So much so that he asked Deborah to pass on his number to me, as he had a few projects I might be interested in, and wanted me to come meet him at his Westwood apartment! The thought of this was terrifying. The big honcho, second in command at Saban, the creative gateway to the fast-growing company, my girlfriend's ex-husband, wanted to see me. He had a few projects I might be interested in! I wondered to myself whether Shuki was under the illusion that I was working on other assignments that might preclude me from being interested in his project. Did he have any idea that at that point, I had rewritten *one* script that had been produced and was basically a washed-up actor just trying to stay ahead of my mounting credit card bills? I suppose that this was the universe's way of telling me it was time to get a grip on reality and decide whether I wanted to live in my crappy apartment in Hollywood for the rest of my life or pursue something I was actually decent at, something that could provide me with a career.

At the time that this all went on, *Mighty Morphin Power Rangers* was starting to take form, but it was not on anyone's radar. This meeting was going to be about a movie Shuki and his then-girlfriend, Shell Danielson, came up with, but that was all I knew. Frankly, I wouldn't have cared what the story concept was. I was out of my *Silk Degrees* re-write money, and I needed work and was ready to do just about anything to survive. My job at the time, managing an apartment complex in Hollywood for free rent, was just barely allowing me to scrape by, and I HAD to make a move. And so, off I went to meet the man.

I was scared shitless when I met Shuki that day. After all, I was in what can only be described as a bizarre relationship/non-relationship with his ex-wife, and although HE had called the meeting, it was still a bit daunting. I had never met the guy, and the whole thing seemed kind of "too good to be true." Who hires his ex's current dude to work for him? It's mental. Whatever. I was overthinking. "Go meet the guy," I told myself. Deborah seemed to think Shuki walked on water, one step behind the Messiah, so how bad could he be?

The moment I walked into Shuki's Wilshire Blvd. condo/music studio, any fear I had was dispelled. Rarely had I met a kinder, more mellow, soft-spoken individual. He genuinely seemed interested in my life and what I was up to. He had a great sense of humor and seemed truly appreciative that I had come all the way over to his place just to hear his idea. The movie he wanted help with was called *Susie Q*. It was the story of a teenage girl who dies in a car crash on the way home from her prom back in the 1950s and comes back as a ghost present day. I thought it was a great premise and immediately agreed to rewrite the script they had. For my trouble, I would be paid $5000, and as a non-union writer, that would be that. Five grand! That was insane; nearly double what I had gotten for *Silk Degrees*. I could almost quit my job at the apartment building—almost. (I waited a bit just to be sure I didn't screw up the script and that Shuki wanted to hire me again.)

Shuki DID hire me again, to write a movie called *Someone to Die For*. The pay was much the same, which was fine. The script came out pretty good. The movie got made, and it was the final little bit of luck that I needed to board that interstellar flight bound for the Power Ranger Galaxy.

I received my next call a few months later. Once again, it was to go to Shuki's place and help him with something he was writing. I figured it was going to be another movie and another few grand, which was great, as I was starting to run low from the last script and it was going to get ugly quickly. Thankfully, I was still managing the building and didn't have to worry about being out on the street. But it was getting to the point where life's little necessities like Kraft Mac and Cheese and Ramen Noodle cups were starting to become life's little luxuries, and that was not a place in which I was comfortable.

Shuki had moved from this condo in Westwood to a house overlooking the San Fernando Valley off a windy road that led up to Mulholland Drive from Studio City. The new place was insane. It was done in this whole Moroccan style, complete with a hookah room, a full music studio, a screening room, and even an aviary full of birds. The house was decorated impeccably, and it fit Shuki perfectly. He seemed to be happy to be out of the smaller apartment and was bouncing between his studio and his office where he was working on polishing scripts for the new series Saban was starting soon: *Mighty Morphin Power Rangers*.

After a tour of the house, Shuki confessed that he usually had his other half, Shell, there to help make sure the grammar was correct in the scripts he was writing and lock down the story points, etc. For some reason, she was not there, and he needed help with a *Power Rangers* script he was writing. The episode was called "Foul Play in the Sky." The premise was that Kimberly was going up for a sightseeing flight with her Uncle Steve, who was a pilot and owned a small plane. Of course, Bulk and Skull weaseled their way onto the plane and Rita roofied Uncle Steve so that he was knocked out and couldn't fly. Bulk and Skull freaked, and Kimberly had to land the plane just in time to do battle with the dreaded Snizzard, who could only be destroyed by Kimberly's pink power bow, which she had luckily had brought with her on the plane ride just in case.

As I read through what he had so far, it looked okay but needed some massaging and dialogue help. I spent the afternoon going through it, and when I was done, I presented it to Shuki. He loved it, was very grateful, and suggested that I might like to play Uncle Steve in the episode. Of course, the show was non-union, but at that point I was pretty much a "non-actor," so I figured, "non-issue." A few weeks later, we shot the episode, and it was a ton of fun. Everyone was incredibly kind. Shuki was directing, so the set was super mellow, and things went off without a hitch.

One of the show's producers happened to be a former pilot in the Israeli air force, so they shot actual flying sequences at a tiny airport in Van Nuys, California, with the producer doubling me in the plane. Little did I know at the time, but that producer/pilot would later become one of the great nemeses of my career. I'll come up with a faux name for him down the road. He's not important to this part of the story. What is important, is Shuki had been made aware of my ability to act (to a point), and more importantly, to coach acting when I was asked to. After all, I had spent the last four years studying under the best teacher in the city. There were a few pearls of wisdom I had accumulated over those years that were somewhat helpful to actors struggling with a line here or there. Ironically, I'm not sure there was much I really did, as the actors that day were the best of the bunch and didn't need any help from me in the acting department. But I was happy to offer them a few well-received suggestions. Whatever happened that day, Shuki was pleased with my contribution, and it brought me one step closer to being invited into the Saban Entertainment family.

CHAPTER 7
"WHERE ARE YOU GOING?"

It was a perfectly pleasant weekday afternoon on Vista Street in Hollywood. I was trying to study lines for a monologue I was to perform in Howard's class the following Monday. The phone rang, and it was Shuki, with what I would learn was his usual greeting, "Doug. This is Shuki. What are you doing?" I told him I was doing nothing, knowing that he would then know he was not interrupting and tell me why he was calling, which so far had always been for a good reason. At first, I figured it was another movie script, which would bring another 5K or so. Great news, as always. However, that was not the case. Not even close. "Doug, we hired this kid for the *Power Rangers*. He's gonna be there for like 14 episodes." I continued to listen. "This kid…he is fucking incredible. He jumps around and flips and kicks ass. I've never seen anything like it." I couldn't imagine why he was calling to tell me all this. Truth be told, Shuki did get really excited about good news and loved to share it with the people around him. This still didn't explain why he would call ME.

Out of curiosity, asked, "What's he been in? Anything I would have seen?"

"Not unless you're taking karate lessons in West Covina," was his reply. I didn't get it at first. "He's never acted before in his life, Doug." I was starting to get where this was going. "What do you think about taking him on and coaching him on set? We'll put you on an hourly rate, and whenever he works, you'll be there."

My mind was spinning at this point. I was pretty sure I was up to the task. Between Howard in L.A. and Clifford in New York, I had accumulated two different but excellent ways to help actors break down a scene and create a roadmap to success. Nothing is foolproof, of course. Human beings are all different. Some of them, no matter how hard they try or how long they study, just don't get it. Their brain is wired so differently that they just cannot find a way to break down the walls required to let themselves be free and give a good performance. Acting is all about giving yourself permission to stand in front of one person or 5,000 people and share your innermost feelings, thoughts, and desires. That is NOT for everyone. And there was always a chance it wouldn't be for this new "Karate Kid" they had hired. So, when it came to the opportunity in front of me, although the money was pretty good, and it meant the chance to be on a set every day, there was a chance, however slight, that the kid could be one of those people who just could not get themselves to perform. If that were the case, I would forever be labeled the guy who failed to get Wonder Boy to give a passable performance. Or he could be a natural and pick it up right away, as some do.

The real challenge was time. I couldn't spend the customary three months teaching him the techniques he needed to grasp. I would have to pare it all down to its most basic concepts, pass these on, and hope for the best. One thing was for certain—there was no way I was letting the guy, whoever he was, turn up on set with zero coaching and be thrown to the wolves. The other Rangers were fifteen episodes in, so regardless of their level of acting prowess, they were all getting by.

"I need to see him at least a couple of times before he starts," I told Shuki.

"Great. So, you'll do it?"

"Absolutely. It should be fun."

As it turns out, it was way more than that.

A few days later, there was a knock on my apartment door. Jason Frank, 19, had been scheduled to arrive 2 p.m., and he'd arrived exactly at that time, all smiles, shuffling feet, and "aw shucks."

"Mr. Sloan?" he said. "I'm Jason. Shuki sent me to learn how to act."

After telling him never to call me Mr. Sloan again, I opened the door and let him in. Jason entered the room with an energy that, even when subdued, was palpable. He was clearly a world-class athlete. This we knew from his awards and achievements. But there was more to it than that. I could tell that his head was swimming with thoughts, ideas, questions. But all of it was being kept beneath the surface, wrapped up in this seemingly shy, very polite, very handsome package. Yes indeed, this kid had the look, the "pixie dust," as I like to call it. It's that inexplicable thing stars have that you just can't pinpoint, but it's there. As I watched him take a seat, I noticed something a bit mind-blowing. Jason Frank had the longest eyelashes I had ever seen on a dude. It was remarkable and was one of many things that drew you in to him. (I didn't say anything eyelash-related at the time, but Shuki and I had a laugh about it later as he too had noticed it.)

Jason sat down on my couch and took out a notebook. Inside the book were all his scripts for the big multi-part episode that would introduce him to the show. As I read through the material, I quickly realized he was being thrown into the deep end. The writers clearly hadn't considered what it meant to ask a complete beginner to carry a five-episode arc on a hit TV show. I mean, Jason knew nothing about acting and was quick to tell me so. And that's probably what saved him in the end.

"It's actually a good thing," I said. "That way we don't have to spend any time undoing bad habits you would have picked up along the way. I'm showing you a simple way to understand technique that help you go on set and perform these scenes with very little chance of screwing it up. But you HAVE to work at it. Acting is like anything: if you don't practice, you won't improve."

He just smiled. "Not a problem." (I later remembered that Jason was a martial arts master at 19, an achievement that would have taken years of concentrated study and practice. There was never going to be an issue of not putting in the work. Big relief there.)

We looked at the scene Jason was supposed to start with on his first day. It was in the school hallway with the character of Kimberly, and he was supposed to rescue her from Bulk and Skull, who were being their usual harassing selves. The scene didn't seem like much; short, simple, two characters. The truth was it was set up perfectly for Jason to be successful on his first day. Why, you ask? Well, first off, there was the flurry of non-contact martial arts moves his character used to send Bulk and Skull running for the hills. It was the beginning of the scene and provided an immediate outlet for the nervous energy that would surely be running through him (his very first time being in front of a camera) and allow him to be more real and more relaxed when the dialogue began.

> SIDE NOTE: There is a scene in the Green Ranger mini-series where Jason (the character played by Austin St. John) and Zach are working out with a punching bag in the Youth Center. In the beginning of the scene, Austin is supposed to execute a flurry of moves on the bag and basically kick the thing's ass. Once he finished, the conversation would continue with Zach. It was very noticeable (to me, at least) that Austin had exerted so much energy hitting the bag that when he got to the dialogue, he was so relaxed that he didn't think about his lines and just had a conversation. He's fantastic in that scene, and I have no doubt that it was a result of Austin releasing all the nervous energy that had been built up before the cameras rolled.

The next stroke of luck was that Paul Schrier (Bulk), Jason Narvey (Skull), and Amy Jo Johnson (Kimberly) were in the scene with Jason. Coincidentally, at that time, those three happened to be the best actors in the cast by a long shot. They were all confident, well-trained, and knew their parts. This was great for Jason, as acting is a lot like tennis. When you play with someone of superior skill, it forces you to reach beyond what you thought you were capable of, and helps you rise to the other player's level and give a performance you didn't believe you could have. Jason was going to be in good company on day one. All I had to do was give him some basic techniques he could use to keep up with the others. And they had to be *very* basic techniques that he could learn in a couple of weeks.

Right about now, I can hear the actors out there exploding with indignation at that last paragraph. How dare I insinuate that ANYONE could, in a week, successfully prepare to work as a professional with a full crew and a cast of other actors! The truth is that 99 times out of 100, they can't. However, there are those rare occasions when someone with zero experience can come in and just knock it out of the park, or at least survive the day. Most working actors carry emotional encumbrances that interfere with their performance, be it on stage or in front of the camera. There's so much pressure to be good, to not lose the job, to not let down your fellow castmates, and on and on and on. However, there are those who, with a combination of natural talent and the mental fortitude necessary to block out all the "noise," can just, well, act. I'm not saying that Jason Frank fell into the category of a complete natural. But he did have the mental ability to focus his energy and trust that Howard's technique, which I was teaching him, wouldn't let him down. From what I could see, it never did.

As Jason and I started to read through the material, with no instruction at first, Jason did surprisingly well. He was frustrated if he forgot a line or messed up somewhere, but I wasn't concerned. I was just trying to get a feel for where he was in terms of barebones natural ability. I told him not to worry about getting it perfect. I was just wanted to hear the scene out loud. It was more for me than him. When we finished, I gave him the first piece of the puzzle that

I had learned with Howard Fine, which, although it seems simple enough, is something that not enough actors take the time to establish. Answering these three simple questions is vital to successfully performing the scene, and they must be answered before you even walk onto the stage or set.

1. Where have I just come from?
    a. It makes a huge difference if you are coming from a New Year's Eve party as opposed to a funeral. The whole scene hinges on this fact. It changes your behavior, how you approach things, how you deal with what is to come as the scene unfolds.
2. Where am I going?
    a. What environment are you entering? Is it safe, dangerous, familiar? Who else is there? Why are they there?
3. What's the first thing you want from the other character(s)?
    a. You must know what it is you want from whoever happens to be in the scene with you. Are you there to confront them? Are you there to seek forgiveness? To comfort them? This is crucial as it informs the entire scene moving forward.

Jason wrote this all down furiously, not wanting to miss a word. It was clear that having these rules were, for him, the beginnings of the sturdy safety net he so desperately wanted. So, we started the scene again. He told me that in the scene as Tommy, he was coming from his last class and was looking for his next, feeling a little lost and a little overwhelmed. I told him not to *play* lost or overwhelmed. This is where actors get into trouble. You can't play lost. You must instead do something active, like search. Then you have a real moment. He immediately got it. So, he was coming from one class going to the next when he sees Kimberly being harassed by

Bulk and Skull. What's the first thing he wants from Bulk and Skull? He told me it was to "warn" them.

"Good," I replied. "What about Kimberly?" I asked.

"I want to *reassure* her."

Also, good. He started with that as we read the scene again, and it was 1000% better.

From there, we continued breaking down the script, with me giving him more and more basic acting techniques that he could use to make a battle plan for day one. We were there for several hours, as there was a lot of work we needed to get through. But his level of concentration was astounding. By the time he left my place, he had a plan and was eager to get home and study. I will never forget that for some reason, when he left, instead of shaking hands, we hugged. I've always been someone who hugs my friends, so this wasn't an issue for me. It just caught me off guard for a moment, as this was the first time we had ever met. However, Jason had a look in his eyes that told me he was genuinely relieved and grateful for what we had shared and the progress he had made. I guess from that point on, he considered me a friend. And from that moment on, I considered him the same. And I was going to do everything in my power to make sure that my new friend succeeded, no matter what the future would bring.

CHAPTER 8
FIRST DAY OF SCHOOL

Every time you walk onto a new set, it feels like the first day at a new school. I will never forget the sheer terror I felt walking on to the *Y&R* set for the first time. I was scared out of my mind that I wouldn't remember the words or the blocking or, well, anything. For me, going to the *Power Rangers* set was much less stressful. I was there with one job to perform, and that was to will Jason Frank through his first day of work. The basic premise of the miniseries was that a new kid named Tommy (played by Jason) shows up in Angel Grove and seems nice at first. Then Rita casts a spell on him, and he turns into a complete a-hole. Later, the curse is lifted, and Tommy becomes the sixth Ranger. Flipping from villain to hero was something that a lot of new actors would have a great deal of trouble with. But as we read through the work for the day in his dressing room, Jason seemed to have no problem with it. He had already been through hair and makeup, where I later found out the talk of his eyelashes was the center of conversation that day.

As we put down our scripts, the hour when shooting would start was closing in. Jason confided in me that he was incredibly nervous. I told him this was an excellent sign and to use that in the scene with Kimberly. It was about his first day of school, after all. She's a pretty girl. It *would* make you nervous to speak to her. Bulk and Skull, although more goofy than threatening, would also make Tommy uncomfortable. "So, let that emotion be a part of what you do in the scene," I told him. He seemed to like this idea. We ran the scene a couple of times and were then called to set. So, off we went.

Being an acting coach on set is a very strange job. A friend of mine from class was doing the same job across town for Neil Patrick Harris on *Doogie Howser* and had told me it was a fantastic job as long as the crew was cool with you. And they aren't always cool with you. That's when it becomes a sucky job. The director is there to direct the scenes being shot, and this includes the actors. If I'm a director, I'm thinking I'm supposed to work with the actors on their performances, so what the "F" do they need an acting coach for?

Then the paranoia sets in. *Does the director not think I work well with actors? Do the producers think I suck? Will I ever be asked back? Should I call my agent?*

For this five-part opus of *Mighty Morphin Power Rangers*, the director was Bob Hughes. Bob at the time was in his forties and a guy who knew a lot about making movies and TV. He was very secure in his role and welcomed the idea of having someone there to look after the performance of this new character. That had been a concern for Bob, since the show was shot in blocks and totally out of order and Jason would have to go from "evil Tommy" in some of the scenes to "good Tommy" in others. This could become confusing for any actor. After I promised Bob that I'd stay out of the way, he seemed to be completely on board with the idea of having me there.

Under normal circumstances, the next person on the acting coach "hate parade" would be the First Assistant Director. On *Mighty Morphin Power Rangers*, it was a guy named Larry Litton. He was a sarcastic, loud, blustery, bear of guy who could usually be found with the stub of an unlit cigar jammed in the corner his mouth. The first AD has many jobs, mostly to do with the schedule and making sure the crew marches forward and completes the work for every day of the shoot. This is a simplified explanation, as there are a myriad of events that can throw a wrench into a shooting schedule, including, but not limited to, weather, illness of a cast or crew member, injury to a cast or crew member, animals or children in a scene, a director who doesn't know what they're doing, an actor who doesn't know what they're doing, and the list goes on. Regardless of these things being out of his control, the first AD better figure out a way to fix it.

When you work on a union production that has a reasonable budget, if you go over your allotted time for the day, you just throw money at the problem and finish the work. On *Power Rangers*, that was never an option. You had to make your day. So when I showed up on set, Larry must have been thinking, not only does he have a new actor to deal with, but he's got some six-foot-five dickhead acting coach who is probably going to knock into the boom mic with his giant melon head every time he walks on set to "help" the new actor.

Thankfully, Shuki had prepped the LZ, as they say in the military (prepared the landing zone), so my arrival and presence on the set was at least accepted, if not welcomed with open arms. All I had to do was stay out of the way, watch the boom mic, and make sure Jason was doing good work, and all would be peachy in Angel Grove.

The first take is always the wide or master shot, which is good for new actors. It allows them to release all that energy before the camera moves in for medium and close-up shots, and they have to keep relatively still and within the camera frame. When they called first positions, and the actors and crew were ready, Jason was focused like a ninja. He winked at me right as they called action and went into the scene without a hitch. He performed his lines admirably, kept up with the other actors, and was ready for take two. I looked at Bob the director, who smiled and kind of shrugged, his way of saying, "I guess we're going to be okay." I gave Jason a minor adjustment for the second take, which was not to "swallow" his lines, as it was tough for sound to pick up some of what he was saying.

Take two? No problem. He took the adjustment and off he went. *This is going to be a freaking breeze,* I thought. Here's where I shake my head and laugh to myself at my own blind optimism. When was any of this stuff ever a "freaking breeze?" The answer is "Never." It is never a "freaking breeze." It's probably best to just shake my head at my own naivete and press on.

After that day of shooting, we reconvened in his dressing room. Jason was desperate to know if he had done okay. Did he hit all the moments in the scenes that he was supposed to? Did the director think it was good? Did the other Rangers say anything? How was Evil Tommy? I told him that if there was an issue, we'd still be out there shooting (probably not true, see above re: not spending money). But Jason did great. I was super proud of him. He was relieved and let out a deep breath.

For me, the fact that he was humble, even vulnerable about all of it, was, I thought, a good sign. The last thing we needed was for him to decide that he had conquered acting in a single day and refuse any future help on the matter, help that he was going to need as the scenes became harder and required more of him. But he seemed fine, which was a relief.

As the five-part mini-series pressed on, we found ourselves working everywhere from alleyways to the Youth Center/Juice Bar, to the Command Center, and even in a Dark Dimension. Through it all, Jason continued to study and kept improving. During those long days of filming, I was fortunate enough to make some great friends on set, including Bob Hughes, Larry Litton, Ian Rosenberg (Director of Photography), Yuda Ako (Production Designer), and on and on.

Most of the creatives on the series were extremely talented and treated the production as though it were every bit as important as a 100-million-dollar feature film, which was made more impressive by the fact that no one at that moment knew what was to come. The show hadn't premiered yet. The men and women I now worked with were ALL IN on this crazy little kids show. Regardless of what anyone thought of the production values, the writing, and the directing, there was a great deal of pride taken in the production of *Mighty Morphin Power Rangers*. There were limited resources, sure. But no one was going to let that get in the way of making the best show they could. It was kind of infectious being on that set, at least in the beginning. Of course, nothing good lasts forever, and the vibe on the set of *Power Rangers* was no exception.

CHAPTER 9
FIRST IMPRESSIONS

I try to be extra careful when I meet actors for the first time, especially on set. I feel like I'm a decent judge of character, but when you're talking about a group of human beings who can impact your financial future, you must be careful to pay attention to little clues and red flags along the way that could lead to trouble down the line. Every set has its pain in the butt. Some have several. It's not unheard of for a show to have several high-maintenance actors unite in an effort to get someone they don't care for fired. That's why I always keep a close eye on "who's who in the zoo."

During the weeks I coached Jason Frank, I was able to spend a little time hanging out with the other Rangers and get to know them. I've never really shared my initial reactions, mainly out of respect. But I figure enough time has passed that I can give you all a basic idea of the impression the original Rangers made on me at the time. This has no bearing on who they are today, as I have lost touch with most of them, but this was what I saw back then.

Amy Jo Johnson. While walking down the dressing room hallway one afternoon, I heard the music of an acoustic guitar and a sweet voice singing along with it. It was a song I had never heard before and later learned was an original Amy Jo wrote, and it was super good. I knocked on the door and told her as much. Singer-songwriters, especially when they are starting to write their own material, never get enough credit. In a way, songwriting is the most soul-baring thing you can do as a musician. You're opening your heart and sharing your deep dark secrets with the world, all while trying to sing on key. And people can be cruel. It's a tough road that takes bravery and talent and a lot of practice. Clearly Amy Jo had both.

I had spoken with AJ a couple of times on set about my days in Howard's class and my time on the soap. But this visit was all about the music. As the conversation progressed, it quickly became evident that this was a passion she took very seriously. We spoke of artists we loved, songs we loved, the five desert island albums each of us would take if we were stranded and had to choose, and on and on. I doubt she will remember this, but for me, it was a really great moment in my career and a valuable lesson. Actors are passionate people. They love to talk about things they are really into, whether it be rescuing animals or painting or music or any other pursuit that identifies them beyond the role they are playing. Those are the best conversations you have on set, not the ones about the job they already have and are always worried they are going to lose.

> SIDE NOTE: Years later, I had almost the exact conversation with another gifted songwriter in the jungles of Puerto Rico on the set of a Disney Channel movie. I was sitting on a couch that was part of the set of *The Princess Protection Program*, a Disney TV movie I Executive Produced and re-wrote, when Demi Lovato plopped down next to me, clearly exhausted. Just fifteen years old at the time, Demi was obsessed with songwriting and spent most of the time she wasn't shooting or in set school in her trailer on a portable keyboard writing material for her first album. Just as Amy had been, Demi was focused and open, and her creativity was through the roof. I've often felt that if Amy Jo had had the push of the Disney Music

machine, she might have had an incredible career in that arena. Unfortunately, she came along a little too early for that.

Anyway...

Amy Jo was a sweetheart. She was all love and rainbows and was the best actor of the bunch by a mile. My only concern with her, as I recall, was what would happen when the Rangers all discovered that this was actual work, and the shiny newness started to wear off. Once there is the realization that you HAVE to be there every day, and in this case, you're barely making enough money to survive, it suddenly becomes less fun and more drudgery. My hope was that she would be able to navigate that without any significant damage to her psyche. I knew there would be trouble with some of the others. I just hoped Amy Jo would remain her brilliant talented self through it all and not be turned off to acting altogether.

Austin St. John. Unfortunately, I never got to know Austin as well as I would have liked. In the beginning, I was there as Jason's acting coach and was pretty much focused on making sure he got through his scenes and stuck to what we had worked on the day before. What I DO remember about Austin is that he was always incredibly gracious to Jason Frank on set. Keep in mind, Austin was just barely 18. He was basically a kid who was the star of a hit TV series and suddenly had this other guy to contend with who was coming in to assume a leadership role as well. There was another "rooster in the henhouse," so to speak. But to Austin's great credit, if it bothered him, you never knew it. He was always friendly and helpful to Jason and seemed to welcome another martial artist to the group. After all, that's what Austin was, first and foremost. And he and Jason seemed to bond over that. There are stories that surfaced later about he and Jason hating one another and wanting to fight it out in the octagon or steel cage or something like that. I attribute that to the fact that Jason Frank was easily misled by gossip and people whispering in his ear about something some other actor had said about him. I really don't think there was a moment I remember where things got SO tense that anyone was ready to throw down, at least when we were filming. If it did, I never heard about it.

Austin's acting, if you considered the fact that he was NOT an actor when he landed the series, was surprisingly decent. I remember being impressed at the time when I was told he was a high school kid teaching martial arts who they found at the open auditions. I mean, this kid was completely raw. The good news was that like Jason Frank, Austin had the athletes' mentality, the belief that hard work brings results. And so, he took that into his scene work as well. Austin studied his butt off, from what I could tell, to get better as an actor, and it showed over time. He kept improving and didn't seem concerned with much besides being the best he could be. This is not to say he wasn't competitive. He was. But he was just competitive enough to raise his game without disturbing the chemistry of the cast. The very first intro of Tommy was a fight between him and Austin in a local tournament, putting their skills on display right next to one another. It was competitive on the day. But it made the scene work, and when the cameras cut, there was laughter and camaraderie. I loved this for Jason because it made him feel welcome and part of the group. I was always grateful to Austin for that. I was seriously bummed out when I heard he left the show. He was meant to be a Power Ranger, plain and simple. Replacing him was not going to be easy.

Walter Jones. Walter was another of the original Rangers with whom I would loved to have spent more time. He was all energy and fun. He literally brought a room alive when he entered it. I'm pretty sure that's what Saban saw in him when they hired Walter to play Zack (that and his Hip Hop Kido—a fusion of hip hop and martial arts he created for the show). He was a naturally funny guy and always had a ton of charisma on and off set. Writing for him was fantastic because you knew that whatever scene you needed him to be in, he could handle it. He was a great athlete, great performer, acrobat, dancer—he pretty much had it all. The great thing about him as an actor that I remember to this day is that he always listened to the other actors in a scene. He didn't just say his lines, he reacted off what the others said. It seems so simple, but so many actors get caught up in their own performance that they forget there's another person in the scene.

One Walter story I always thought was funny goes like this: When shooting the morphing sequences, it was necessary for him to hide his left hand, because, I'm not sure how, he lost his middle finger as a child. Just before a shooting one of those sequences, Walter somehow got hold of a Caucasian colored false middle finger. When the cameras rolled, he performed the scene with this giant prosthetic front and center, flipping the bird. From what I was told, it was all his idea, and he thought it was hilarious. I would love to find that take and see it again all these years later.

As with the other Rangers, Walter was not happy with the wage the Rangers were being paid, which at the time was $600 a week. And keep in mind, they were doing four shows in ten days because of the footage and the block shooting format. He really felt they were being treated unfairly, which I have to say is not something I can argue with. He ended up leaving the show with Thuy and Austin. I think for Walter especially, as hard as it was to leave, in the back of his mind he knew there was a great deal of opportunity out there for him. He probably wished that he could have been in the *Power Rangers* feature film, which I believe would have allowed him to really shine as an actor. In the end, Walter went on to work a ton after he left the series. I was always happy to see him in other shows. He deserved it.

Thuy Trang. Thuy is one of the great tragedies in the *Power Rangers* Universe. Thuy was one of the most centered, genuinely happy people I had ever met, a true pleasure to be around. Her family had endured a horrific journey from South Vietnam, where Thuy almost died in the hull of a cargo ship bound for Hong Kong and was lucky to even make it to the U.S. She had experienced more than most of us will ever endure before she was even an adult. In the time that I was there working with Jason, I had a few conversations with Thuy that today I feel blessed to have had. She was an inspiration. The performances she gave were among the trickiest of anyone in the cast. Her character of Trini was the least well-defined. She was a late addition to *Power Rangers*, replacing another actress, so I'm not sure how much attention was really paid to finding where Trini fit in the group. Thuy's solution to this was just to be herself. Literally. Her character, as far as I could tell, was nearly the same as the actor's; both were gracious, regal, kind, smart, and fiercely loyal. As a result, her character became less of a stereotypical archetype and more of a real person. And all the credit there goes to her, because it sure wasn't in the writing. I never got to ask her whether her approach to the role was intentional. Regardless, it worked very well. Let it be said that there is NOTHING harder for an actor to do than to play themselves. It requires a complete lack of self-consciousness, which few actors can achieve.

As most *Power Rangers* fans are aware, Thuy Trang passed away tragically in a terrible automobile accident in 1997 on the way from San Jose back home to Los Angeles with several friends. The news was a complete shock, of course. At the time, I was working on the Disney Channel Movie *Johnny Tsunami*. I remember hearing what happened from Scott Page-Pagter, the ADR Producer on *Power Rangers*. He and I had remained great friends, and this was an unfathomable pill to swallow. Thuy will always be one of my favorites. Never a complaint. Never anything but a huge smile. Such a shame. Such a waste.

Okay, so that's the Rangers. It's probably time to move on with our story and…oh, wait. I'm forgetting someone. Aren't I? Yep. That's right. I AM forgetting one Ranger. All right, fuck it. Let's rip that band-aid off right now and talk about…

David Yost. Okay, so I am going to write this as honestly as I can, with the full knowledge that I will probably make some people angry at me and start a whole thing about me having an issue with David. The truth of the matter is, I don't know where I stand with David these days. The few times I've tried to speak to him at *Power Rangers* events, he pretty much ignored me and refused to engage.

When I went to introduce him to my wife, who is the love of my life, David did the same to her and basically iced her out. I don't know whether he is harboring things from 1995 that he believes I did or said. I do know I would love nothing better than to speak with him and clear things up, whatever those things may be. For now, let me start with our younger selves and tell you what I remember about that time.

When I first met David as Billy the Blue Ranger, I was Jason's acting coach, so I didn't really have any meaningful interactions with David on any sort of work level. But I was able to observe his behavior and how he got along with others. Jason Frank had warned me that David could be a bit standoffish and a bit of a complainer, and that even at that early stage, he was not well-liked by the crew. This was in the beginning of Jason's time on the show, keep in mind. Over the years, their relationship had so many ups and downs and bizarre and unspoken complexities, it became hard to keep track of whether the two of them were getting along or not at any given moment.

From what I observed at the time, David was much more complicated than just being a "whiny little a-hole" (as he was described by one crew member). David had a wall up, emotionally, a big, strong wall that must have taken years to build, or so I assumed at the time. I had no clue he was struggling with other things that had nothing to do with the show, things that in today's world would have been much easier to deal with and help him through.

Having been an actor myself who also struggled with letting go and tried desperately to keep a lid on my emotions (the worst thing an actor can do), I spotted it instantly in David. Over time, I also saw him become increasingly uncomfortable playing his character, Billy. I heard him say on many occasions that the Nerdy Billy in the overalls and glasses thing was just a stereotype and that Billy didn't need to be a nerd to be smart. As the show progressed, David wanted his character to transition to a more subtle, less obvious Billy. Smart kids could be cool too, right? Of course they could!

David did have a point, and a very valid one at that. If you looked at it through the lens of 2025, he was dead on. But this was 1994, a time when subtlety didn't exist in kids TV shows, and it certainly didn't exist on *Power Rangers*. Additionally, Billy was beloved for what he was in the show—a nerdy guy who was super smart and gave all those smart kids out there someone in the *Power Rangers* world they could relate to. Changing him into another Jason or another Tommy would have completely thrown off the balance of the cast, which was pointless and not going to happen.

We will get more of the David Yost saga later. But for now, I will say that he was, to me, the least pleasant of all the actors I met in those very early days on *Power Rangers*. I'm sure I was among the least pleasant people he met in those early days. Suffice to say that we were both much younger and had a lot to learn about social interaction. I will say, however, that there were times that I really enjoyed hanging with David. He could be funny and fun and cool as shit. We just got off the rails somewhere, and I still would like to figure out why.

CHAPTER 10
A PIG SURPRISE

The first three episodes that aired of *Mighty Morphin Power Rangers* got an average reception in the Nielsen ratings and were absolutely blistered by the critics. I can't remember there being a single review that spoke well of the series. Nor can I remember Haim or Shuki giving a crap. By the end of the first week, *Power Rangers* was a smash hit with ratings that in today's landscape would be impossible to achieve. Back then, there were many fewer ways for kids to entertain themselves, so the networks and cable channels enjoyed viewership in the millions daily. But none of them were bringing in Power Ranger numbers. It quickly became obvious to the folks at Fox Kids that they needed to complete the initial order of 40 episodes and add 20 more to the schedule. Haim always kept it a bit hush-hush in terms of the plans moving forward, but the rumor at the time was that the show was going to be on for a while, so they needed to start writing their butts off to meet production demand.

My phone rang.

"Doug. It's Shuki. What are you doing?"

As usual, I replied that I was doing absolutely nothing, regardless of what I was actually in the middle of doing. Shuki informed me that he wanted to get me into the writers' rotation for *Power Rangers* and to do that, we were going to write an episode together. This, of course, meant that I was going to write a script based on one of his ideas and he was going to give notes and I was going to re-write it and he was going to give more notes until it was ready to be sent to production. The good news was, I got to keep all the money. Yep. The entire $2500 would be going right into my pocket. Now, that may seem like a pittance for writing a 30-minute episode of a hit TV series. But in my mind, I was getting paid half of what I had been getting for screenplays and only having to write 22 to 28 pages. SCORE! EASY MONEY! And God bless Shuki Levy for letting me keep it all. He did not have to do that.

> SIDE NOTE: As easy as I thought it would be, what I didn't realize was the VERY time-consuming and sometimes frustrating part of writing any *Power Rangers* script. This had to do with "writing out the footage." This task entailed sitting in a room with a VCR and stopping and starting a tape of the Japanese footage for that episode to log the time code of exactly what action you wanted to use and include it in the script. You then had to go back and write placeholder dialogue for the Japanese fight scenes, which would later be rewritten by the ADR staff as if none of your dialogue was ever there. This was always the grueling part. Later, when I became the showrunner, I delegated that duty to whoever was my assistant. At first, they wouldn't mind. They were getting to write on a real TV series. But after a couple of months, the look on their faces told the real story. Thankfully, in the end, both of my assistants from those days went on to become writers on the show, and one even became a showrunner himself. Just goes to show that sometimes you must endure being locked in a room with hours of Japanese TV footage you can't make heads nor tails of, to get ahead.

Speaking of Japanese footage, the package arrived at my apartment that night with a videotape of the Pudgy Pig monster from Japan. Along with that, there were two more VHS tapes with additional footage of a Goldar (Rita's gold wolf-looking henchman) fight and the appearance of Scorpina (a character from the Japanese footage we hadn't used yet). Pudgy Pig had already been used in another episode, but there was a mandate to conserve and even repurpose footage, as they would soon be running out of usable material.

As I said before, the original idea from Fox Kids had been to produce 40 episodes, with the network just praying that they made it to air before the affiliates started to drop them. When the show blew up, and the exact opposite happened, Fox ordered more episodes quickly, which left the production fishing around for anything they could use to maintain the ratio of Japanese footage to scenes shot in America. And that ratio HAD to be within an extremely low standard deviation, especially on the American footage side. As it stood, they were at a ratio of 50/50 American to Japanese and they stayed pretty much dead on to that. That way, production had the ability to keep to their schedule of shooting four shows in ten days.

When I look back on that episode, it was an incredible pain in the ass. It felt like the script was a jigsaw puzzle and I was piecing together bits of footage from several episodes to create a coherent storyline. I'm not convinced we were successful, but we quickly found out that plot holes and nonsensical cuts from one scene to another, were as common on the show as bright colors and cartoon music. The truth was, whatever you could get away with before the network figured out didn't make sense was okay with Shuki and Haim. And if it really came down to it, Haim would pick up the phone, call Margaret Loesch, and ask her to tell the executive who was making all the fuss about a scene that made no sense to stand down. And they would. I think that Margaret knew that at that point she had to keep Haim happy. *Power Rangers* was in the stratosphere, and there was no use pissing off Uncle Haim (that's what we called him) for no reason. Haim was protective of his brand and also didn't want anyone slowing down the money machine. So, pretty much everyone marched to his drumbeat.

"Pig Surprise" ended up being a "surprisingly" decent script. There were some funny lines in there and some nice moments. There was also the mishmash of footage that made the story kind of fall apart at the end, which to this day is a bummer for true fans of the show. But being a *Power Rangers* fanatic could often be a disappointing endeavor, as I later learned when I mistakenly visited a Rangers fan site with my real name, and heard thousands of angry gripes and hate speech about the show and me personally. (My favorite thread was one entitled: "DOUGLAS SLOAN MUST DIE," on the Ninja Storm message board, which I will cover extensively in Book 2. There's a whole story surrounding this call for my head, which illustrates how incredibly passionate *Power Rangers* fans are and how little patience they have for what they perceive to be screw ups.)

The next week, Shuki and I wrote another script together, the "Crystal of Nightmares." This was a bit of a different affair, as it involved the teens going to a resort in the mountains to study (stock footage) and Rita's henchman Goldar turning their dreams into nightmares and causing them to lose their confidence. Once again, it was a Goldar fight that was pieced together to account for the lack of any footage, so the end was not the best. But it's what had to be done back then while the deals were being made to bring more footage from Japan and solve the content crisis.

I went out to the set to watch them shoot the episodes, as they were both in the same block, and what do you know, my friend Bob Hughes was directing. It was great to see him, as it had been a while, and he genuinely seemed happy to have me there. We got to talking and I distinctly recall asking him what he thought the plan was for Jason Frank. The Green Ranger footage was running out, and there was going to be no way around the fact that they needed that material for Jason to remain on the show. Bob claimed he had no idea. I later discovered that he knew that there were several things Haim was working on to allow everyone to forge ahead. But

Bob wasn't giving up any information. He was a real secret squirrel when it came to company goings-on. I must commend him for this and realized on that day that Bob was someone you could let in on a sensitive bit of information and know that it would stop with him.

CHAPTER 11
MUTANTS AND SHARKS AND FLEAS, OH MY!

I had successfully passed the test of writing my first two episodes and was going to be given the chance to officially enter the rotation of writers on the *Power Rangers*. Not that any of us ever really saw one another, but there was definitely a group that the higher-ups liked to use. And there were others that certain higher-ups didn't want to use but had no choice because other higher-ups demanded they be hired. These scripts, from the "B" team, were usually rewritten many times before they made it to production. Thankfully, once Shuki had okayed the "final" script, he didn't really seem to notice if we polished up the dialogue and fixed any plot holes. He was so busy once it was delivered that he had no memory of the episode and had moved on to another emergency.

If I was going to become a regular writer on the show, I first needed to go down to production headquarters and meet with the person running the day-to-day creative. Obviously, this person was NOT Shuki. He had decided that this task was NOT something he wanted to commit to on a full-time basis. The whole idea of keeping track of all the scripts, when they had to be delivered, the last-minute fixes and all the rest of the business that is normally associated with a creative showrunner, would take far too much of his time, as he was still creating music for movies and TV shows and helping Haim continue his plans for world domination. Shuki would remain the creative force behind the show, but for the big decisions, not the day-to-day. As a result, they assigned one of the executives in the company to take over. My instructions were to go to the production office and meet with the executive to discuss my next writing assignment.

Ellen Levy Sarnoff had been with Saban Entertainment for close to a decade and oversaw creative development for the kids' division across the board. She was responsible for some big animated series and their successes, so she seemed like the logical choice to handle the creative on *Power Rangers*. Ellen was a magna cum laude graduate of Wesleyan University, spoke three languages, and had the reputation of being a brilliant and creative executive. When I first met her, I thought she was a complete lunatic, in the best way imaginable. Her desk was strewn with bits of script on different colored paper that were cut into strips so she could literally "paste" them onto a master page whenever she wanted to make changes to a script (yes, she would literally "cut" and "paste"). Having worked at a computer store during my acting days and knowing what you could do with Final Draft or whatever the screenwriting software was around back then, I was a little confused as to a) why she didn't just have them get her a Mac and do things that way, or b) why, if it was such an issue, one of the P.A.'s or her assistant didn't do it for her. I could never have kept track of all the scraps and pieces she had scattered about. But I soon learned that she knew exactly where everything was and had a kind of a system that, at the time, worked for her. Ellen didn't know how to use a computer when I first met her (many people didn't) and from what I could tell, she didn't really want to learn. She was a brilliant, successful executive. This was the way she preferred to work, and it seemed like it got the job done in the end. Who was I to question it? The person most obviously bothered by Ellen's approach was a condescending, uptight production coordinator who huffed and puffed every time she was handed a script as though she was being asked to clean out a cat box. More on that person later.

Ellen and I bonded instantly. She was hilariously funny, very kind, insanely smart, and so supportive. She had also worked with my father at some point in the past and had really nice things to say about him, including the fact that she remembered him as being very "handsome." Weird to hear that about, Dad, but okay. Anyway, we started looking through available Japanese footage so that I could find my next assignment. This was how the writing of episodes began, even for the regular writers. Several video cassettes arrived, each with a different monster from the Japanese footage, and you would pick the one you thought you could make work. You then came up with some ideas to pitch to Ellen, who would take them to Shuki for his approval, etc. Once you had your concept approved, you would write an outline. Then you would hammer out a script, and finally, the dreaded footage had to be time-coded and dialogue written out to go with the monsters and the guys in the spandex suits.

The monsters I looked at on that day were a giant flea, a poisonous dancing jellyfish, and a menacing giant lizard. I immediately felt like the flea was going to be the way to go. The story, to me, was obvious, even though I remember turning in several other pitches along with the pet adoption premise—

1. A flea circus comes into town and sets up in the park, gathering crowds from far and wide. One of the fleas is especially talented, and can ride a tiny bicycle, pull a wagon, and even break dance. We learn that the flea circus was created by Goldar, who planted the shrunken down flea monster into the attraction so that it would land on one of the Rangers and wackiness would ensue.
2. One of the moms was opening a new salon and did a day of free haircuts to promote her business. Her assistant gets kidnapped and replaced by one of the bad guys,

dumping the shrunken down flea onto the head of one of the Rangers, and the same wackiness would ensue.

In the end, those were just not quite strong enough ideas. The pet adoption pitch that eventually was used felt much more like an MMPR episode. So, I began the process, and within a couple of weeks handed in the script. Ellen had some notes, of course, but it seemed like she was pleased. Phew!

About a week later, I received another VHS tape. This time, it had just one monster on it—the "Slippery Shark," a giant hammerhead-looking thing that had a boomerang-shaped fin for a weapon. Additionally, it could travel underground with just its dorsal appendage sticking up. I remember thinking that as PR monsters went, it was not terrible. And the fight footage from Japan depicted the Red Ranger and the Green Ranger not getting along, arguing in costume about what we assumed was how to capture the Slippery Shark. It seemed obvious from the footage what the show was going to be, and there really wasn't much deep thinking that went into it. The characters of Jason and Tommy had to get in an argument and turn against one another, which would lead into the arguing spandex characters.

I came up with several ways that the two characters could have gotten into a fight. I think one was Tommy believing that Jason was trying to steal Kimberly. Another was a karate championship they were both getting ready for and started taking a little too seriously. In the end, Shuki said, "Fuck it. Rita puts them under a spell." What seemed so overly simple at the time was, in retrospect, the right way to go. It was too early for Tommy to have bad feelings about another Ranger, or for any of them to have ill will towards another. They were a team, and although we as humans argue and spat all the time, these guys knew that their friendship was too important to allow petty arguments to get in the way. So, Rita's spell it was. She's always up to something, that out-of-sync rascal!

This was the first episode that I had written with Tommy in the show. Jason had been off the series for a few episodes, but was back, much to the delight of audiences, I'm sure. This was also the first time I met Worth Keeter. He was directing this block of episodes, and even though he had directed other episodes, we had not run into one another yet. Worth was a great guy. He hailed from North Carolina and had that calming Southern vibe, where everything just moves a bit slower and easier, or at least that's how it seemed to me. Worth had been in the business a while and had experienced a lot. He had a seemingly endless supply of crazy stories from previous productions on which he had worked. Unfortunately, the only one I can remember and do justice to, would not be politically correct to repeat in today's world. But back in the day, when things were a bit looser, I laughed my ass off when I heard it.

As I was still Jason's coach, I was expected to be there for the whole block and watch my episode come to life for the first time. I even recall being asked for a few line changes on set, which I was only too happy to provide. Worth was super collaborative, and I remember that being a fun time. And my script was being shot, with Jason acting in it, was really cool.

Fortunately, I was given another script to write while the Slippery Shark episode was shooting. The footage for this one was interesting, and I remember trying to put the puzzle together in my head the first time I watched it. Rita creates a group of mutant Rangers that the real Rangers must fight. But it wasn't that simple. In the Japanese show, the original five Rangers, without Tommy, fight the mutants for about a minute or two of screen time. There is no mutant Red Ranger, but a giant crawfish monster that is the leader of the group. Then, the Green Ranger appears midway through the fight, as does the phony Green Ranger, and they all start to battle. In the end, the monster grows, they call the Zords, and that's the story. What was evident immediately was that no obvious story connection was going to be possible between the Japanese footage and what we were going to create. No one wanted to do a crawfish story. The idea of a crawfish monster growing out of a table covered in them while being enjoyed by the Rangers was ridiculous. I brought it up once as a joke, and Shuki looked at me like I'd lost my mind.

This episode was the beginning of what would become a string of challenging scripts we needed to write for the show. Even with the mega success of that first year of the *Mighty Morphin Power Rangers*, there was a problem that was unavoidable. There simply was no more Green Ranger footage. We had used every frame of it. Meanwhile, Fox Kids had, as you remember, ordered another 20 episodes. They pulled the trigger the moment the show became a hit. Great news in many ways. But we needed to figure out a way to bring Tommy and the Green Ranger back into the fold. We couldn't just say goodbye to him. He was fast becoming the most popular Ranger. Kids would be devastated if Jason Frank wasn't on the show. We needed to find a way to keep the "Green Dude" around.

Of course, Haim was way ahead of the problem. So far ahead in fact that, it never actually became a problem. In his infinite wisdom, Haim had gone right back to the source and contracted TOEI, the Japanese production company responsible for the Rangers footage we were using. He made a deal with them to shoot a bunch of additional material featuring the Green Ranger that we could use to finish out the season. They were only too happy to oblige and even sent the rubber monster suits over for us when they were done using them.

Once the costumes arrived in a giant shipping container, it became evident that we were going to need a dedicated "monster wrangler," someone to keep track of each costume, including what condition it was in and make sure that the right creature got to the set on the right day. They promoted a Key (senior-level) Production Assistant to fill the position, a hilarious little curly-haired guy from New York named Jon Countess, who was a cross between Lenny Bruce and Mighty Mouse. Jon brought great energy and commitment to his new job as monster wrangler, almost growing attached to the creatures he cared for. He took the job very seriously and made sure that if there was a creature on the call sheet, it arrived on set in the best shape possible via his old VW bus. It was a crapshoot every day as to whether that van was going to fire up on its own or need to be jump started. But Jon and the monsters always made it to set.

One day there was a massive battle scheduled that included about a dozen of the monsters. So, naturally, Jon packed them into the VW van and belted them into seats so that they couldn't move around. From the outside, it looked like a van full of actual creatures, passengers on some crazy bus ride to hell. On that day, a California Highway Patrol officer pulled Jon and his bus full of monsters over before Jon even made it to the freeway. The officer asked Jon why he was driving a bus full of monsters. Jon's response was, "You see them, too? Thank God! I thought I was the only one!" The cop apparently thought this was hilarious and let Jon go about his business after taking a few shots with the monsters for his children. I would have given anything to have seen it. Great line.

When the new footage began arriving from Japan, it was indeed very Green Ranger-centric, ergo the episodes would be very Tommy-centric. I remember thinking that now would be a great time to produce a character-based episode that gave Tommy something besides the usual martial arts, Tommy and Kimberly love story, and the evil Tommy stuff. I pitched to Shuki and Ellen, who was running creative on the show at that time, that Jason Frank was evolving as an actor, and we should give him something he could throw himself into that felt real (as real as *Power Rangers* could get). They thought it was worth a shot, so, like any good Power Ranger writer, I started with Ms. Appleby. (Kidding, of course. I mean, she was a fine actor, but…never mind.) As I was saying, I came up with the idea for Ms. Appleby to give the kids the assignment to ask their friends what their biggest fault was. Once this was established, the students would attempt to correct the fault their friends pointed out. It was a simple story, but was based on their personal character traits, something most kids could relate to.

Tommy asked the other Rangers what they thought his major flaw was, and it became clear that they all felt he was forgetful at times. The script went on to show examples of this to set up the story. Of course, this was a bit of a reach, as we had never once witnessed Tommy being absent-minded in any of the other episodes. So, we needed to hammer home that this WAS a character trait of Tommy Oliver. No one seemed too bothered by the fact that this came out of nowhere. It also ended up being a great way to give all the Rangers a chance to interact with Tommy in a meaningful way, as they tried to help him find a solution to his "brain farts."

> SIDE NOTE: At this point in time, Jason Frank had started to allow his inner JDF to emerge. He was still a polite, kind, sweet kid, but there was also a sarcastic little shit hidden inside who had started to poke its head out—not in any bad way, just funny and, at times, surprising. JDF was hilarious. If you watch the end of the mutant Ranger episode, the teens are all laughing at Bulk and Skull when they open a gift meant for Ms. Appleby and Silly String explodes all over them. Jason and the others were supposed to get a big kick out of this and have a good hearty laugh. Jason, I could tell, felt like this was lame and over the top and wasn't really going to go there, although the director kept insisting. Finally, Jason unloaded a maniacal phony cackling that was completely beyond what had been asked of him. He also had this crazed look in his eyes. I was off set watching and was laughing so hard I had to leave. I figured they would reset the camera and do another take. They didn't. They kept it. If you look at the episode, at the very end, you can see and hear it. Jason looks crazy! What I didn't know at the time, of course, was that this was merely the very tip of a massive iceberg that ran deep into Jason's psyche and would awaken bit by bit over the course of the show. What was funny then would eventually not be quite as enjoyable. As Jason pushed the boundaries of what he could get away with, he began to pull away from the series and the friends he worked with.

Anyway, the script came out better than I could have hoped. It had a lot of good character moments in it and even offered a lesson for the viewers at the end, which was that your faults are part of what make you who you are, and if your friends are truly your friends, they will accept you regardless. I was excited as hell when they started to shoot.

Terry Winkless would oversee this block of episodes. He was another director with a lot of previous experience and was also very talented. There was something about the way he set up shots that was super clever and had a quirky, different feel, which I thought was true to the spirit of the show we were doing. After all, it was a live-action cartoon, and there needed to be a little weirdness in the way it looked. Terry nailed that.

In terms of openness and willingness to interact, at least with me, Terry was miles away from Worth Keeter or Bob Hughes. He was sarcastic with a dry, sharp wit that never rested. And, whether this was intentional or not, he came off as a bit condescending, again, at least to me. But remember, I was the acting coach and a writer. I was mostly there to get in the way. I'm sure he saw this episode as a nice opportunity to work with the actors, and there I was, with Jason, doing the very thing he was probably psyched about doing. I never really had the chance to ask him about that, but I did notice that things became a lot easier once I was made a producer on the series. Dynamics do tend to change quickly in the TV and movie biz when your credit appears *before* the show begins instead of *after*.

So, in large part due to Terry's great directing and Jason Frank and the rest of the Rangers totally nailing their parts, it turned out to be one of my favorite episodes. Bulk and Skull were hilarious as usual, and Ms. Appleby was great. It was the first time I really felt like I had gotten something I'd written on film that I could be proud of. And, as this was Episode 59, and the penultimate show of season one, I was excited to see what the next year would bring. In keeping with the weirdness and unpredictability of my journey at Saban, it was freaking crazy.

CHAPTER 12
I JUST WANT TO DO CYBERTRON!

As the season ended, it had become glaringly obvious to more than just Haim and Shuki that there was something special about Jason Frank. He was a star, pure and simple. It didn't take a genius to figure out that JDF had the goods to make a go of it beyond the spandex and martial arts world of *Power Rangers*. Jason could carry a show of his own, and that must have been exactly what my bosses thought as they started to develop the idea of Jason having his own series. Smartly, Haim was stocking up on footage from other shows that aired in Japan for future use in the U.S. I think Haim figured he was going to keep getting shows on the air, and since the footage was relatively cheap, why not? The first order of business was that *Power Rangers* needed a companion series. Clearly, an hour of Saban in that afternoon Fox Kids block of shows would mean more money going into the Saban coffers and the time to strike was right then and there. So, using the footage from a Japanese series called *Metalder*, the idea for *Cybertron* was born.

In the source material, *Metalder* was a lone hero who went to war against a machine army and blew a lot of stuff up. It was A LOT darker and more violent than *Power Rangers*, but it was cool enough and had a great setup for Jason as a lead character who wouldn't have to share screen time with five other Rangers. Shuki and Haim decided to shoot a presentation pilot with Jason Frank in the lead to take advantage of his growing popularity and act as a sales tool for the series. I really can't remember who wrote the script for the pilot, but I'm pretty sure Shuki had a hand in it somewhere along the way. And I must have been around as well, because somehow, I was recruited to play Jason's long-lost father Tyler Steele (seen in flashbacks). Jason's character was Adam Steele, a young martial artist, heartbroken over the disappearance of his father and determined to learn his dad's fate by using the technology of *Cybertron,* a robotic fighting machine/suit similar in many ways to Iron Man. The pilot presentation told a completely different story than what ultimately ended up being *VR Troopers*. Yes, there were some similarities, including the sensei, played by the late Richard Rabago; the Villain, Richter (later Zichter due to legal clearance issues with the name Richter); and scenes of Adam sitting on top of a mountain at a pagoda by himself, recapping the episode in voice-over. But that was kind of it. The comic relief was a goofy pair of guys (one played by Jamie Kennedy who went on to have success as a comedian and actor) who carried around a video camera and recorded everything in sight as their "schtick." They were clearly meant to be the Bulk and Skull of the show and even had the same music during their scenes in the pilot. The villain, Cyrus Richter, had a son, Percy, also a martial arts expert, who was Adam's nemesis in the real world. Finally, there was Mia. She was the daughter of the sensei and was meant to round out the cast and bring the girl appeal. There was no talking dog or flying car, and the character of Percy ended up being quite different in later incarnations.

Bob Hughes shot the seven-minute pilot presentation with the plan that he would run the series if it got picked up. Presentations are incredibly hard to execute successfully. First, you are usually starting without a full-length pilot script that you can pull scenes from and shoot. You have to capture the essence of the show you are trying to sell and make sure that the viewers understand what it's about and how cool it's going to be. They were lucky to have Bob Hughes helming the project. Bob is a great director and storyteller and got some amazing images and performances with the limited time and budget afforded him. The other thing in their favor was that there was all that action footage from Japan that they could cut into the piece. And they did…quite cleverly and quite liberally.

My part in the pilot was a flashback Christmas scene where my character gives a young Adam (played by a child actor) a toy that looks like the *Cybertron* robot. We then hug, I utter a few lines, and that was it. You can find this presentation on YouTube and check it out for yourself. The one time I saw it I was so horrified by my bad acting that I never watched it again. It was awful. At that moment, I vowed to return to the stage one day (sound or theatre) and give a far better performance to at least prove to myself that I hadn't wasted seven years of my life chasing an unachievable pot of gold.

And so, with the pilot shot, the process of editing it together, scoring the music, and adding the visual effects began. Once finished, it would then be taken out to the syndication market to sell. Fox Kids was not going to be involved with the series as directly as they were on *Power Rangers*. I'm not sure exactly why, but I believe that one possibility pointed to the fact that they felt it was too dark and too violent and would never pass the Broadcast Standards and Practices department, which at the time was run by a woman everyone called the Church Lady because of her tough stance on anything that could traumatize the audience or cause them to try to imitate their TV heroes. Apparently, *Cybertron* was sure to do that, with the robots blowing up and their heads and other appendages flying towards camera before they died a gruesome death.

> SIDE NOTE: BS&P, which stands for Broadcast Standards and Practices, was a department that was there to police the network's shows to ensure that they didn't violate any of the

violence, morality, or ethics rules set up to protect the company from litigation. For kids TV, the rules were even more intense. The key phrase that we all came to know and love was "imitatable behavior." If kids were watching a show where someone jumped off a roof and landed safely, this was something our viewers could imitate at their own house and was therefore discouraged. Our characters weren't allowed to hit anyone in the head, neck, or face. That was a serious no-no. Our Rangers always had to be wearing seatbelts, proper safety gear for skateboarding or any other action sport, and the list goes on. And this was true for any network that aired shows for preschoolers all the way up to adults.

The Disney Channel was no different. While working on *Princess Protection Program*, Selena Gomez and Tom Verica shot all day in an open-air 1960s Jeep. I was off set that day, and when I ran into our producer later that night, I was informed that the work that had been completed in the Jeep was an issue. The footage looked great, except for one problem: neither actor was wearing a seatbelt. The reason, as it was explained to me, was that this vehicle, an older model, had no seatbelts. So, no one thought it would be an issue for Disney. I was pretty sure it would be an issue, and it was. But thanks to our brilliant producer, Danielle Weinstock, we were able to make a deal to create CGI seatbelts that looked every bit as real as seatbelts would have, had they been used in the scene. So that was one of the theories as to why the *Cybertron* presentation was not gaining traction at Fox Kids. You can go against a lot of folks, but you can't go against the Church Lady, wherever she may be lurking.

There WAS another completely alternate theory floating around about *Cybertron*'s difficulties finding a home, one that I personally found fascinating. The thought was that Haim had decided that with the success of *Power Rangers*, it would be in the company's best interest to fund the series not by the licensing fee they would receive from a network, but by selling it to individual markets and stations and compiling that income from those presales to pay the cost of the show. I have a feeling it may have been a combination of a lot of things. What I do know is that in the end, Fox Kids put the show on the air, and it seemed to me that they let a lot of stuff pass that would never have flown on *Power Rangers*.

While *Cybertron* was slowly being put together and sold into syndication, Saban needed to keep Jason Frank occupied in order to keep him in the family. So, of course, back he went to *Power Rangers*. Although Jason was happy to continue working, he was completely freaked out that things were taking so long to come together on *Cybertron*. He had developed a quite detailed, if not humorous (just the way Jason deflected things that were important to him), paranoid fantasy that they were going to keep him chained to *Power Rangers* and recast *Cybertron* with another actor. When we would talk in those days between the pilot and the ultimate decision to rework *Cybertron*, he became obsessed with the idea of being in the show. Even though *Power Rangers* was hugely successful, Jason didn't seem to care. He would repeat again and again, "I just want to do *Cybertron*, man. I just want to do *Cybertron*." Every time I saw him—in the parking lot at the stages, in my apartment for coaching or his dressing room in the morning—that had become his mantra. As I had no idea of the ultimate plan, all I could do was tell him that as far as I knew, that was exactly what he was going to be doing. But, in the meantime, at least, he had work on *Power Rangers* which allowed him to continue his acting journey. His response was always, "Yeah, but I just want to do *Cybertron*." One day he saw me walking to my car from inside the production offices. He ran full speed down the stairs and out the door, just to tell me that he "just wanted to do *Cybertron!*"

This period was the first time that I was witness to Jason Frank becoming well and truly fixated on something. This obsession, I felt at the time, was excessive. It was also the first time I saw a real vulnerability in him. No matter what I said to Jason, the fact that it always took this long to sell a show, or that he was better off on Rangers for the time being, or that he was going to be a huge star, none of it mattered. It was as though any information passed through one ear and out the other, with no stop to apply logic in between. All I could do at that point was listen to him, hug him when he broke down in tears, and tell him everything was going to turn out awesome and that I had his back.

CHAPTER 13
SERIOUSLY DUDE, I JUST WANT TO DO CYBERTRON!

As time dragged on...and on...and on...the Tommy character was literally exploding in popularity on *Power Rangers*. The last of the new Green Ranger footage was gone, but there was another season arriving from Japan that featured a VERY cool White Ranger who would be used in the U.S. version of the show. Of course, it became instantly clear to the higher ups what needed to be done with this new character. Not only that, but the talk of a full-length *Power Rangers* feature had become very real, and appeared to be a done deal. The studio couldn't ignore what this weird little TV series was doing in the ratings every afternoon, and they were not going to squander the opportunity to capitalize on that in movie theaters.

As all this was going on, the ever-growing audience for *Mighty Morphin Power Rangers* was frustrated with Jason Frank leaving the show and returning to the show over and over. They wanted Tommy back permanently. He had clearly become the most popular of the Rangers and the fans wanted him there on an ongoing basis. Jason had received a call from Shuki telling him that the plan was to bring Tommy back as the White Ranger and then that character would star in the movie and be the leader of the

Rangers in following seasons. They would also be pumping tons of money into publicity for the White Ranger, even securing a spot for Jason in the White Rangers costume, helmet off, on a future cover of TV Guide.

> SIDE NOTE: TV Guide was the small magazine that came out every week listing what was going to be on TV for the next seven days. Getting on the cover of TVG was a major win. And for Jason to be considered for a solo cover was unreal. He was on a kid's show. It was his first job ever. And he was going to be on the cover? To put it into perspective, that same year, Jerry Seinfeld, George Clooney, and Michael Jackson were a few of the stars to appear on the cover of TV Guide. Not bad company.

For anyone else, all this news would have been mind-blowing. It was a bit like winning the young actor lottery: Hit show, big Hollywood movie, TV Guide. I, for one, was over the moon. I felt like in some small way, I had helped Jason become a serviceable actor and as a result helped launch him into the stratosphere in our little world of kids TV. See if you can guess what Jason said to me when he called me right after he hung up with Shuki. Let's say it together everyone…and…action! "Doug, man, I just want to do *Cybertron*. I just want to do *Cybertron*." And…CUT!

Sorry to be a buzzkill, but this is the part of our story where we must put away all things warm and fuzzy. I had to throw down some tough love to my buddy. I hated to do it. But Jason needed to hear what the reality of his situation was. First, we had to get him off of the *Cybertron* thing. Fortunately, I had been thinking about this and was waiting for the opportunity to spell it out for him.

"Dude, I promise you, you do *not* want to do *Cybertron*. You have to trust me on this," I insisted. "No matter who's on that show, the footage is crap, there's not that much of it, and that show is never going to be what *Power Rangers* is. I'm thinking it's two years and out for that series. You'll be looking for work again, I promise you. You'll miss out on the movie, and some other a-hole is going to be on the cover of TV guide."

There was a silence on the other end of the phone. "Yeah, I guess so. But…"

I cut him off. "Jason. Buddy. By the end of next year, you will be a movie star. No joke. You will have starred in a feature film that will be the hit of the summer. It will open doors for you that you can't even imagine right now." Silence. "If I was your manager or agent, I would do anything I had to do to keep you on *Power Rangers*. Anything."

At the time, I didn't feel as though I was making empty promises to him. We all knew what was coming. The movie was going to be seen by everyone. Jason would be the star of a huge summer blockbuster. His stock was bound to skyrocket, introducing him to the world of movies and nighttime TV. The possibilities were literally endless. He could finish up his commitments to Haim and Shuki and move on with a real agent pushing him and unlimited opportunities.

Of course, I was wasting my breath. Jason wanted what he wanted—what he had been promised (in his mind). He desperately wanted his own show, and it was weighing heavily on him. I think he knew in his heart that he was not going to be in the new series, and it was tough for him to let go of the idea of that whole thing, regardless of what the realities were.

This whole series of events is a hard scenario to get your head around unless you'd spent a lot of time with Jason David Frank. He seemed like such a badass. And a part of him WAS a badass. However, for all his bravado and fierce fighting abilities, deep down, Jason Frank was an incredibly sensitive artist. He was also a child at heart. Not that he was childish—more that there was an innocence in him. It was not unusual for him to break down during our many conversations when he felt like things were going sideways and he had no control of his life. (The sight of tears welling up in Jason Frank's eyes was compounded by the fact that they would gather on his insanely long eyelashes and just sit there before they fell. It made the whole thing so much more dramatic and so much sadder.) Day after day, I let him talk it through and get it all out, which he needed to do. He had been under a ton of mostly self-imposed stress, desperate to know what his future would bring. It was literally driving him insane. Now, at least the question had been answered, and he could begin to heal. He couldn't see it yet, as his mind was all clouded with other garbage, but this turn of events was going to put him on top of the world. He had no clue what that even meant or what was in store for him. Young actors rarely do.

> SIDE NOTE: Again, years later I was on the set of *Princess Protection Program* while they were re-setting the lights for a scene. Again, Demi Lovato sat down on the couch next to me and commented casually that she was going to be going to New York to perform a song that she had written at some big gathering for Disney Channel and their partners. I had heard about this, because it required a slight tweaking of our schedule to allow for the trip. There would be hundreds of important people at this event, and clearly they were rolling Demi out as their next big star. I thought back to the time before Jason's career took off and how similar this moment felt. I asked Demi if she was ready for it, if she knew what was coming. She was still a kid, just fifteen at this point, and she had no idea that her life would never be the same, just as Jason didn't before the White Ranger happened. She was in no way ready for what was to come in terms of how famous she became and the stress she would endure under the pressure of superstardom.
>
> There was a year there where I fully expected to get a phone call telling me that Demi had passed away for one reason or another. Ironically, I DID receive that call years later, but it was with the news that we had lost Jason Frank. Demi seems to be thriving, which is something for which I am truly grateful.

Regardless of anything that's been written or said about her, the mistakes she may or may not have made while navigating her celebrity, she was always very sweet and super polite with me, and I adore her to this day.

Not too long after his phone call with Shuki, Jason approached me at the stages and said he had something he wanted to give me. Hmmm. *That's weird,* I thought. We had been through so much insanity and turmoil that the idea that he had something to give me instantly gave me pause. I had been tapped to work as the staff writer on *VR Troopers,* the show that was previously *Cybertron,* and I still wasn't sure how he felt about that. (As I said, we're jumping around chronologically. It will all make sense. I promise!) The opportunity came up after the decision was made to recast the new show's lead and keep Jason on *Power Rangers.* But I wasn't sure Jason fully understood that. Was he going to "give me" a well-placed kick to the gut for what he could perceive as me playing both sides?

We met out in the parking lot, and it was in this moment that I learned something very important about Jason Frank's inner psyche. It was another piece of the complicated puzzle that comprised this incredibly talented but sometimes tortured soul. He sat me down on the curb and pulled out a small box with a bow on it and handed it to me. I was taken aback, so caught up in my paranoid fantasy of getting a kick in the gut from the Green Ranger that I had completely written off the idea that this could be a nice moment. I opened the box, and inside was a beautiful gold cigarette lighter (I was known to smoke a bit back in the day—thankfully, that habit is long gone). On the lighter was an inscription which read, *"Doug. Thank you so much for all your help. Love, the Green Dude."* I, of course welled up. Jason did as well. We hugged for what seemed like a long time. I then proceeded to fire up a Marlboro Light with the new lighter to calm my nerves.

As I took the first drag, Jason went on to tell me that he was so glad, so relieved, that he didn't take the new show (not his choice, but whatever). He knew *Power Rangers* was the right move and he was totally psyched to go to Australia to film the movie. Now, some might say that he was just putting on a brave face and trying to get past all the hurt and pain he'd put himself through. But this was NOT the case. I had watched as Jason's brain cause him to obsess over *Cybertron* to the point of complete distraction. On that day, I learned that once Jason was over something, it was gone. He didn't dwell on *Cybertron*/*VR Troopers* for even a second. Once his brain made the switch, the turnaround was immediate and absolute. Stupid me: I thought he would lose his mind having to watch another dude get the role on *VR Troopers*. The idea of him watching the show start production without him worried me. Not to mention the fact that I was going to be working full time on the series. I was expecting a complete meltdown, not a beautiful engraved lighter, a gift that was truly from the heart. But this was how Jason was wired. He was genuinely excited about the future, the movie, the series continuing afterward. He was taking meetings with big-time movie people. Fox Kids was about to air the umpteenth return of Tommy, which everyone was excited about. There was a buzz around the company that the series was going to get another order of 60 episodes. Haim had even invited Jason to dinner to make sure he was aware of his importance to the company.

So: Jason was cool, I had a new fancy gold lighter, and I was moving into the next phase of my time with Saban. All was right in Angel Grove, and I could return to my new little office next door and do my best to help Bob Hughes turn this new show into a great companion piece for *Power Rangers*.

CHAPTER 14
INTRODUCING BZ AND LITTLE BZ

On a TV series or movie, there are many types of producers. In TV, there are supervising producers, executive producers, co-executive producers, and the list goes on. The executive producer on a TV series is also known as the showrunner. He or she is the person who oversees the creative vision of the series. Someone must have, in their brain, all the answers to what the right or wrong creative choices are for the show. From the season arc, the individual scripts, the shooting of the show, the editing, mixing, and beyond, the EP, as they are also called, is the person who is the last line of defense against anything that does not belong in the world that has been created for the series. This has been my job for close to 30 years, although technically that was NOT my job on *Power Rangers* at Saban.

I think the reason I'm decent at this whole TV thing is that my attention span is that of a teacup Chihuahua. It always has been. As a result, I've done pretty much every creative job involved with a production from editing, to directing, to writing, to acting, to scoring and songwriting, and the list goes on. It's a bit freakish, the things that have been lodged in my brain over the years. And I have no idea how they got there.

I recall when producing *DreamWorks Dragons*, I was sitting in a sound playback, where the final mix of an episode is played for the producers and network executives. In the middle of the playback, I asked them to stop, as something felt "off" to me. It was something in the music, a particular instrument that was out of tune. And, sure enough, when the harp was isolated, it was hitting a couple of seriously sour notes. Let it be known that these little flubs would have had zero effect on the success of the show. No one would have even noticed or cared. But that didn't matter. My job was to be there as a backstop for ANYTHING that was incorrect and fixable. That's the job of the executive producer. Other producers are part of the writing room, others are executives at the production company who are getting a credit (I've even seen a network executive take the executive producer credit, which is SO lame), while a specific type, the line producer, is in charge making sure that the show is delivered on time and for the money that has been allocated to the budget. The line producer's role is important but probably the least associated with creative decisions.

There's an old saying that line producers spend most of their time trying to get the word "line" out of their title. Over the years, I have found this to be more of a dopey quip than a fact. The line producers I have worked with were so busy focusing on their jobs that they didn't have time to get involved with the creative. Some even told me they were glad not to be a part of it, as their job was black and white, numbers, "yes" or "no," never "maybe." It's a pressure-filled position, but not one that has to deal with the misguided studio exec who wants to see changes like putting Band-Aids on a male actor's nipples so that they aren't seen under his tee shirt, or refusing to allow the application of makeup that's supposed to make a character appear unattractive in a particular scene because it would have made the character *too* unattractive.

On *Power Rangers*, the line producer was a former Israeli fighter pilot who had come to the U.S. and worked his way up in the film business to the point that he was now in charge of the logistics and budget for *Power Rangers*. My initial dealings with him were scant, as I didn't really become a full-time part of the series until after I had finished with *VR Troopers*. He seemed like a nice enough guy, although there was a layer of arrogance that was hard to ignore, and at times just made my whole body tighten up. And maybe he had earned the right to be arrogant. After all, if you fly fighter jets during a war, you get to be at least a little cocky.

The first couple of years I was working at Saban, I didn't think much about him. I knew that he had a mini-me kind of guy who was the production manager on the series. They dressed alike and were never seen too far apart from one another. One of them was always rushing around with a walkie-talkie in his hand like he was supervising the delivery of a donor heart for Haim himself.

It was kind of funny in the beginning. The mini-me production manager was an aspiring writer and had been given a couple of opportunities to write for the show. His scripts were average. Not great. Not terrible. The issue with the guy was that he wanted to argue about every note given to him by Ellen Levy Sarnoff who, as part of her job as creative producer, supervised the writing on the show. It drove her crazy as I remember, but he was mini-me to another producer, so it was a weird dynamic for her. But this person, it was obvious, felt like he had every right to keep Ellen in hour-long meetings that should have been five minutes because he wanted to "discuss" every note. The truth was, the script was going to get rewritten anyway, so why even bother?

I will get into much more depth regarding BZ and Little BZ later. For now, what I wanted to establish was how I will refer to them in this book, as giving them any sort of recognition by naming them was never going to happen. I had a lot of ideas, but what seemed most appropriate was BZ and Little BZ, a shortened version of the name Beelzebub, a moniker for Satan in the Christian faith. Beelzebub was one of the seven deadly demons. The name seemed to fit BZ quite well once I experienced the totality of his arrogance and the absolute cruelty with which he could treat people. So, that's it on these two for now. BZ and his mini-me, Little BZ. They will be back later and will not disappoint.

Oh, and Freddie Mercury, you genius frontman for the brilliant rock band Queen and arbiter of all it means to be an artist, if you are looking down from above, I apologize for using this word that is, in modern days, attributed to your masterpiece "Bohemian Rhapsody," but you know how it is, darling. Sometimes things simply cannot be avoided.

CHAPTER 15
HOW ABOUT A PEACE CONFERENCE?!

With all the talk of the feature film and Jason Frank being back in the fold, all six of the Rangers felt (rightly so) that this was their chance to adjust their contracts and start earning union wages. With that would come great health coverage, pension contributions, and everything else that goes along with being in the Screen Actors Guild.

The six of them agreed, much like the *Friends* cast did later, that they would go in as a group and demand a raise. However, David Yost, Jason Frank, and Amy Jo decided at the last minute, for whatever reason, not to push for the raise. I never got a straight story as to why this happened. I know that Jason Frank had been promised certain side projects that would earn him extra money, and that AJ and David, for whatever reason, usually sided with Jason over the other three Rangers. So, maybe that was it. I can only speculate. I just know that the idea of being in a giant movie that was going to open in theatres all over the world was a really hard thing to risk. Also, I truly believe that it was impossible for a young person in their early twenties to comprehend the enormity of what changing their minds would mean and how it would affect Thuy, Austin, and Walter, who chose to stick to their guns and push for more money.

SIDE NOTE: If you look at the episodes that were on the air around this time, you will notice several new characters who were given an unusual amount of screen time as compared to the usual guest actors. Two that come to mind were Richie and Curtis. Richie was a good-looking lad who worked at the Juice Bar beside Ernie. He was a handsome Latin teen with a great smile, and that was about it. Nothing much beneath the surface, but how would you know? It's not like he was asked to flex his acting chops. Then there was Curtis, Zack's cousin who played the trumpet, had a dance background, and was kind of a poor man's, well, Zack.

There has always been speculation that the reason these guys were brought onto the show was to steer viewers away from the idea that Tommy was coming back as the White Ranger. And, in part, this might have been true. However, the feeling I got at the time was that Richie and Curtis were there as more than just red herrings. The issues of pay raises among the actors had begun to escalate and become a real pain for Haim. I feel like Richie and Curtis were also there to throw a bit of fear into the hearts of the actors who were threatening to leave if their demands weren't met. It was like bringing in a first-round draft pick rookie quarterback to get the veteran starter to sign his contract and stop making waves.

The issue for me back then was that these two had none of the charm or charisma that the original guys had, even after the multiple episodes in which they appeared. And the idea that anyone would think they one of them would become the new White Ranger seemed like a stretch. But, hey, it was *Power Rangers*. Anything could happen and often did. Not in this case, though. Shuki and Haim could have easily thrown them in there as the new Rangers if the others left. But Curtis would have merely reminded the audience of how great Walter was in his role. As for Richie, the kid was a charmer and had the looks. If he ever figured out the acting side of it all, he would have been competition that Tommy didn't need. And Tommy was the leader. He was the star. Any new Ranger would have to be a sidekick with no hope of ever usurping Tommy's status as the high commander.

As shooting continued and the movie talk escalated, Walter, Austin, and Thuy did not back down. They shared the same agent who was pushing them to hold fast, convinced that Saban would come around. In any other normal Hollywood negotiation, that would have been decent advice. However, the actors and their rep had a couple of things going against them. First off, the three actors were not the most popular Rangers on the show. Jason and Amy Jo had become the central focus of the series by this time. It was clear that as popular as the others were, they were not Tommy and Kimberly. Second, the actors and their rep were dealing with Haim Saban. "He's a different cat," as one of my favorite guitarists of all time, Steve Lukather, likes to say when someone is out of the ordinary. Haim doesn't respond well to threats and in fact seems to take them as an opportunity to prove his point by crushing the one doing the threatening. Add to this the fact that the actors had legally binding contracts they signed with no coercion or pressure, and the fact that Haim had replaced the original Yellow Ranger from the pilot for the same reason. Clearly, Haim would not be afraid to do the same with Thuy, Austin, and Walter.

Haim once told me that there are two things kids love more than anything in the world: dinosaurs and robots. "We have both," he said. "Why does it matter who drives them?" He then went on to remind me that in *Super Sentai*, the Japanese show that supplied *Power Rangers* its footage, they changed the cast every year, and it had been on the air for 30 seasons. "30 seasons! Can you believe that?" Who knew that would be a harbinger of things to come?

So, with a boatload of steely determination and not a drop of visible perspiration, Haim stood his ground. The three Rangers stood their ground—and then the ground collapsed beneath them.

Goodbye Trini, Jason (Austin's character, not Jason Frank), and Zack. Hello Aisha, Rocky, and Adam. Boom! It seems like it happened overnight, but of course it didn't. There was a huge search, kept under wraps, and Steve Cardenas (Rocky), Karan Ashley (Aisha), and Johnny Yong Bosch (Adam) were the three actors they found. These three would soon step into the biggest roles on kids TV and then appear in a huge feature film that would commence shooting in a few months. That's quite a tall order for any actor. Unfortunately, these three weren't truly actors yet. But the team needed to find out exactly how far they were from being serviceable in their new roles. So, it kind of made sense that I got the call.

Shuki asked me to take the three newcomers outside the soundstage in Valencia and onto the grass at the edge of the parking lot to run lines and see where they were in terms of their acting abilities. Of course I was happy to, as the curiosity was killing me. I figured they needed to be at least at a certain level, or they were going to get swallowed up by the enormous presence that was Jason David Frank and the experience of Amy Jo Johnson and David Yost.

When we sat down on the grass, all three of the new Rangers were polite, considerate, and seemed truly excited to be there. It quickly became evident that Karan Ashley was not going to have any issue fitting right in. She had some very real acting skills and brought a little sass to the role, something that was lacking with the former lineup. "This might work out after all," I thought. If the guys were half as good as Karan, we were fine. Unfortunately, half as good turned out to be a monumental "overreach."

Johnny Yong Bosch might be one of the nicest, most polite human beings I'd ever met. He was soft-spoken and kind, with the heart of an artist. However, it was clear that he was way out of his element at that time in his development as a performer. Johnny was there because he was a martial artist. As for his skills as an actor, there weren't many. Nor was there any reason there should have been—he had never studied acting. A week before, he'd been training in the art of Kung Fu, and now he was sitting on a patch of grass listening to some idiot (me) try to teach him the craft of acting in the hour they had allotted before a costume fitting. It was as though I was a tennis coach trying to prepare someone who had never held a racquet for their first match at Wimbledon thinking there was a chance they would even be able to return a serve. What made it even more frustrating to me was that Johnny had that martial arts/athlete work ethic. Had he been given the same time as Jason Frank to get up to speed, Johnny probably would have picked it up very quickly, as I'm sure he would have worked tirelessly to do so. But there simply was not that time. Johnny was going to struggle for a while, and there was really nothing I could do to help him in such a short amount of time. I felt terrible about it, but what could I do?

Steve Cardenas was another one. Like Johnny, he was a talented martial artist, a black belt by the time he was 16 (if I remember correctly), and a gifted athlete. Like Johnny, Steve had zero acting experience. However, where Johnny was relaxed, almost sleepy in his performance, Steve had this visible nervous energy that for me was hard to get used to. As nice a guy as he was, Steve was like a nervous puppy who was SO desperate to do things right that it came out as this weird combination of trying too hard and shutting himself down in fear of doing or saying the wrong thing. I had never experienced anything like it before and never have since. Looking back, I feel like the poor guy just had no idea what he was getting himself into when he auditioned. A movie or TV set can be an incredibly intense place. If you aren't familiar with that, it can also seem completely crazy. Then when you add in the fact that it was the *Power Ranger* set, where it was not unusual to see a guy lugging several giant rubber monsters across the parking lot, or a five-foot-two Japanese man with orange hair dressed in the Pink Ranger's spandex skirt, smoking a cigarette in front of the production offices, or a very scary-looking bodyguard in a dark suit with sunglasses standing outside the door carrying a sidearm, and the place was the capital of crazy town USA. Not to mention the fact that these actors were expected to replace the original Rangers, so there was an insane amount of pressure on them.

Steve, at that moment, at least to me, was unteachable in the time we had. Again, I felt terrible about it. But, as an acting coach, you must be able to estimate people's limitations and decide whether they can achieve what is being asked of them. In this case, I didn't think Steve or Johnny could deliver what was being asked —and it was truly NOT fair to them. And it certainly wasn't their fault.

I place the blame for this squarely on the shoulders of those who hired them. The whole process was rushed, and it wasn't these kids' fault that they got their dream job and signed on the dotted line. Who wouldn't have? I would have at the drop of a hat. And what kid even thinks about the fact that they may not be equipped to handle the job they've been hired to do? Most folks don't understand that acting is an art, performed by skilled people who have had years of training and practice. It's not any different than driving a race car or playing a musical instrument or reaching the finals at Wimbledon. Through the years when it was my responsibility to choose guest cast members, I always put acting as the number one criterion. The martial arts stuff could be left to stunt doubles. I guess what I'm saying is that none of this was the new trio's fault. It was the situation, and it was going to be interesting (one way or the other) to see how it played out.

I reported back to Shuki and let him know that I felt bad about all of it, but I wasn't sure what could be done. Time was not in abundance, and that's exactly what we needed with Steve and Johnny if we were going to get them up to speed, especially for the feature.

I should have known how he'd react, but it still caught me off guard. In his inimitable style, he just laughed and said, "You worry too much, Doug." He explained to me that it would work itself out just like it did every time.

I thought to myself, *In the Wonka-esque world of Shuki, it probably does every time.* At that moment, I had the luxury of laughing along with him, as I was meant to be writing *VR Trooper* scripts and not coaching actors. They would have to figure it out somehow. Shuki was probably right. I did worry too much.

The next order of business was how to get Jason, Trini, and Zack out of Angel Grove and get these three noobs into the command center to be *Power Rangers*. Of course, the three OGs had left on not-so-great terms and refused to film any scenes that would facilitate their characters' departure. I didn't blame them at all for that. But it did leave us having to figure out how to get the task done without them. A meeting was called and a bunch of ideas were thrown around. The initial thought was a bit of an obvious one. Have them lose their powers so they must give up their roles as Rangers. BORING. OVERDONE. UNIMAGINATIVE. Thankfully, this was impossible to accomplish without the original three, as we wouldn't be able to see them actually lose their powers and react.

Someone, I think, suggested that Zedd capture them and turn them into creatures that would appear later in the show to fight the Rangers. The problem there was that they'd get blown up at the end, and that wasn't cool. Neither was the idea of Zedd stuffing them into a trash can and sending them to the far reaches of the galaxy. Seems like their families would have missed them or Zordon would have found them, or the Rangers would have never let that happen in the first place.

Finally, the idea of an international youth peace conference came up. At first, it sounded ridiculous. Even today, it sounds ridiculous. But, let's face it, there weren't a lot of options. You had to think about the fans, so for whatever the reason the O.G. three left Angel Grove, it had to be one that didn't end in explosions or death by freezing in a trash can while orbiting around Jupiter or some other planet. It needed to be noble and worthy of these three beloved characters.

The peace conference was a simple solve. It made the three exiting Rangers seem like they were leaving for a very good reason. Jason, Trini, and Zack would be chosen out of all the teens in Angel Grove to travel around the world and discuss issues of hunger, war, ecology, and anything else that needed the point of view of the young crowd. They would be gone a long time, and this humanitarian mission was couched as one of the few things that could supersede being a Power Ranger. So, the script was written—unfortunately, not with much finesse, which added to the corny premise. I was a little surprised they didn't put one of the A-team writers on it. But I'm pretty sure some behind-the-scenes political wrangling factored into deciding who would write the script.

To pull the episode off, cheats would have to be used in filming. Library footage of the Rangers was helpful. So much existed of them just standing together in the Command Center, they could use a wide shot from overhead to set up that they were all there, shoot closeups of Tommy, Kimberly, and Billy, and then cut to stock footage of the three that had left the show. Once it was time to Morph, the sequences were stock shots, and once in the Japanese footage, there was a library of lines from the original Rangers that could be re-cut, flipped around, and stuck in to make the scenes work. The final onscreen goodbye, which turned out pretty well (if not a little clumsy) took place in the park, with photo doubles silhouetted against the setting sun and voice actors delivering their dialogue. The whole thing was a hodgepodge of basic film school trickery that, in the end, worked out fine. Problem solved. Now it was all a matter of prepping the new Rangers to take on their roles, not only as TV stars but movie stars.

Okay, NOW that we have the Rangers all settled and in the right places, it feels like it would be a good time to walk next door (virtually of course) to look at my time on *VR Troopers*. I was there for an entire year, after all, and it is part of this story, if only that it shows what it was like to be on the show that WASN'T *Power Rangers* while Power Ranger was on top of the world.

CHAPTER 16
TROOPER TRANSFORM!

I realize that I am jumping back in time a bit to begin the *VR Troopers* story. But let's face it, it's been 30 years, and trying to put together any sort of precise timeline, to me, is a complete waste of both your and my, well, time. The important thing is that all this stuff happened at one point or another, and the exact dates are not that critical. If exact dates feel like they ARE important, I'll mention them. Let's just go with that. Okay, crank up that imaginary crazy "back in time" music and the wavy visual FX as we take you back to...

I was summoned to meet with Shuki in his office on a day I was going to be there coaching Jason anyway. The production had moved from Culver City to Valencia, a growing suburban sprawl north of Los Angeles. The stages were much larger, there was a ton of office space, and the unions didn't normally venture that far out to disrupt non-union productions. It also gave the two knuckleheads BZ and Little BZ a free, secure place to park the fleet of trucks they owned and rented back to the production. Fortunately for them, "Operation Transportation Compensation" and the extra money that went into their pockets was safe for the moment. I always wondered if Haim knew about their little enterprise. He must have. He knew everything else that was going on. Why would this be any different? I imagine Haim had a certain admiration for the kind of thinking it took to rake in enough extra money to make the whole thing a dream job, with the certainty that Saban was completely unaffected and in fact reaping the benefits of the cost savings BZ's company provided.

Shuki's new office in Valencia was a former swing set from another production that was left behind. It was a 1,000-square-foot office set that looked like it belonged in an East Coast mansion or top-flight New England law practice. The walls were beautifully paneled, the carpet was plush, and there was real leather furniture that crackled when you sat down. It was gorgeous, which is what BZ must have realized when he insisted the set remain exactly as it was and that Shuki use it as his office, furniture, props and all. Who was Shuki to refuse? It was a beautiful, dark, private space, and best of all, Shuki could do one of the things he seemed to love most in the world—smoke cigarettes. There was no smoking allowed in the building as per the fire codes, but Shuki figured that armed with the "As Seen On TV" ashtray he brought from home, with its tiny smoke-sucking fan, he was going to burn 'em to the filter until someone told him to stop. No one ever did, of course. But you always knew he was in the building when you walked down the hall and heard the whirr of that little ashtray and smelled cigarette smoke. BZ was especially proud of this setup. It had clearly earned him a gold star with the boss and probably helped keep his trucking empire going without disruption.

That day, I finished with Jason and headed down to Shuki's office. As I took a seat on the plush leather couch and watched him take a long drag from his cigarette, I was secretly praying to myself that I wasn't going to be assigned to coach the new Ranger actors. Don't get me wrong—to this day, I love helping young artists find the spark inside themselves that leads to successful performances. My time with JDF had been among the best of my professional life. He was a fantastic student with tons of natural ability and charisma. I just couldn't say the same for Steve and Johnny, as I'd had barely had an hour with them. I knew that if I was going to be their coach, all other work would have to stop. No more scripts. No more story meetings. Nothing but basic acting classes and standing on set giving line readings, hoping that any day the lessons would kick in. That would have been a giant step back for me.

Of course, I was prepared to tell Shuki I would be happy to do it and accept my fate with grace in the moment, waiting until the ride home to pound the steering wheel on my crappy old Chevy Blazer while screaming expletives at the split plastic dashboard with the foam poking out. Thankfully, this meeting had nothing to do with the new *Power Rangers*, or Rangers at all for that matter. Phew! This meeting was about the status of *Cybertron* and how I would be an integral part of that project moving forward.

There were challenges with the original concept, especially from a toy perspective. Bandai, the company that had been making and selling the *Power Rangers* toys for decades (they still do to this day), was not going to be involved with the new series. I don't have 100% confirmation on why that was, but I can certainly offer a few thoughts on the subject.

Toy lines rely on primarily one thing for their success—the story that they tell, or that the original intellectual property (TV show or movie) tells. Where *Power Rangers* was colorful and positive and fun, the footage for this new series was dark and gloomy. The robots and vehicles were all black and gray and looked like military issue machines. In the *Metalder* footage, there was one hero who was red, blue, and silver, but that was about it for shiny and colorful.

The next issue was the strong belief that the new show would not survive with only one character in the lead. Kids relate to the characters on the screen because they are someone or know someone who looks, or behaves, like that. If you were a kid and you sat down to watch *Power Rangers*, you were pretty much guaranteed to find someone on the screen who had the same or similar characteristics as you. There was the brainy guy, the cute gymnastics girl, the Kung Fu master girl. All bases were covered. And if they discovered a hole, they'd fill it right away. If Saban rolled out a single lead series with one single hero, chances are it would struggle. Kids love being part of a team. This is one of the things that made Rangers so successful. This is what would make *VR Troopers*, the show *Cybertron* evolved into, successful. The characters would hang out in their regular lives, but when it was time to fight, they would do it as a team in the VR world.

And what about the toy line? One hero and a scant few vehicles was not going to make a great follow up to the candy-colored barrage that was the *Power Rangers* line every year. Successful toy lines, at least for action properties, rely on the ability to create dozens of figures, weapons, vehicles, and environments to make them worthwhile to manufacture. Before they are even geared up, toy companies know when a line will become profitable and how much it will require to do so. Otherwise, the toy company can't cover the cost of the infrastructure that a toy line requires to succeed in a crowded and competitive marketplace. Ironically, Bandai already had the molds for both shows that were eventually used to create *VR Troopers*. The official story was that the molds were lost or destroyed at some point, and it wasn't worth creating new ones. This seems to me to be a pretty decent theory. It would be Occam's Razor of the *VR Troopers* toy mystery. It's the simplest explanation that requires the fewest examples to prove it. But what if...

What if Haim wanted to get in bed with another toy company, one in the States? Why would he do that, though? Well, wouldn't it be smart to create a rivalry with Bandai so that somewhere down the line, Haim could perhaps strong-arm the Japanese company on the next royalty agreement for Rangers or the toys for another series that fit their agenda. Additionally, Kenner, the company set to manufacture the *VR Troopers* toys, had been around forever and were candidates for the Mt. Rushmore of toy companies, along with Mattel, Hasbro and LEGO. It would be unlike Haim not to explore the idea of branching out to make this new connection in case something went awry down the road with Bandai. Mr. Saban is incredibly forward-thinking and, I believe, was constantly running simulations in his head that all accounted for every scenario as it pertained to world domination. He really was/is that brilliant. Of course, this Kenner thing is ALL speculation, although there are enough grains of truth to make it a plausible explanation.

Ironically enough, Kenner had similar fears about the toy line. They wanted the show to have more characters, more vehicles, and more robots, which is what sent the series off in the direction it did.

Shuki informed me that I was to begin writing the pilot once we had all figured out what the new premise was going to be. After that, we would be going into production. This was no longer going to be a star vehicle for Jason David Frank, or anyone for that matter. It was going to feature a cast of three, two guys and a girl, which changed everything.

Haim and Shuki, after consulting with Bob Hughes, had decided to cut in yet another Japanese series to go with *Metalder* so they would have the footage needed for the show to expand. Enter *Spielban*, a Japanese offering starring two heroes that had produced 44 episodes available for us to use in our show. "What about a second season," you ask? Not to worry. There was always another show hidden in a vault somewhere they could crack open and find great footage, which is, in fact, what they did for season two.

The big challenge moving forward, was that *Spielban* and *Metalder* were two completely different shows. We had to figure out how to connect the two for the battle scenes and make it seem as though they were all one big melee. Bob Hughes was set to run the show and had proven to be pretty much a genius at making this kind of cinematic shell game work. Apparently, he had assured Shuki and Haim it could be done, and they had no reason (aside from logic and sanity) to think that it couldn't be. And so, these two totally different series, having nothing to do with one another in their original forms, would become one American kids show.

As Shuki filled me in, it became clear that along with the good reasons Saban had for keeping Jason Frank on the *Power Rangers*, there were excellent reasons not to move him over to *Cybertron*, or whatever it was going to "morph" into. The show was not going to be the star vehicle it started out as. So, why would they put Jason in an entirely new show where he was sharing the screen just like he was in Rangers? And for that matter, why would they put him in a series that was going to be the companion piece for Rangers and had a pretty decent chance of falling short of the success of its predecessor. It was the right thing to do to keep Jason on *Power Rangers*. But we've covered that ad nauseam already.

In that meeting, I was told I was going to write a two-part pilot script, which would throw out much of the old 7-minute presentation and introduce several new elements. After much brainstorming and back and forth, it was decided that the new show would include a talking dog named Jeb, a flying car, and two more "Troopers," Kaitlin and J.B., would be sourced from the *Spielban* footage. This revamped version would also get rid of Tao's daughter and the son of the Zichter character. The entire premise of the show was discussed. Virtual Reality had become a big thing in the tech world. It was seeping into entertainment and all sorts of industries slowly, and people were starting to see the potential in it. It was decided that these three teens, who'd met at a dojo owned by Tao, would enter a portal where they could talk to an older professor (himself a VR program) and receive their orders to fight the sinister Karl Zichter, who was hell-bent on taking over the V. R. space with his army of robots for his own nefarious reasons. His henchmen were actually henchwomen, lifted directly out of a Robert Palmer music video. As we continued to rework the idea, the characters all came together and seemed to round out a nice diverse cast.

I remember at the time that my one big concern was the fact that audience would quickly realize that these heroes weren't facing any actual danger. In Virtual Reality, nothing is real. It's all just a fabrication by a computer and, as a result, you can't get hurt or killed in that space. We needed to come up with a way to add some jeopardy, which is why we decided that if they were captured or blown up in VR, they would remain there forever. I guess people bought it, as the technology was so new you could pretty much make up anything—who would question it? After reflecting on it all these years later, I'm not sure that kids would have given a crap either way. Blow some stuff up and cut to the talking dog giving the raspberry (CG tongue), and everyone is happy.

So, after much discussion, meetings, rewrites, and more rewrites, the two-part pilot was ready to shoot, or at least as "ready" as any script became around that place. There were always tons of last-minute changes. The show was going to begin shooting in February of 1994 on the stages in Valencia, California. Shuki had determined that there needed to be a full-time writer on the series to work with Bob on laying out the season and polishing up the scripts other writers turned in. In TV, it's important that one writer or "voice" touches up all the scripts before they are shot. This is to give maintain continuity in the way the characters act and speak and ensure they remain consistent throughout the run of the show. Shuki informed me that I was going to be that person for *VR Troopers*.

And there it was. It happened. I was going to be gainfully employed as a staff writer on a real TV show. My salary would be $1,000 a week. Holy Crap! Talk about a freaking roller coaster of emotions. I cannot describe the feeling that went through my body at that moment. $1,000 a week? That was insane money. INSANE! I had never made anything close to that except on the soap, and this opportunity had the possibility of lasting for years. I could have job security, get a new car (my Chevy Blazer was near its end), afford to take my "not-girlfriend" (still Deborah) out and pick up the check...this was the single greatest moment of my life! The following day, I would be in a new office, in a new building, working on a new show. Woo-hoo!

CHAPTER 17
WE ARE VR!!!

As I previously mentioned, Bob Hughes was the man in charge at *VR Troopers*. He was very funny, very smart, and a very talented producer in every way, from the budget to the schedule to the creative, which is unusual in our business. He was truly a guy who wore a lot of hats and seemed to make it work. He had also done a very smart thing by hiring a brilliant Unit Production Manager by the name of Danielle Weinstock (who I later recruited to work with me on *Princess Protection Program* for Disney). At the time, Danielle was just starting her career but was already a force of nature, which was great for Bob, who was almost Zen in his approach to the work. To this day, Danielle remains one of the people I respect most in this crazy business. She never dodges a question, always gives it to you straight, and has ZERO problem with conflict if it arises. In fact, sometimes she seems to enjoy it. She is also insanely funny and has this hilarious way of cocking her head to the side and raising her eyebrows if something is just so ridiculous she can't find words.

Back to Bob Hughes. Bob was Irish through and through and very proud of his heritage. He loved all things Celtic, including a band called the Young Dubliners, a popular Irish rock group that happened to feature my friend Randy Woolford on guitar. They would weirdly become part of the big puzzle later on in the *VR Troopers* era. Bob and I spent at least one awesome night at the L.A. House of Blues on St. Patty's Day, rocking hard to the sound of the Young Dubs.

Bob understood that this was my first staff job on a show and allowed me to fumble my way through until I figured out what my role was. He was very inclusive, loved to talk story and made me feel as though I were a partner and not just a hired hand. As with many jobs in the industry, a staff writer can be any number of things. They can just be there to bounce ideas off. They can be there just to do research. Or they can be there to write, write, write, which was the case for me on *VR Troopers*.

As *Troopers* was a new series and the first follow up to *Power Rangers*, there was a lot of attention on us. Haim and Shuki were very present in the lead-up to the first season. Haim even piled into his stretch limo and had himself driven up to Valencia to check on pre-production and go to meeting or two. This was a bit unnerving for everyone at first. Seeing the big boss in the flesh, slumming it at the production offices, was kind of bizarre. But that m'fer was so damn charming and so damn smart that he completely disarmed us all, and we looked forward to seeing him after a while.

There were a couple of Haim appearances that were particularly memorable, at least for me. The first was a meeting of all the writers being considered to write for *VR Troopers*. At the meeting, Haim was supposed to impart his expectations for the show and hear suggestions from the group on how best to write the stories we were going to tell. There were about 10 of us around a large conference table on a Saturday morning and in walked Mr. Saban. He was a tiny bit late, allowing him to enter the room at the perfect time to make an impact without keeping us waiting.

Haim sat down at the table in his perfectly tailored suit (yes, even on a Saturday), holding a cup from Starbucks in one hand and a crunchy biscotti cookie in the other. He apologized to all of us for being late and for not bringing lattes for everyone. He then asked,

"Would anyone like this one?" Clearly, he was NOT serious. I'm sure that Mr. Saban was looking forward to downing that caffeine blast to help him through the early Saturday morning meeting and was just asking to be polite in his funny, weird, Haim way. We all clammed up, of course. Who in their right mind would take a latte from Haim Saban's hand and drink it in front of him and a room full of other people who could all have used a latte at that moment?

And yet, a hand went up. At the end of the table was a guy I had never met before, a writer I hadn't worked with, who came in with a real attitude upon his initial arrival. He had instantly tried to establish himself as the alpha dog at the table and had no problem putting people down. He even called *Power Rangers* "The biggest piece of shit in the history of television." That had raised a few eyebrows. The guy was certainly not afraid to say something stupid. Whether he understood it to be stupid was another question. And this proved itself to be true once when he took Haim up on his offer and relieved the boss of his drink along with the biscotti. Haim, of course, was completely unfazed by this, and I think he found it amusing. The rest of us were, however, in utter shock. What was this moron doing?

As the meeting progressed, every time that idiot bit into that biscotti and slurped Haim's latte, the whole room put their heads down. Not this guy, though. He proudly devoured Haim's crunchy Italian biscuit and sipped that frothy latte in front of all of us without the least bit of shame. The guy was clearly a nut. Finally, the meeting was over, and the biscotti and latte had been consumed. Then it happened. The final insult. This clueless writer with some kind of death wish handed the cup to Haim for him to throw away. I mean, what the crap was going on? Was this some kind of sick prank? Were the rest of us being tested? Were we supposed to mob the guy and give him an Aaron Sorkin "Code Red" beating ala *A Few Good Men*? Was this guy even for real?

Now, there are those who would tell you that the guy was trying to show the boss that he wasn't scared, that he wouldn't cower in Haim's presence like everyone else in the room, me included. Maybe that was the case. But, dude, seriously, read the room. What the "F" were you thinking? Clearly, he wasn't. What a meeting.

What I find interesting is that the writer in question literally disappeared from the industry. He never wrote on our show, and as far as I know never worked on any other series or movie. And I have checked over the years. There is no mention of him on IMDB anywhere. He just kind of vanished. This provides a great button to the story and begs the question, "What happened to him?" Was it…

1. Haim's military trained security staff took the guy out to the California desert and buried him with box of biscotti and a Starbucks gift card? OR—
2. Haim warned his friends in the industry about this little prick and ruined his chances of ever getting work again? OR—
3. The guy's agent found out about his client's misstep, dropped him, and the dude quit the business and spent the remainder of his life spent avoiding the aroma of Starbucks lattes and the crunch of their surprisingly edible biscotti?

I would vote for number three. First off, Haim would NEVER waste important resources over a lost latte and a breakfast snack. He would also not waste his time ever thinking about this poor misguided clown again. Haim had a lot of other fish to fry, and seeking revenge on this dude was not among said fish. Taking over the world of kids' television must take priority in a case like this, and I believe that it did. Onward.

The other time I remember Haim coming to the stage was for an early production meeting during the week. It was held in the upper conference room which they were just getting into shape after the place had been sitting empty for quite some time. Haim arrived with his bodyguard in tow and greeted everyone individually. The thing I immediately noticed was that he was wearing the most expensive looking suit I had ever laid eyes on. I mean this thing must have been well over $5,000 and was tailored to perfection. It was this incredible deep blue, almost black. I had never seen anything like it. He looked immaculate.

As he was about to take his seat, Haim noticed that one of the ceiling tiles was out of the grooves that held it in place, allowing a view of the structure above with pipes and wires visible. He clearly thought that this was not acceptable and wanted someone to reposition the tile before we started the meeting. And what idiot volunteered? That would be me. Yep, for some reason I decided that since I was the tallest one there, I would pop that baby back into place so that Haim could concentrate on more important things, specifically our meeting. So, armed with nothing but good intentions, I reached up to the ceiling and with a little jump, popped the tile back into place. What I hadn't anticipated was the paint dust, pieces of tile, clumps of dirt and all sorts of other crap that fell to the ground when I readjusted the panel. Only most of the messy, dusty junk never made it to the ground. It landed on Haim…all over his very expensive suit, front, back and sides. I immediately felt my face getting flush red, and if truth be told, I got a little dizzy. I think Bob was in the room, and in his fun-loving way, gave me a hard time for ruining the boss's suit. To Haim's credit, he brushed off the mess without a saying a word.

When he was all cleaned up, Haim looked at me and remarked that it was lucky I was a "creative genius." It was the perfect way to disarm the situation. A funny, nice compliment that pretty much let me off the hook and moved things along. I was starting to get a good picture of Haim, although I later learned that he could be much less easy-going about something if it was important to him. But in this case, the suit meant nothing. Clearly, he could have cared less. He probably had a spare in the limo. And he didn't want me to sweat it.

Troopers was starting to shape up to be a decent, quirky little show. We found an amazing cast, led by Brad Hawkins as Ryan (changed from Adam), Michael Bacon as J.B., and Sarah Joy Brown as Kaitlin. They each brought their own strengths to the table.

Michael was a serious martial artist. He was very tall, so it was even more remarkable to me how fluid, and at the same time compact, his moves were. He looked every bit the part of a black belt. His acting was a bit suspect. Again, as is the norm with Saban, they wanted him for his fighting skills and figured the acting would come later. Thankfully, he caught on quickly and was never a hindrance or someone we had to write around. I thought he did a great job as J.B.

Brad had that pixie dust that I like to talk about. He was good looking, but in a down-home, Texas kind of way. He was all-American, with his blond hair and aww-shucks attitude. He had a big smile and southern charm for miles. Dude was confident as hell but never let on that he had it all covered. I loved that about him. Also, Brad was a great athlete—flexible, fast, strong. It was not an issue to train him up to, at least on screen, keep up with Mike, who was a beast in the dojo. I always admired these two. Brad for allowing himself to be coached, and Mike for sharing as much knowledge as Brad could cram into that beautiful head of his.

Sarah Brown was and still is an incredibly gifted performer. Her ability to access her emotions at the drop of a hat was equal to Amy Jo's. Her physical skills got better with every episode, and there was never a time we couldn't cut a scene together because she was lagging too far behind the boys. But the thing she did that was really amazing, and it sounds simple, was to listen. In every scene she appeared, she was focused on what the other characters were saying, really taking it in and processing it, then answering accordingly. This was a true gift to the other actors, as it kept them in the scene and focused as well. As a result, acting was never an issue on *Troopers*, at least with the main characters. They were fantastic.

In every series or movie I've done over the years, I have a "favorite hire" in the cast. This is not necessarily the actor with the biggest part, but it's someone who I was really rooting for and ended up getting the part. In *Troopers*, it was the hiring of Michael

Sorich as Woody. He was a voice actor who had done some amazing work for the company, and this was the first time he was to appear in one of the shows on camera. He was super excited and could not have been more gracious and thankful for the opportunity. It was so great to see.

Finally, there was Jeb. Jeb the freaking dog. This was a talking dog who sounded like Jack Nicholson and would comment sarcastically on anything and everything that went on in the episode. Kerrigan Mahann did the voice, and it was very well executed. That wasn't the issue. The problem was the actual dog. Of course, this being Saban, there was no money in the budget for a trained studio animal. But we needed a dog that could at least follow a few simple instructions. Our stunt coordinator Phil insisted that he had the perfect pooch. He did. Sort of. His dog Zeb (I know, it's confusing, but Jeb was the character's name, and Zeb was the dog we cast) was a dopey looking, if not completely adorable, Redbone Coonhound. If you are not familiar with the breed, they are, as the name says, part of the hound family, bred to chase their prey up trees and make sure they stay cornered there by barking nonstop until their owner shows up. This trait was alive and well in Zeb. It was almost a daily occurrence to be sitting in the office and hear that loud deep bark coming from outside or the set. Sometimes it would just continue. This was when Danielle Weinstock would peek her head into my office and do her tilted head/eyebrow thing. At the end of the day, Zeb WAS smart enough to play Jeb, and we were able to get by with him sitting still and eating peanut butter to make it look like he was talking. I'm not sure the Jeb character ever rose to the desired comedic effect. My thought was that since kids had no clue who Jack Nicholson was, it probably only amused us adults. But the dog was in the show until the end, so WTF did I know?

> SIDE NOTE: One of our Assistant Directors, who later went on to become a director, was a guy named Al Winchell. Al was incredibly sarcastic and had a very quick wit. What he didn't

have was patience for the work grinding to a halt because one of our directors was trying to make logical sense, on the set, of a moment that would never make any sense because it was in our show, and our show sometimes didn't make any sense. The reality was that most of the time Al was right. They had what we needed in the can, and it was time to move on. He would allow the directors just enough time before he would announce on the bullhorn, "Dog Talks. Car Flies. Moving on," which was his way of saying that logic didn't play a huge part in the show, so let's not go down that rabbit hole. To this day, when I see Al, these are still the first words out of our mouths. Great guy.

So, we had our cast. We had two really good directors who came onboard, one of them being Worth Keeter, my old friend from *Power Rangers*. The other was John Weil, who was a high-energy fellow, completely obsessed with getting every detail correct when shooting his episodes. Dog talks, car flies, moving on might have been coined on one of his blocks of shows. But he did a great job, and that's what matters. Our Director of Photography was a quiet but brilliant guy named Jim Mathers (who coincidentally was the brother of Jerry Mathers of *Leave it to Beaver* fame). Our other Assistant Director who worked every other block of shows was Eric Mofford. He was a guy with a perpetual smile and an amazing way of guiding the crew through the hours of stress and strain, making sure that things always stayed even keeled and fun. Eric was the first AD I ever worked with long-term, and I will forever be indebted to him for helping me get through the jitters and beginners self-doubt that we all struggle with on our first show. And so, with the key players in place, we were ready to go into full-blown production mode. Unfortunately, the universe had other plans, and *VR Troopers* would be delayed.

CHAPTER 18
DOUG, RITA MUST BE UP TO SOMETHING!

I was now living in a one-bedroom apartment in the same building I had been managing before I was able to afford to pay rent. To me, I was basking in the lap of luxury. I had a bedroom that was not in the same room as my kitchen, which for those of you who have been where I was back then, you'll understand is a HUGE deal. With Deborah's help, I had done some minor decorating that made it feel like I was living in a real home for the first time in years. There were things on the shelves, knick-knacks, bric-à-brac, and even a few well-placed tchotchkes. The small apartment was really coming together. My only concern was that if there happened to be an earthquake, it would all fly off the shelves, smash into a million pieces, and I'd be cleaning up for weeks.

Speaking of, for those of you who are interested in seismic geology, a "blind thrust" earthquake is one that occurs along a fault that isn't mapped on the surface. These types of seismic events are considered among the most destructive, as they often occur in urban areas, kind of like the San Fernando Valley just west of Los Angeles. I think we all know where this is going.

I awoke on the morning of January 17, 1994 at 4:30 a.m. to find myself on the floor of my bedroom, face down. Car alarms were wailing up and down the street, and the ground was shaking so violently that I literally could not bring myself to my feet until it stopped. The Northridge Earthquake had just "blind thrusted" my sleeping ass from my bed and onto the carpet in a matter of 20 seconds. Disoriented and in the dark, as all the electricity was out, I scrambled to my feet and was about to head into the living room to assess the damage when the first aftershock hit. It was a 6.0, so that was no joke. I stood in the doorway between the living room and bedroom until it subsided. It was then that the phone rang. I was pretty sure it was going to be either Deborah or my parents, so I quickly picked it up. What I heard instead was, "Doug, It's Shuki. I think Rita must be up to something." Looking back, that might have been the perfect thing to say at that moment. I was literally shaken to my core, so that little bit of levity was just what I needed. He went on to tell me he had tried to call Deborah and his daughter to check on them, but since the office-style phone system at Deb's house was on the same electrical system as everything else, it wasn't working. Shuki was worried. I told him that I could try to call her, but that I would probably get the same result. We agreed that I would go over to Deborah's house as soon as I was able and make sure that they were okay. I was much closer to them than he was, so it only made sense that I was the one to make the trip.

I looked around my apartment to find that pretty much all my knick-knacks, bric-à-brac and well-placed tchotchkes were strewn across the floor as if a bomb had gone off. I, of course, immediately and stupidly stepped on a sharp piece of one of the knick-knacks and screamed out in pain as blood began to seep into the carpet. My first official earthquake injury! Yay! I was able to locate a roll of duct tape and used it to wrap my foot up with paper towel so I could get on with the business of getting dressed and heading over to Beverly Hills to check on Deborah and Tamara.

I threw on whatever was close by and went to grab my car keys. Normally, they were sitting on the kitchen counter, as this was the first place I stopped when I got home, usually to go through the mail and just chill out. But the keys were gone. They had vanished into the void that was once my comfy little Hollywood hideaway that currently looked like a set from the movie *Twister* after take number 47 of the final tornado scene. I frantically searched high and low. Maybe I hadn't put the keys on the counter. But where, then? Where the "F" were these effing keys? I looked at the kitchen sink, which was filled with broken dishes and several shattered items that had been on the kitchen shelf. I don't know why, but at that moment I decided to stick my hand into the garbage disposal just to make sure. There they were. My keys had fallen off the shelf and landed in the disposal. Phew. Mystery solved. And so, I was off to be the hero and report back to Shuki that the most beloved person in his universe, his daughter, was safe and sound.

CHAPTER 19
PERSPECTIVE

Walking into the garage of my building I found that it was full of dazed tenants, all milling about, grumbling about something. It was then that I realized none of them were able to get out of the garage. The gate was electric. It also weighed hundreds of pounds, and there was no way to manually lift it. And just like that, I was stuck. I wasn't going anywhere for the moment. Son of a bitch! I look back at that moment when I was so frustrated with my stupid duct-taped foot and my desperate need to get my car out of the garage and onto the road to my girlfriend's/daughter of my boss's house, and I cringe.

This was a freaking disaster, a major earthquake. If my apartment was that bad, there were others that were far worse. Of course there were, particularly those built earlier and closer to the epicenter. 57 people died in that quake. 9,000 more were injured. Who was I to be so pissed off that I couldn't make points with my employer by checking on his family, one of whom happened to be my girlfriend? Whatever. You can't change the past, and I'm sure a lot of people did and said things that day that they look back on with some remorse. So, I headed back up to the apartment to begin the clean-up.

Eventually the power was restored, and the true scope of the Northridge Earthquake was revealed on TV. It was horrendous. All I could do was watch in disbelief as I tried to salvage anything I could from the mess on my floor. What a freaking day. Whatever Rita was up to, she took it a little too far that time. F'ing Rita.

It was a bit of a challenge getting to after that. The commute to Valencia required me to take the 5 freeway north. The problem was the freeway collapsed in the earthquake and there seemed to be no other way to get to the Santa Clarita Valley. This could become an issue.

> SIDE NOTE: The inconveniences suffered by commuters to and from Valencia in the months following the Northridge Earthquake were meaningless compared to the terrible loss of LAPD officer Clarence Wayne Dean. He was riding his patrol motorcycle in the early hours of January 17th and had the misfortune of being on the Newhall Pass interchange south of Santa Clarita and north of Granada Hills moments after the seismic event. It was dark on that overpass and not realizing that the roadway had collapsed, with no time to stop, Officer Dean fell 50 feet from the roadway and died on impact. Clarence Wayne Dean was a U.S. Marine and a 26-year veteran of the Los Angeles Police Department. That overpass, which has since been rebuilt, now bears his name, the Clarence Wayne Dean Memorial Interchange. Every time I drive by, I look to the sign with his name on it and try to give a thought for Officer Dean and his family.

I quickly learned that traffic had been rerouted to a service road that required some side street navigation but allowed folks to pass. It could take hours, but you'd eventually get back on the freeway and to your destination. At this point, my crappy Chevy Blazer was really, truly on its last legs. I was just starting to receive a regular paycheck and made a note to myself that I would need to figure out alternate transportation, and it should be something more worthy of a Hollywood writer. The thing about an earthquake is that there seems to be a definite shelf life for the initial terror that it unleashes on people. And this is in direct correlation to the aftershocks. As they grow fewer and are less severe, people start to feel safer putting their lives back together. This was the case with Northridge. It took a while, but the aftershocks, once nearly as powerful as the quake itself, were now tiny tremors that barely got noticed. People started to live normally again, the fear subsiding and the memory of those awful moments fading. And with that, it meant for me, it was time to begin the next chapter of my journey. It was time for the dog to talk and the car to fly. It was time to move on.

CHAPTER 20
YOU'RE GONNA DIRECT TODAY

The first season of the Japanese footage presented us with several cool multi-part episodes we could turn into events for *VR Troopers*. The pilot was finished and well received. So, after a few standalone episodes, we decided to push the boundaries a bit. The first multi-parter we put together was called "Defending Dark Heart." I was beyond happy to write the scripts, which would be directed by John Weil. We were able to make the mini-series because a similar arc existed in the *Metalder* footage from Japan. In the show, one of the Grimlord's evil mutants, Dark Heart, fails to exterminate the *VR Troopers* and is going to be "decommissioned" by the rest of Grimlord's army. The footage was decent, so there were a lot of ways to go with the story.

I remember that at the time, Bob and I both really wanted to weave in a personal story for the characters. We felt it would be the only way to sustain the entire four episodes and keep the audience interested. To this day, I tell writers who work for me that story and plot are two very different things. The story is what the character is going through and how he is personally changed by his journey. The plot is the basic movements that take place in the episode and should be informed by the character story. In "Defending Dark

Heart," we needed to come up with a way for this to mean something more than just another Grimlord goon coming to town and stirring things up. We decided to go back to the idea that Ryan had never given up hope that his father was alive and was perhaps trapped in the VR world. The possibility that Dark Heart was Ryan's father, trapped in the body of a mutant and under Grimlord's control, created a life and death inner conflict for Ryan. He was desperate to make sure Dark Heart survived in case he was his father. We felt like this was a simple and effective way to create some real stakes in the mini-series.

Then of course we had to find ways to give it as much comedy as possible by using a lot of Percy, Woody, and Jeb. The story was serious, and it was imperative that we try to keep it from spiraling into a depressing melodrama. All in all, I think we did okay. I still think "Defending Dark Heart" holds together. John Weil did a great job directing and was really clever at balancing the serious with the comedic.

As production of the first season of *VR Troopers* progressed, the shows were well received in the ratings, often times getting close to Power Ranger numbers in terms of the Nielsens. This was in part because it came on right after Rangers and kids just naturally stayed on to watch another show that had many of the same elements as their beloved *Mighty Morphin Power Rangers*. For a while, I was a happy guy, making my $1000 a week and writing my scripts in my little office, staying under the radar. However, I soon started to get the itch to try something new, something I hadn't done before. Halfway into the season, it came time to start filming the mentor-like character Professor Hart giving the Troopers instructions and assistance with their missions. So, it was basically a day of feeding Julian Combs, the actor playing Professor Hart, his lines while he looked into a locked camera and burned through the episodes we had written. The shoot was on a Saturday, and Bob Hughes kindly offered me the chance to direct it. "Hell yes!" Here was something I could get behind. "Thanks, Bob!"

The Professor Hart shoot went well (many thanks to Jim Mathers. the very patient director of photography), and after a full day we had half of his performances for the season in the can and ready for the effects house to work their magic. I was hoping at the time that I could switch it up a bit, do some camera moves, different sizes, etc. But it quickly became obvious that would have gone completely against what we were trying to achieve with this character. He was basically our Zordon, so the idea that he would be seen as anything but a dude with a snappy turtleneck and a sick blinged-out pendant around his turtlenecked neck was not going to happen. And rightly so.

This little taste of directing had me wondering what it would take to direct an episode of my own. There were several roadblocks to prevent that from happening. First, due to the block style of shooting, when you directed for Saban at the time, you directed not one episode, but four. If I was given a chance, it would have to be directing a block of shows. They weren't going to break protocol and shoot a single episode just so I could get my feet wet. Second, I was committed to writing and editing scripts for the show. I couldn't just drop out of that process and head off to direct, leaving Bob to deal with the scripts himself. It was a non-starter. So, I kept writing and editing for the show, figuring that it would be impossible to get a shot at the big chair.

I had just put the finishing touches on the scripts for a two-part mini-series that would be the last episodes of season one. I decided to reward myself for finishing and head down to craft service (the donut table) for some mid-morning sustenance. The crew was setting up a new shot in Professor Hart's lab set when Shuki, who was directing, approached me on his way outside to smoke a cigarette.

"Doug. What are you doing right now?" he asked. I told him proudly that I had just finished writing the final episode. Without missing a beat, he said, "Good, you're gonna direct today." He handed me the sides (the script pages for what was being shot that day) and headed out for his smoke, leaving me standing there completely confused and a bit terrified. I was sure I saw him smirk on the way out, undoubtedly at the look of complete and utter surprise on my face. I walked around the corner and saw the entire crew standing there, waiting for someone to tell them what to do next. "How the hell should I know?" I thought to myself. Five minutes ago, I was wiping chocolate donut frosting from my shirt and trying to figure out what I would do for the rest of the day. The thought never crossed my mind that I would be directing an episode of the show.

Looking back, I feel like it was probably something Shuki and Bob set up in advance. They knew I wanted to get in the director's chair and that I had done the Professor Hart footage with little problem. I think they wanted to see if I could handle being thrown into the fire with no warning and just rely on my instincts. I feel like Shuki would never have just left and not told Bob, or that Bob would not have been at least given the heads up.

> SIDE NOTE: Shuki was (and I'm sure still is) someone who could do just about any job related to filmmaking. As a result, he always had fifty things going on and would bounce from his studio to his office, to location, to outside meetings continually. It was not unusual for him to just stand up in the middle of a meeting and excuse himself, never to return. He was spinning a lot of plates back in the day and somehow managed it all. The point I'm trying to make is that it is not out of the question that, on the day, Shuki could have just gotten bored, spotted me at the craft service table, and decided that this was his way out of a long grueling day of shooting followed by fighting the traffic back into the valley on a workday. What I think is more likely is that Shuki had heard from Bob that I had an interest in directing and figured that this was a good way to throw my feet into the fire and see if I made it through.

When I sat down in the director's chair and told Director of Photography Jim Mathers what had just happened, his smile turned into a chuckle. He was amazingly kind, filling me in on what had been shot and where we needed to get to in the scene. I quickly jotted some ideas down on the script pages in front of me and figured out how many shots I needed to get the scene done. I showed the list to Jim. He simply nodded and started setting up the first shot. I have never met a calmer, more stoic person in my life. Jim never gets angry or excited on set. He just goes with the flow, offering advice where he can, doing the great job he does with little fuss. I'm certain that my surprise day of directing would have gone very differently without Jim Mathers behind the camera.

At the end of the day, I thanked everyone and headed back to the office. Bob Hughes told me he had watched a little and I had done well. Another director would most likely finish the job. There were script rewrites to be done, and I needed to focus on that. But he made sure to let me know that he would do whatever possible to get me back in the director's chair soon. Since we were coming to the end of season one, I assumed the possibility would be something to look forward to next season, if there was a next season. In the meantime, I needed to get over to the *Power Rangers* set. There was something they needed my help with.

CHAPTER 21
YOU NEED IT WHEN?

"How long does it take to write a *Power Rangers* episode?" This is a question that I have been asked countless times over the years. The simple answer is that it varies. A lot depends on the source material, the amount of actual footage, and the writer's experience. If it's a new freelancer who has never written for the show, we usually give them a couple of weeks to get it done. If it's someone who has been around and knows the ropes, probably a week once the outline is approved. Sometimes, however, a situation would arise that required a much quicker turnaround. And, when I say, "much quicker," I mean…well… here's the story:

Having completed my work for the day on *VR Troopers*, I walked up the stairs to the *Power Rangers* production offices, located right next to the Trooper building. The call for my assistance had come from Ellen Levy Sarnoff, who was still running the creative on *Power Rangers* and oversaw the scripts. She had an office at the stage in Valencia but was also still being consulted on everything else "kid-related" going on in the company. So she split her time between Valencia and the Saban offices back in town. I had a hard time figuring out how she managed it. But she always did so with grace and humor.

When I entered Ellen's office, I was not surprised to find her desk littered with the scraps of a script that she was cutting and taping into a master document, then taking to the copy machine to pull it all together into one readable script. I sat down in the chair across from her desk and could instantly see that, underneath her ever present smile, she was more than a little frustrated. What I came to learn over the course of time and on that day, was that BZ and Ellen had been having a rough go of it. I think that Ellen's way of doing things, her scattered approach, her cutting and pasting, were driving the hyper-organized BZ insane. He hated the fact that she looked like she was flailing and might not get him the scripts on his timetable. And clearly, in addition to treating her poorly himself, he had poisoned his underlings against Ellen. More than a few times I saw them huff and puff in dramatic frustration over having to copy script pages for her. The worst was Jabba. It never occurred to me at the time that this person bore any resemblance to the Star Wars character, because she didn't really. It was her horrible attitude that earned her the moniker. She was a vile, unpleasant creature who, under the protection of BZ, would walk into Ellen's office with a scowl on her face and literally slam her hand on the table as she picked up the latest script pages to take to BZ for his perusal. Jabba knew she was protected by BZ and could get away with some questionable behavior. She wanted everyone, regardless of their place in the hierarchy of the production to know she was protected and that she had no respect for Ellen.

So, after she filled me in, Ellen and I moved past the BZ BS and got into the reason I was there. *Power Rangers* was one script short for the next block of filming. For some reason there had been a mix-up, and the story hadn't even been conceptualized yet. All they had was some footage of a striped tube monster battling the Zords and not much more. So, there we sat on a Friday, with the director starting on Monday, short one script.

SIDE NOTE: Some of you are probably thinking, "Of course BZ was pissed. He was short a script. Clearly Ellen was to blame. She's the one in charge of scripts. How could a script fall through the cracks?" On the surface, that is the logical conclusion anyone would draw. However, what most don't understand, even some in the industry, is that there are any number of reasons for the delay of a script, and few of them have to do with the actual person in charge of the scripts.

Usually the issue begins with someone very high up on the food chain who, for one reason or another, forgets or doesn't bother to read the story premises sitting on their desk and fails to approve them on time, thus leaving the writers with nothing to write. You might be asking now, "Well why don't you just hurry them along and get the notes. Tell them they're late." As easy as this sounds, it's not. Network executives, heads of companies, and other important members of the TV creative hierarchy do not take kindly to being pestered for anything, especially notes. It forces them to look at a premise or outline or script and decide whether they believe it's good enough to go to the next step.

Most of these folks don't like to commit to any kind of approval until they can gather with others and form a community opinion. That way they are safe if someone even higher up than them looks at the concept in question and thinks it sucks. This can take weeks to accomplish. And, if you are the showrunner waiting for the go-ahead on a story, depending on your boss, you will be waiting as long as it takes them all to get it together because you don't want to bother them too much, knowing all the other crap they have to deal with. This usually is what ends up causing problems between the creatives and production on a series. And the real culprit never gets any of the blame. And that is just one possible scenario.

So, for whatever reason, they didn't have a fourth script to fill out the block that would start prepping on Monday. Ellen put it bluntly to me: "Do you think you and I can write a script in four hours?" I looked at her and knew she was going to attempt this miracle of modern screenwriting regardless of my participation, and if Ellen did it alone, without anyone to bounce ideas off, it would be that much harder. I told her to find a computer we could use that had Final Draft on it and a room where no one could find us. I was not 100% confident in our ability to pull this off. It was a big ask. However, the idea of shutting BZ and his cronies up, if only for a few days, and giving Ellen some breathing room, was a definite motivator.

We flipped on the Mac computer, and I typed *FADE UP:*, then we sat there for a moment and laughed hysterically. What the hell were we thinking? We pressed on. After looking at the Japanese footage about a zillion times, we finally decided that the monster kind of looked like he was made from pool flotation devices or inner tubes. The tubes were blue and white and covered his entire body. Hmmm. What goes with flotation devices? Well, the park where we shot had a lake that was approved for swimming, so that might be a good place to start.

The next hurdle was to figure out how to come up with enough additional footage so that the episode wouldn't break the bank when they shot it. The simple answer to that is to find snippets of footage from earlier episodes that were not used. And if we could string them together with some sort of theme, then all the better. We looked through what we had in terms of remaining footage and realized that there were several water-related creatures that we hadn't taken full advantage of, kind of a seafood salad of rubber monsters. We figured Lord Zedd could send down the Slippery Shark, the Goldfish, Crayfish and a couple of other denizens of the deep one by one to battle the Rangers. We had the costumes and could shoot the fights on the beach at the lake where the rest of the story was unfolding. So, this was the plot. Now we needed a story.

We came up with the idea of a kid named, what else, Dougie,

who was afraid to go in the lake due to his fear of monsters. Rocky, a lifeguard at the lake, tries to help little Dougie get over his fear of monsters. Of course, right in the middle of this, Bulk and Skull decide to try drawing the *Power Rangers* out by strapping Styrofoam shark fins to their heads and swimming under the surface. Eventually all the real monsters show up, and the Rangers must split up to fight on two fronts. They defeat the bad guys in short order, and we conclude our story with Dougie rescuing Bulk and Skull and overcoming his fear of the water. BOOM!

The story seemed to work, which was good because there was no time for an outline. We just had to write it and hope that the higher ups would approve it over the weekend. In total, it took just under four hours for me and Ellen to crank out the script and deliver it to production before the end of shooting for the week. This was a banner day. I remembered how much I loved writing for *Power Rangers*, and I admit, cramming it in BZ's grill felt good. Even though he had a bunch of issues with it, BZ couldn't deny we'd delivered a fully realized script in an afternoon. Ellen and I tried to stifle our laughter on the way back to her office. The good guys won on that day. A legit PR script in four hours. And, at the time, I would defy anyone to have guessed that was the episode if they didn't know the footage. That might have been the most fun I ever had writing in my professional career.

Yes indeed. Despite the fact that BZ was still an arrogant jackass and Jabba was as scary as ever, it felt good to be back at the Ranger stage. There was excitement and magic in those halls. The show was a part of history, and I was a part of that show, even if it was in the smallest way. History was about to be made again, and this time, history wasn't f*ing around.

CHAPTER 22
THE WHITE LIGHT SHINES BRIGHT

The first *VR Troopers* episodes started airing in September of 1994. They were well-received in the ratings, and the popularity grew as the series progressed. I'm told there were even times when Troopers did as well in the ratings as *Power Rangers*. I can neither confirm nor deny this, but I know two days when this was definitely NOT the case. Those two days came a couple of weeks after the premiere of *VR Troopers* when *Mighty Morphin Power Rangers* made a definitive statement to the world that the show was not to be fucked with. I am speaking, of course, of the White Ranger two-part reveal.

The White Ranger extravaganza was a decent enough script, although I always felt like it was a bit of a cheat that Zordon just decided one day to create a new Ranger and give the powers to Tommy. I mean how many other times could they have done this? The guy almost got obliterated repeatedly while using the fizzling Green Ranger powers. He even lost them at least once. Where was your White Ranger then, Zordon? Of course, I KNEW where he was, in Japan, being boxed up to send to the US for next season. Regardless, the storytelling, to me, felt like places we'd been before in the show. There could have been much more of a struggle to gain the white powers and create a new Ranger. But it was Shuki, so you had to figure there was some sort of reason for keeping it simple. Shuki understood that it didn't really matter whether the set up was some complex Shakespearean turn or just a straight-ahead "Here are your new powers, off you go" *Rangers* episode. The audience truly didn't give a crap. Tommy would appear on screen in the second part as the White Ranger, and all would be forgiven. That was the focus of kids across the country. Unfortunately, the directing under BZ's clumsy hand didn't help—overacted and awkward, with moments like Kimberly fainting weakly, which didn't do her character any justice. But, as I said before, none of that really mattered. The only thing of any consequence was that when the White Ranger was lowered from the ceiling, and his mask was removed, a smiling Tommy Oliver was revealed.

And so, on October 17th and 18th of 1994, the highly anticipated White Ranger saga was scheduled to air on Fox Kids. The episodes were promoted like crazy, and Fox was expecting a nice ratings number when the data came out the following day. Well, that was not to be the case. It wasn't a "nice" number. It was a complete obliteration. It was unheard of and, to this day in kids TV, unequalled. The second episode of White Light received a 14 rating. Now, that's not just for kids. That's for households. It meant that across the country, 14 million households were tuned into *Mighty Morphin Power Rangers* that day. This was freaking insane. This meant that this episode had transcended kids ages 2 to 11, who were the primary audience. It meant the viewership for this episode included parents, grandparents, older brothers, older sisters, cousins, neighbors, and the family dog. This was unprecedented. It was pointed out to me at the time, that there were many producers and executives with nighttime shows on the air who would have given anything to have 14 million households watching their offering. But this was *Mighty Morphin Power Rangers*, the "dopey" little show with the rubber monsters and the kids who knew karate. What the hell was happening? Was the world about to spin off its axis? Were these numbers wrong? Were they fixed? What the "F" was the deal?

Of course there was no "deal," no secret explanation for the success of the show. The world was not coming to an untimely end. A lot of things had to happen for those 14 million households to be planted in front of their TV sets watching the return of the White Ranger:

1. Kids in the early 1990s were still watching TV. They weren't obsessed with video games or the Internet. There was no YouTube or Snapchat. It was Fox Kids, Disney Channel, Nickelodeon, and Cartoon Network. That's where kids went to be entertained (or babysat, in many cases).
2. *Power Rangers* was appointment viewing for that generation of young ones. It's what they talked about at school. It's what they played at recess. It's the toy they asked for at Christmas and Hannukah. *Power Rangers* was robots, dinosaurs, bright colors, and character archetypes relatable to every kid at school. And, clearly, *Power Rangers* was all about…
3. Tommy Oliver. His popularity had grown to epic proportions. And although there was no official word on who the White Ranger would be, most of the audience figured it had to be Tommy. And him coming back as a whole new Ranger was a pivotal moment in the history of the series that no respectable *Power Rangers* fan was going to miss.

You could almost hear executives scrambling all over the Fox lot and office tower, trying desperately to think of new ways to exploit this once-in-a-generation anomaly. The feature film, already in development, was immediately fast-tracked. They needed to get that thing going. Now, not being around for the creation of the movie story or anything related to it, I can't really speak to how all that went on. What I can speak to is the effect it had on the actors and their expectations moving forward in terms of financial rewards. It was hard to disguise the fact that *Power Rangers* was "fat stacking mad Benjis" and it would only be a matter of time before the Rangers themselves were at least given a bump up to a living wage. Wouldn't it?

Once the dust settled, several things became crystal clear. First, Jason David Frank was paramount to the continuation and success of the franchise. They were incredibly lucky to have found him when they did and luckier that he resonated with audiences so universally. An unfortunate byproduct of this was that it empowered Saban even more to cut ties with Thuy, Austin, and Walter over their wage dispute. Haim now knew that the series would survive. Those ratings made it clear that as long as Tommy was there, everything would be fine.

Second, the show wasn't running out of steam any time soon, as many industry experts had predicted. As a rule, a live action kids show gets an order of 60 episodes in total. Anything more than that is a gift and a blessing. Well, as it turns out, this would be the gift that kept on giving, and giving, and giving. But I was still working on *VR Troopers* and enjoying the collaborative efforts of Bob, Jim, Scott, Danielle, and our entire crew. As first "real" jobs go, it was pretty chill, and it seemed like the "White Light" might have been burning a little hot at that exact moment.

CHAPTER 23
THE RISE OF DR. POINDEXTER

As we were finishing up season one of *VR Troopers*, there was less and less for me to do. The scripts were written, and the final episodes were being planned out. It was getting to the point where I just needed something to keep busy. The ADR studio was right next to my office, which had its advantages and disadvantages.

Scott Page-Pagter oversaw the ADR (Automated Dialogue Replacement) department. This was a HUGE job at Saban. Every episode of both *Power Rangers* and *Troopers* had hundreds of lines of Automated Dialogue Replacement that needed to be recorded, most to replace the Japanese actors' voices. There were also takes that didn't get good enough sound and needed to be fixed, or an airplane had flown overhead and ruined the sound. Finally, there were the "efforts." If you watch a show, you will immediately notice that when the Rangers or Troopers fight, they expel a large burst of air and shout with each punch or kick. This is called the *kiai*. Every fighter has a different version of this sound, and it is very personal and individual to each. There are several purposes for the kiai. It is said to focus one's energy, while at the same time emptying the lungs of air to protect against a potential gut shot knocking the wind out of the fighter. The Rangers and Troopers, along with the actors doing the voices of the monsters, would form an endless parade that passed through the ADR stage. I was always amazed at how quickly and precisely the Rangers actors did their ADR. Jason Frank was a master. He could run through an entire fight scene, kiais all in the perfect places, not stopping and doing it all in one take. He was just so used to it by a certain point that it became second nature.

Scott Page-Pagter and I had become great friends. We could spend hours just talking about music, scuba, whatever. I visited the ADR department often, which I'm sure was a bit annoying for Scott at times since he was pretty much always trying to work. As I spent more time there, I started to get that twinge I get when I'm missing doing something I'd once been completely obsessed with and was now completely out of my life. As it turns out, acting was the thing I was really missing. But I was a writer now. No more foolishness. I had a steady job and needed to focus on that. One day at lunch I was lamenting my feelings to Bob Hughes, and Scott's eyes lit up.

"You should play Poindexter," he said. I started to object, but he interrupted. "No. It's perfect. You love that character. We'll get some thick glasses, and you can do something crazy with your hair. It'll be great."

I told him that I would at least put myself on tape for the audition and see what everyone thought.

"Nope," he said. "You're doing it."

I was completely blown away by this. All those years of acting, all the studying and auditions, and here I was getting to create a fantastically bizarre character, completely outside of my wheelhouse, without having to go through the dreaded audition process.

Brad Hawkins and the rest of the *Troopers* cast were super excited that I was going to be in an episode. I think part of them really wanted me to see what it was like in their shoes; the long hours, physical scenes, working with the dog. I didn't care. I was just happy to be performing again. And, since I had long since let my SAG membership lapse, working on a non-union show was a non-issue. I told myself that I was going to take this thing all the way or not at all. I asked wardrobe for the highest "high-water" pants they could find, the prop department for the thickest glasses available, and hair and makeup for the greasiest hair product they had. It all came together to create this bizarre super nerd-savant who ended up being the most fun I'd ever had in an acting role. Working with the Troopers was awesome. We laughed our butts off time and time again, mostly at the idiotic way I looked as Poindexter. And I gained a whole new perspective on what it meant to be an actor on a Saban kids show. It could be grueling. But once again, I go back to the analogy of film school. Working on those series as an actor was like getting paid (very little) to train and learn in front of a camera while being part of a team of professionals with the same goal. Finish the work. Try not to let it suck. Make the day. Wake up and repeat.

> SIDE NOTE: There are wide ranging opinions as to whether film acting is different from stage acting and whether there are different skills one must acquire for each. I tend to land right in the middle of the argument. Acting is a VERY personal endeavor. Everyone takes a different road to get where they're ultimately going in this business. It is also a very difficult road for many people. There are actors who study for years and years, perfecting their craft, learning about the history of theatre, Shakespeare, Tennessee Williams, David Mamet. And I applaud them for their desire to honor the art and to soak up as much as they possibly can on the road to what will hopefully be a successful career.
>
> There are others who don't give a crap about all of that and just take a few cold reading classes or sit in a scene study class and watch but don't participate. This is not what I would recommend. Most who choose this route never get near to steady employment as an actor. However, occasionally, one of these carefree individuals somehow makes it through the invis-

ible wall and becomes a star, perpetuating the idea that stardom, or even becoming a working actor, is easy to achieve.

Case in point: We had a guy in our class, when I was with Howard, who rarely got up on stage to do a scene. In fact, I only remember one time in the years I was there that he performed a full scene with a partner for Howard to critique. However, when other students put up a scene with the small part of a waiter or some other walk on, he was always happy help out and play the part. He seemed to love doing it, always at the last minute, always with no rehearsal. The thing was that every time he walked on stage, he was freaking hilarious. He wasn't trying to be. He just was. He was only being himself, having fun with no pressure to perform, because it wasn't his scene, so what did he care? The truth was this guy had the pixie dust. The same that Jason Frank had, the same that Selena Gomez has. This dude didn't need to try to elicit a response from an audience. All he did was say the lines, and his inherently goofy, glorious personality did the rest. It was remarkable. And guess what? He booked dozens of national commercials in a year and had auditions pretty much every day, while the rest of us toiled over our scenes, stressing, sweating, bleeding for our craft. For him, he just let it happen. One night at class, he was lamenting the fact that he had an audition the following morning but was thinking of blowing it off. It was "too early," and he just didn't think it was worth missing out on those extra hours of sleep. After a barrage of "Dude, you better get up," and "I'll drag your ass there if I have to," he went to the audition and booked a series that ran for five years. Dude went on to become a successful actor and still just says the lines and lets the pixie dust fall where it may. I've run into him from time to time up in Vancouver when I'm shooting a movie, and he's there doing one as well. We always have a great laugh, and I marvel at how success hasn't changed him a bit.

The reason I tell this story is to illustrate that no one can predict what it will take to have success as an actor. Christopher Meloni, famous for *Law and Order: SVU* and now his own show, was also in that class and worked harder than any of us week in and week out. He was brilliant and never took his foot off the metaphorical gas pedal, getting better and better with every scene. Same with Peri Gilpin (Roz on *Frasier*). She was on stage every week, toiling over what seemed like the most difficult scenes she could find. For most, it's work, work, work. Practice, practice, practice. That's normally what leads to success in any endeavor, be it creative or athletic or, well, anything. Acting is usually no different.

I've said it before. That was the thing about those Saban shows. It was a great place to practice your craft in a professional situation. The money was shit and it was hard to watch the actors get screwed week in and week out with their measly paychecks. But there was improvement in those who studied and used the time to work on the things they weren't as good at. Years later, I'm happy to see that many of them have found ways to capitalize on the thermal nuclear event that was *Power Rangers*.

CHAPTER 24
FIDDLER ON THE LOOSE

During my undergrad college years, I decided for some reason that I wasn't busy enough with a full class load, my fraternity, the tennis team, and a full-time girlfriend, so I decided why not join a rock band? So, I did and after a few weeks of rehearsal, we were out playing the clubs in southern California. It was so fun working with such amazing musicians, and one of those was a guy named Randy Woolford, an incredible guitar player who later in his career became the lead guitarist for the Young Dubliners.

As I mentioned earlier, when working on *VR Troopers*, Bob Hughes told that he was a huge fan of the Irish rock band, which was on the precipice of huge success. They had a record deal with Scotti Brothers (the company that put out "Eye of the Tiger," the Rocky song) and would regularly sell out the House of Blues. The band was a great combination of Irish folk and modern rock. They had a fiddle player and a guy who could kill it on the mandolin, but they also had a monster of a drummer, and as I said, my old friend Randy on electric guitar. It was fantastic. I joked one day with Bob that we should write a show around the Young Dubs. His eyes lit up. Strangely, we did have some footage of a fiddle playing mutant. There had to be a way to incorporate that into a story. Bob, to my surprise (I was still giddy after having seen the Dubs on St. Patrick's Day at the House of Blues) was totally into the idea. In fact, he wanted to direct the show if we managed to pull it off. All we needed was a solid story and the band to agree to do it.

The idea came about quickly. Kaitlin would have a cousin, Keith, from Ireland, in town with his band on a tour of the U.S. Grimlord would kidnap Keith and turn him into a fiddle-playing monster who the Troopers must fight, but not destroy, as they would be wiping out Kaitlin's cousin in the process. The script turned out to be halfway decent, if not a little corny (what else was new), and we started to discuss how we were going to make this all happen within the confines of our little low budget kids' show. Keith Roberts, the lead singer of the Young Dubliners, had an incredibly sly wit and outgoing personality that made him the only one who would be able to pull off the lead role we had written for the episode. He was just naturally funny, and we figured he'd be able to do it. The first problem? Keith was NOT the fiddle player in the band. In fact, Keith didn't even play the fiddle. He'd never had to. However, he could play the guitar, very well, so we were hoping this would help. Bottom line—we needed him to be the character who was turned. We would have to ask Keith to mime playing the fiddle in the show. I wasn't sure this would go over too well with the band, as they were all about representing themselves honestly and openly to their fans. But we would try. If they said no, it would be a deal breaker, which would suck, since the script was already written.

Another issue facing us was that we couldn't just give all the lines to Keith. The band all had to chime in along the way as bands and good friends do. How was this going to work? None of these guys were actors, and on stage they stayed mostly in the background, so we had no clue what they were going to give us when they were in a scene with lines. We were going to have to count on the fact that they could pull off the few speaking parts they had, relying on good directing and their natural Irish charm, of which there was an abundance…at least with half the band. The other half weren't even Irish. This meant that the non-Irish band members with lines, none of whom were actors, had to say those lines in an Irish accent. This included my friend Randy. So, we had a lot to discuss with the lads if we were going to make this work. We were pretty sure they were going to say "no" to the fiddle thing. I was convinced, in fact, that it was going to solve all our other problems by cancelling the whole deal.

To my surprise, Keith laughed and, in his Irish accent, said, "Sure. Why da fook not?" Funny enough, this was their answer to everything we requested of them. Their fans would know it was for the show and wouldn't "give a cold shite" as long as their young Dubs were playing the songs they loved on TV. The band always seemed to be of the mind that any exposure they could get was good. They'd appeared on all sorts of telethons and morning shows over the years. They still do as far as I know, having recently appeared on a rock and roll cruise with a slew of other bands. The boys just love to play, which is pretty much a prerequisite of being in a band these days when the only way to make real money is live performances.

And so, with all the music rights worked out and the script approved, the Young Dubliners were set to appear as themselves on Episode 47 of season one of *VR Troopers* entitled, "Fiddler on the Loose." (I know, kind of an obvious title. But sometimes when there's low hanging fruit, you just gotta grab it and be thankful for the snack.)

I was still concerned about the idea that they were going to be asked to deliver lines normally reserved for real actors, but for some reason, Bob Hughes felt there was no way it was going to be an issue. He told me several times to stop worrying and that it would be great. Keith would be great. The band would be…well… great. And as it turns out, Bob was not wrong.

As we were shooting the episode, I would watch the scenes on the video playback and think, "Hmm. That's actually not terrible." Not much of a compliment, I realize, but I didn't want to get too excited. There have been many instances where what I saw on set was NOT as good as I remembered it and actually horrible once it got to the editing room. Bob kept saying, "It's gonna be great!" I kept thinking, "Don't get too excited."

The shoot went smoothly as most of Bob's shoots did. A few weeks later, we gathered to watch a cut of the episode. I was happily surprised. It was great. Keith was fantastic. The band all delivered their lines like pros. The story was engaging, and the music was, of course, awesome. The episode was great! Even Randy with his fake Irish accent came out looking okay. There was nothing here to be worried about or ashamed of. Thanks to Bob, Jim, Danielle and the rest of the crew who put the logistically difficult episode together, it was a success. And to this day, Randy insists that the band even loved it.

CHAPTER 25
RISE OF THE RED PYTHON

As it turned out, the mathematics of *VR Troopers* season one, in terms of the schedule of shows to be produced, left the Red Python miniseries as the final two episodes of the season without any other shows to pair it with for production. We had done 50 shows thus far, and with the three- and five-parters, it just worked out that the last two were the only ones left. We would have to a shoot a two-show block. If I had known that ahead of time, I would have pushed to direct them. Turns out there was no need to push. Bob had already cleared it with Shuki, who was fine with me stepping up and directing the two shows. After all, I had written them, so I was familiar, and it was only two instead of the normal four. Holy crap, I was going to be directing my own scripts! The cold chill of mortal terror immediately ran up my back. I was committed now, and that meant I had to get to work right away so as not to screw this up. I didn't want to let Bob down knowing he had gone out on a limb for me. I could NOT mess this up.

One thing to know about me is that with anything I do, regardless of whether it is work, a hobby or whatever, I come in hot right out of the gate. When I get into something for the first time, I am all in, obsessive beyond what is normal or healthy. This is part of my neurological function that is tied to the whole, must accumulate "things" scenario, where I'm always searching for the next thrill or comfort or anything to release those endorphins and give me a sense of well-being. I had directed the Professor Hart shoot and the scenes for Shuki that day, and I was pretty much obsessed with the idea of directing. It's all I thought about, which is basically the state you need to be in to successfully direct a TV series. Over the years, I've noticed that the best directors I've worked with are relentless in their pursuit of making sure that every little detail is accounted for, and they will not rest until they are. That was not going to be a problem for me with the Red Python mini-series. I was down for making this thing as cool as I could with the resources provided.

Casting the role of the guest star, Amy, was the most important place to start. The shows revolved around her character, so she had to be completely relatable, attractive, but also smart and her own person with her own life. The idea of having her work in an animal shelter allowed us to instantly establish all these attributes. And I love the fact that there was absolutely ZERO romantic chemistry with Ryan throughout the mini-series. You would expect that there would have been, as it was the perfect opportunity. But we never went there. It was just two people meeting for the first time, primarily concerned with the well-being of a displaced animal and proving that just because one person is male and the other female, they can exist in the same universe without wanting to take it to the next level.

This is going to sound insane, but I cannot for the life of me remember the name of the actress we cast as Amy. I tried to look her up, but the role on every website is mistakenly listed as Wendy Lee, who was the voice actress who played the Red Python in the footage. If you are out there reading this, actress who played Amy, I apologize profusely. But I promise you, I did try to find you.

> SIDE NOTE: Finding actors for guest starring roles on Troopers and *Power Rangers* was always a challenge. We had to hire nonunion talent, as none of the Saban series were SAG shows.

Therefore, most of the people we saw for the parts were just getting started or had been trying to break in but hadn't been able to. I give all the credit in the world to Katy Wallin, our Casting Director, and Thom Klohn her Casting Associate. Those two were absolutely the best of the best at finding talent who, although they were new, could do the job. I think they worked tirelessly to continually update their files with new actors that we could choose from. Katy and Thom DO NOT get the credit they deserve when it comes to the success of both shows.

I've often wondered what lead me to cast the girl we did in the role of Amy. I recall that Katy Wallin was surprised and not totally convinced that I had made the right choice. I look back now, and I can see why she may have felt this way. There were other actresses who were more physically right for the role, more athletic, graceful, lithe. I just think for me, at the time, the casting process was 100% instinctual. If someone came in who I felt drawn to, or was interested in watching, be they male or female, that was the person I was going to choose. I didn't think much further ahead than that. If that person was a decent actor, I was all in. Maybe I was pushing back a bit against the whole martial arts comes first thing that we had been adhering to for so long. But I wanted actors whenever I could get them. This is not to say that we were looking at a young Meryl Streep. But the woman was solid and had clearly had some training. This was imperative to me. Let the fight guys figure out how to turn her into a "Karate Kid."

In the end, I thought she did a great job. She was super nice, a joy to be with on set, and very professional. Weirdly, I never saw her in anything again, so I'm assuming she did not pursue acting as a career. But she could have. She was great.

The Red Python episodes were short on comedy, and that needed to change. We had exhausted the Percy angle at this point, as it had been an entire season of him trying to learn the identity of the *VR Troopers,* and we needed something else to bring the funny.

We had always wanted to do a *Risky Business* spoof using Jeb the dog in the Tom Cruise role, alone in the Dojo and having fun just doing naughty stuff. As it was the last episode of the season, I figured, "Why not?" The second unit would shoot it, as Zeb the dog belonged to Phil, the second unit director who also trained Zeb. So, we asked them to just go wild. Do what you want. Don't hold back. For me, the sequence turned out just okay. I'm not sure what the kids watching the show back then thought, but for me, I really wanted to see that dog slide into the Dojo like Tom Cruise did in the movie. I mean, THAT'S the signature visual of that whole montage in the film. Every spoof that's ever been done begins with some version of that. I was told that there was no way to accomplish it, so I hadn't pushed. I was fully aware that although there were any number of methods they could have employed using a green screen and Visual FX, there were time pressures that kept it from being a reality. I probably should have checked into that before I put this idea into my own head. My fault completely.

They shot that whole scene in an afternoon, and that alone was a remarkable feat with our pal Zeb. The little vignettes they did were pretty funny. Hopefully the kids laughed. In terms of Jeb in that episode, I felt like the interaction between him and Amy was the funniest. And the line about Tao being out "stocking up on eye of newt" made me laugh when I re-watched it recently.

The one thing that I look back at that makes me just absolutely lose it laughing is the fake paw. The props department had constructed a "stand-in" paw that was supposed to be Jeb's paw whenever he had to type or touch something they couldn't get the actual dog to do. The only problem was that this faux foot looked more like a mummified hairy spider-alien appendage than one of Jeb's actual paws. The real dog had a smooth, almost silky short coat. This thing had whatever the opposite of that is. I'm not certain they even tried to get close to the actual paw when they made it. (Now that I think of it, I'm not 100% sure the paw was constructed by our team. It could have been purchased.) But let's face it—dog talks, car flies, moving on. The paw was just another hilariously bizarre part of the show that no one ever seemed too concerned about.

Of course, Dr. Poindexter would have to make an appearance in the miniseries. If I was going to go down, I was going down swinging, a man in charge of his own destiny. I truly loved that character and wanted to put on the glasses and hair grease just one last time. I was unsure if there was any comedic value left in him (if there had ever been any to begin with), but I just wanted to get in there with my buddy Brad, who was the only one in the scene with Dr. Poindexter and have a laugh. We did have many laughs. While *The Young and the Restless* was my favorite acting job, to this day Dr. Poindexter was my favorite character to play. It was short (thankfully) but super fun. And it gives me something ridiculous to show people when they ask about my acting days.

Speaking of acting stints, there was another one in the first episode of Red Python that I should mention. For some reason, in this episode I became obsessed with the Skugs (Grimlord's foot soldiers who appear as humans and transform to fight) showing up in ways we hadn't seen before. I just wanted to do something different with it. In the first episode, I thought it would be fun to have a cliché New York, Staten Island gangster dressed in a ridiculous suit along with his whiny girlfriend come to the animal shelter pretending to be there for a pet adoption. When it turns out they are looking for a "Python" to adopt, the ruse is pretty much over (not that it wasn't the moment they appeared on screen). The problem was, I needed a solid, trained actor to play the gangster dude. Everyone I knew at the time was in SAG, and I didn't want to ask them to work nonunion. To my surprise, one of my very best friends at the time, we'll call him Jackie Lajeunesse, stepped up and asked me if he could play the part.

Now, this dude was as authentic as they came. He was from New York and had kind of a mysterious if not a bit shady background. For starters, his father owned a dry-cleaning business. No, for real, on Long Island. And Jackie always seemed to have money, which he peeled off a roll of bills like Robert DeNiro in *Goodfellas*.

Although he had no job that I could identify. It was hard to say if Jackie was connected, but he sure had that aura. He was usually armed with a pistol he kept in his ever-present long trench coat and got around L.A. on a big red Honda motorcycle. When he would pull away, the trench coat would fly behind him like a character from a Guy Ritchie movie. Jackie had hair that was so perfectly quaffed, it would have put the Jersey Shore guys to shame. He was perfect for the role, and I couldn't believe how lucky I had gotten to have him. We found a very funny woman to play his girl, and we were off to the races. The scene is ridiculous, looking back on it. But it was fun to shoot on the day, and it was a new way to bring in the Skugs—always a plus.

During this time, I had finally traded in my beat-up old Chevy Blazer for the car of my dreams. I found a 1982 Porsche Targa with 80,000 miles on it, and I think I spent $17,500 on the thing. Of course, I would quickly learn what a total piece of crap it was when it had me running back and forth to the dealership for expensive repairs (I would have been better off keeping the Blazer—at least Chevy repairs were affordable). The engine once even caught fire.

At the time we were shooting, the car was still new to me, and I was having the time of my life driving it (when it ran). I figured, why not use it to introduce some Skugs. So, when Ryan comes to a roadblock on his motorcycle, he turns to see a black Porsche pull up and roll to a stop. No one even got out of the car. The Porsche just transformed into a quintet of Skugs. That might be the first and only time an inanimate object directly became the Skugs, and probably broke the convention we had set up. But who cares? It was super cool (or at least I thought it was at the time). I look back now a bit embarrassed that I was the douchebag producer who was flaunting his new toy for everyone to see. Of course, the car I was so obsessed with owning would slap me back to reality by becoming a source of irritation and embarrassment.

In the end, the Red Python episodes came out well. I was happy with most of the mini-series. Of course I would have done a few things differently. But I think all directors will tell you that's the case after completing a shoot. The relief of being done was enormous. It was fun as hell, but there is SO much to think about when you direct a film or TV episode or anything with actors and a big crew. Everyone looks to you for answers to hundreds of questions every day. And you need to know what to tell them. This is why it's super important for directors to hire the absolute best department heads—production designer, director of photography, casting, hair and makeup, etc. You find the best people you can and let them do what they do. They're working because they are good at their job. Let them get on with it and help guide them when you feel something should be different than what they are proposing. It's a delicate balance between delegating and collaborating. Some directors feel completely the opposite. They need to control absolutely every single hair ribbon, picture frame, shoe style; anything that appears on screen. I think this eliminates the opportunity to be surprised by a better idea. I enjoyed working with smart, talented people and incorporating their brilliance into the mini-series. They gave me every opportunity to deliver a show of which I could be proud.

So, there I was—my directorial debut finished, and my writing for season one finished. Perhaps if there was a season two, I would get another shot at directing. Let's face it, there HAD to be a season two. No one was talking yet, but it seemed like a foregone conclusion. Little did I know that none of it mattered as it pertained to me. As with all things Saban, the unexpected was about to happen, and although I would go on to direct again, it would be under VERY different circumstances.

CHAPTER 26
WELL, THIS IS FREAKING AWKWARD

I ran into Shuki in the parking lot when I arrived at work a couple of days after my *VR Troopers* directing gig. He told he needed me in a meeting over at his office on the *Power Rangers* set. I had no clue what the meeting was about. I knew they were finishing the season, and once it was complete, the actors would be heading to Australia to film the feature. Maybe he was going to tell me there would be a second season of *VR Troopers* and he wanted to make sure that I was going to continue? Of course, I absolutely would. I loved my job and could not have been happier working with Bob, Danielle and the rest of the crew. I had just seen Bob enter the *VR Troopers* building and head up to his office. So, I didn't think he would be in this meeting. But it was not unusual for Shuki to keep things between just us when it came to big news about my future. I just needed to do was tell my brain to shut up. All would be revealed in a matter of moments. Yeah, good luck with that. The next time my brain shuts up will be when they place my ashes into an urn.

I walked down the hall towards Shuki's office and could hear the familiar sound of his Ronco smokeless ashtray coming from inside. I also heard multiple voices. One of them, I realized, was

Ellen, chatting away, her easy breezy self, loving her job and excited to hear what Shuki was going to suggest moving forward. Unbeknownst to her, that excitement would quickly turn to despair. I should have known something terrible was coming when I turned the corner into the room and there sat BZ, also in attendance, clutching the notebooks that contained all his budgets and schedules. The serious look on his face which, along with his perma-mullet, gave him the appearance of a pissed-off turtle. His lower jaw jutted out and he was tense as hell, all of which told me that this meeting was going to suck big time. I had learned that if BZ was tense, he knew what was coming and it was probably something he had cooked up. And, most likely, it was nothing good (except maybe for BZ himself).

The meeting went quickly and with few pleasantries. Shuki looked to Ellen first and said, "Guys, we're going to change things a little bit. Ellen, you're going to go back to Burbank. Doug, you're gonna take over for Ellen. You're in charge of writing on *Power Rangers*. BZ, you keep doing what you do. Okay? Meeting over." With that, Shuki stood and walked out. Through the wall, I heard his Town Car start up, pull out of its parking space, and speed off.

Okay, so let's break this down. Shuki drives all the way to Valencia just to "cap" Ellen and does it in front of me and BZ. There's no discussion as to why it is happening. No debrief afterward. Literally, it was a five-minute affair that could have been about anything under the sun. But it was not. It was a public execution, done in questionable taste, with BZ looking on like a starving hyena waiting for the scraps of Ellen's dignity to gnaw on.

I wasn't all that surprised that Shuki had bailed once the bomb had been detonated. Shuki HATED any kind of conflict. This was something he told me on several occasions. He also hated hurting people's feelings. Or at least I believe that to be true. He's a musician, an artist. He doesn't have the cutthroat gene that allows him to go in, take someone's job away from them, then meet up for Starbucks a few minutes later. He would much rather have been at home in his hookah room, pulling on a lovely bowl of "fruity tobacco" and relaxing after a hard day of composing. He was, at this moment, doing the next best thing, relaxing in the back of his town car amid a cloud of cigarette smoke, undoubtedly glad it was all over.

I looked at BZ, who was now wearing what can only be described as a victory smile. He glanced over at Ellen, waiting for her to speak. I believe this was his way of silently telling her, "See? You see the power I have? You should have taken my creative notes." And the fact that I was there, I was pretty sure that was his doing as well. He must have insisted to Shuki that I be present for Ellen's dismissal. He would have made up an excuse, but for BZ, the reason would have been so that I understood what had gone down and knew not to mess with him.

I was just trying to absorb the broad strokes and decipher what this all meant in the moment. Was I suddenly, with the wave of a hand, the new "cut and paste" dude? And what did BZ have to do with all of this anyway? Why was he there gloating like a child who just told Mom his older sibling had gone *Edward Scissorhands* on the family's goldendoodle? Whatever this was, it was difficult to process.

Ellen and I walked to her office and closed the door. I immediately told her how sorry I was, that I knew nothing about any of it and I wasn't even sure it was right to accept the job.

"Don't be ridiculous!" she said. "You have to accept it. At least then there's someone in here we can trust. What if they need a script written in 4 hours?" We both tried to see the humor in it. But it was not easy.

What happened next was something that I will always remember, no matter where my life takes me. In that moment, Ellen did what VERY few of us would have in a similar situation. As she packed her things, she made sure to explain, in detail, every single aspect of what her job entailed and what MY job would entail as the creative producer on the behemoth that was *Mighty Morphin Power Rangers*. She let me know what would be expected of me and basically how to stay out of trouble in what was a very demanding and tricky position, especially with you-know-who and his army of undermining minions only a few feet away. BZ had successfully campaigned to remove Ellen from the position. Ellen was a high-ranking executive with years of experience and hit shows to her credit. BZ was a line producer. Yet he was able to send her packing back to Burbank and make her feel terrible in the process by hatching that BS meeting, which, by the way, I later confirmed was his suggestion.

Clearly, I was taking on a job that was well beyond my experience. On *VR Troopers*, I was the "script guy" and did a decent job with that. But there was always Bob Hughes, who was really in charge of things. He was the backstop and a friend I could go to if things went sideways. Now, there was no more backstop. It was more like the "Moon Door" *in Game of Thrones*, a hole in the floor of a castle that opened to reveal a several thousand-foot plummet to the rocks below. I now had a backdrop instead of a backstop. Down the hall was a guy, who, if you didn't get things done his way, would make sure you were fired as soon as he could hatch a plan to pull it off without looking like he had anything to do with it.

As I walked back to *VR Troopers* to fill Bob in on what just transpired, I started to think about just what made BZ tick. I mean, what I had just witnessed was a vicious thing to do to someone as kind and professional as Ellen. And it didn't seem to bother him in the least. BZ really was like some kind of robot assassin with no feelings who just mowed people down if they got in his way. Part of me thinks that this was something he couldn't help, drilled into him long ago, at least as far back as the military. He absolutely could not function in an environment that wasn't on time, on schedule, and by the book. It HAD to run like a military operation or he would implode. BZ was unable to deal with the uncertainty of not knowing the precise minute a script would arrive or if it had too many things he didn't want to pay for from his budget, or if there were too many extras or guest cast or if it the script was too long. BZ wanted four scripts delivered on the day he had specified in a meeting several months ago. They all needed to be the correct length, inexpensive, and reasonably producible in every way on the first go-round. This is, of course, UNREASONABLE to expect on any level. The preparatory period for any show is so that these things can be ironed out and adjusted in subsequent drafts of the script. BZ always claimed that the writers knew the rules and had deadlines they agreed to follow. They had to be held accountable. "Really? That's all that had to happen to fix the entire broken system?" Who was going to hold Shuki accountable, or Cheryl Saban, or Haim when he was reading and giving notes? Would that be you, BZ? He always seemed frustrated by the fact that the scripts were just late sometimes. His go to comment was, "If Little BZ could get his scripts in on time, why can't the others?"

The answer to that was simple. They all could have delivered on time if their only requirement was to turn in unusable scripts that were completely rewritten from a writer who discarded any notes in the process. But let's not start with the accusations quite yet.

BZ had played the long game on his quest to ambush Ellen. I'm sure he'd had many conversations with Shuki, Ronnie Hadar, and even Haim over the course of months to make sure nothing would blow back on him. Ellen, after all, was a beloved member of the Saban family, and BZ needed to be sure that his desperate and unrealistic attempt to create order didn't jeopardize his job or trucking empire. But that was the genius of BZ. He let his plans simmer and develop over time, so they seemed like there was nothing even happening, no plan, no dirty dealings. He must have somehow convinced Haim that he had come to the decision on his own, that Ellen would destroy his hit show with delays and the inability to work with BZ and his crew. They had to make a change. Once that seed was planted in Haim's mind, that there was a chance the golden goose was going to be harmed, it didn't matter who it was. They had to go. BZ just sat back and watched with a smile, determined to convince the next person in line to give him a seat at the creative table. At least this was the pattern I observed when it came to BZ and the show. It was like waiting for the end of a long game of chess in which the board would blow up, eviscerating everyone but BZ and his little gang.

Of course, I could be totally wrong about all of this. As I have said more than a few times, this is my opinion based on my memories of what I saw and the only explanation that makes sense all these years later. I may be missing a few details, but I think I'm close on this one. Who knows? And does it really matter now? A wonderful, kind woman had been treated like crap. And I was taking over writing on the most successful show in the history of kids TV. I should have been over the moon. I would surely be getting a little bump in pay, and I was going to be working with Jason Frank and the others to create cool new shows that would hopefully help keep the franchise chugging along. I should have been screaming it from the mountaintop. But I was not. I didn't say much of anything to anyone about it.

Ellen was a good and decent human being, and what was done to her—removing her from the show with no explanation in front of the person who most likely made it happen (BZ) and the guy who would be replacing her (me)—was just crappy and humiliating. If Ellen Levy Sarnoff is reading this, and I hope she will at some point, please know that you were all class and grace during that time. Ellen, you were the better person in every way, a true example to me of the way to handle adversity, and I thank you for that. I could NOT have transitioned into that job without your love and support.

CHAPTER 27
TOUCHDOWN ON THE DARK PLANET

So, suddenly out of nowhere, I was back at *Power Rangers*, the newly appointed creative gatekeeper of the series. In truth, they brought me over to appease BZ. He wanted to install someone he could pressure to deliver scripts on his timeline. I think he also hoped we would become partners in the creative development of the show, that I would welcome his ideas and help him extend his power base beyond the spreadsheets and schedules he'd been stuck with during Ellen's reign. Ellen had kept BZ out of anything creative, and that had eventually lead to her ousting. BZ saw himself as king of the *Power Rangers* castle. He hated sharing the throne with anyone and wanted every person on that crew to "bend the knee" to him and him alone. With Ellen gone, he was one step closer to absolute power.

I needed to figure out how to proceed in a way that would appease BZ, allow us to work in relative harmony, and make him believe that he was part of the creative process, all while still doing what I felt was best, and made the most sense creatively, for the show. It became an insane, ass-kissing mind game I was forced to play, all in an effort not to disturb BZ's ego or incur his wrath.

This, by the way, should never have been an issue. Because this is NOT the way TV shows are set up. The line producer (BZ) is normally charged with executing the vision of the creative producers in whatever way they need. The line producer has a budget that is constantly being rearranged, moving money from one department to the next to allow for unexpected costs. It's an important job and a difficult balancing act (literally), and that's what he was there for—to help Shuki, Haim, me, Scott Page-Pagter, and any other producers involved in the creative achieve our goals and do the best job we could. Or at least that's how it should have been. It was not. BZ had set himself up as the center of power for the production, and with Shuki and Haim as busy as they were and Ellen gone, he could continue to build on that, especially with a newbie like me in the creative producer position.

When I moved into what was once Ellen's office, I put the feelings of guilt and anger about how she had been treated aside and set about trying to create a successful department that could co-exist with BZ's production team. The first thing I needed to do was assuage his fear that we would continue with Ellen's system of script delivery. I immediately told him I needed a computer system for the scripts—two Macintosh SEs and a laser printer. I also needed an assistant/script handler who could help me with meetings, deadlines, and basic organization, as well as taking care of the distribution of the scripts from the first drafts through the final pages.

Of course, BZ was completely and utterly onboard with both the computers and the assistant, anything that would make things run in a more orderly and efficient fashion. And so, I started a process that I had never in my life had to face—hiring someone to work with me. In this case, the person that I would be hiring would be my partner in crime, there with me every step of the way. I like to think of my writing staff, including the writer's assistant, as a team, like any other. I'm the coach, and if I help everyone achieve their highest level of performance well, we could still lose, because let's face it, successful TV shows are pretty hard to come by. But it gives us the best chance not to completely screw things up, and that's about all anyone can hope for. I must say that over the years, my greatest joy in the job space is seeing people working for me succeed and be rewarded for their performance. I have NEVER had a writer's assistant who didn't go on to become a working writer. I have even had a few become showrunners. The one thing to keep in mind when it comes to elevating your people, though, is never do it with an expectation that they will return the favor. Most will not. Once they have moved on and assumed their new positions, they will become way too busy to even return your phone call. In fact, you will probably not hear from them again until they need another job.

So, I interviewed several candidates for the assistant role and decided to go with a shy but incredibly funny woman named Jackie Marchand. Jackie came to me through a friend of a friend, and I just got a really good vibe from her in our meeting. I felt like Jackie could handle the work no problem. I had mistakenly thought that she would be able to start slow, as the office was a bit quiet with the Rangers doing press and ADR for the feature. I figured that most of what she would be tasked with in the beginning would be helping set up the computers and getting the system worked out and running smoothly. What I hadn't even considered was that the day after Jackie started work at MMPR, I was scheduled to leave on a scuba diving trip to Belize with Scott, his brother Gib, and a few other folks. This was something that had been planned for a while, and there was no getting out of it. (Not that I wanted to. I mean, Belize? Come on!). So off I went, leaving poor Jackie to fend for herself in the world of BZ and his sycophants, led by the terrifying Jabba, who had her nose into everything and would surely do nothing to make Jackie's life easier. Additionally, the new computers were set to arrive while I was gone. In her interview, Jackie had told me that her experience with the world of computing had mostly been on Windows-based machines, so she may have a little catching up to do in that respect, as we were going to use Macs. What I didn't know, and Jackie recently revealed to me, was that she had absolutely no computer training back then. She had been working at a shop that sold mostly acoustic guitars and was kind of a throwback to the 1970s. She literally didn't know how to boot up or initialize any type of computer. I'm glad I didn't know this, as she was going to be left to do all the set up on her own, unboxing the machines, booting them up for the first time, getting the software loaded, etc. This may seem like child's play, as you're reading this in whatever year you're reading it. But this was 1994. Back then, setting up a Mac wasn't as automatic as it is now. There were little plastic disks to deal with that had to be inserted into the 3.5-inch disk drive and transferred onto the "massive" 80-meg hard drives in each machine (80 megs! I actually thought we had overbought for our needs at the time). The setup was a process that I had learned while working at a computer store for years during my acting days. To me, back then, it was second nature. But to someone who lacked that experience? Yikes!

When I returned from the dive trip (which was amazing BTW), I immediately knew that I had hired the right person for the job. The office was set up perfectly. The computers were up and running, software loaded. All the tapes for the new season had been catalogued. Jackie had handled it all beautifully, and we were ready to roll.

This is a valuable lesson for anyone reading this who is just starting their career in the entertainment industry. You can only help yourself by going the extra mile. Most bosses don't want to be bothered with the little stuff. They don't want to know how it all works, or how you made it work—just that it does. And all the better if you do it well. The best way to climb the ladder to the job you want is to shine in the one you have now.

CHAPTER 28
OUR SAVIOR ARRIVES (HEAVENS OPEN, ANGELS SING)

When thinking back on those early days, I never realized how truly isolated and on our own little island Jackie and I were. Our office was in the corner of the building, separate from BZ and his crew. BZ had his minions who he had trained not to share information freely with us. Questions regarding anything related to the logistics of the show had to go through BZ and BZ only. Anytime we approached her desk with a question, Jabba would just give that bizarre grin and point us to BZ's office. It was completely foreign to me after having such an amazing relationship with Danielle on *VR Troopers* that someone would take such pride in creating an environment of exclusion and secrecy.

The good news was that Jackie and I were about to be blessed with an amazing new partner in our quest to build a happy, productive work environment. Ann Knapp (later Ann Austen, but we'll use Knapp for our purposes) was coming over from Fox. I'm sure this was partially an insurance policy to make sure I didn't screw things up. She would bring with her a sane, calming, creative voice and tons of experience. At the time I felt a bit like they had snuck one past me and given me a new boss to contend with. In retrospect, it was a brilliant move on Shuki and Haim's part. And it was a definite life saver for me and Jackie.

Ann had spent much of her career as a network executive in one form or another. As such, she was used to being the final word on all things creative for the shows she oversaw. Her job was to ensure every episode was acceptable to all the departments at the network before it ever got close to being aired. Her coming to Saban was huge. She understood how things worked at Fox Kids and would help us avoid making dumb mistakes the network would reject and that would cost us valuable time. She was even friends with the Broadcast Standards department. The Church Lady herself was a regular lunch companion, allowing the two to discuss workarounds for the things the Church Lady felt too scary or violent. Ann had relationships with the creative executives at Fox who would take her place, most of whom she had trained. She was also brilliant with editing notes and just so happened to be a great writer as well. She was a powerhouse who pretty much knew it all but never let on that she did. In fact, if you met her for the first time the way I had, you might have assumed she was a pleasant visitor to the set, there to have lunch with a friend and had gotten lost on the way.

On the day Ann arrived, Jackie stepped into my office to inform me that our new cohort was on her way up from the parking lot. "Shit," I thought. I should have worn a button-down shirt. I looked like a freaking hobo. I could have at least tried to up my game a little to make her feel welcome. Technically, I wasn't supposed to look corporate, though, right? I mean she would be sporting a fancy business suit and be all decked out and made up, but she'd just have to accept that this was production, and we were a little less put together than at the network. I walked to the end of the hall and looked down the stairs to find I was wrong about pretty much every assumption. There, sitting on a step, out of breath, sat a VERY pregnant woman in a simple denim dress. She was holding the hand of a small red-headed toddler and smiling as they made their way up the stairs. Her face was beet red from the heat outside, and she rested every few steps in order to keep a bag of toys and diapers from tipping over and spilling onto the floor.

I introduced myself and we both immediately started laughing. Not a word spoken beyond introductions. Just laughing. The whole thing was so ridiculous. Me worried about being up to corporate snuff. Her, with one and a half kids in tow, on one of the hottest days of the year, and not even giving it a second thought. It was kind of hilarious but at the same time heroic. This young mother, loaded down with every possible piece of baby-rearing weaponry, was ready to get to work on freaking *Power Rangers*. It was awesome. From that day on, we laughed a lot. We also cried a lot. We yelled a little. We did some wonderful work together. But I will always think back to the day she appeared at the sound stages just being her supermom self. It was awesome.

Ann was instantly welcomed in her new role as creative team captain, and every chance I got, I made sure everyone else knew there was a new sheriff in town, and she was all about the creative. Great news for us. Not so much for BZ. As Ann settled in, she, Jackie and I became our own little power trio. The RUSH of *Mighty Morphin Power Rangers*.

The three of us easily bonded for many reasons. We felt a certain kind of pride and excitement in being a part of this huge success that none of us could have fathomed. We also knew we were in a very unusual situation, one that should not be taken for granted.

There was a lot to keep me busy, so there really wasn't a time when boredom became an issue. Somehow, I had become the producer most of the cast came to if there was an issue with the way they were being treated or with something they felt was unfair. I think that with me having been an actor, they felt like I would understand their plight and at least listen to them when they had a problem or complaint. At the same time, if the crew was having an issue with one of the cast members, they came to me to help sort it out.

CHAPTER 29
TOMMY WITH A SIDE OF KORN

One busy afternoon, Ann was at a meeting, and I was in my office working on a draft of a script for the next block of shows. I'd been visited several times by different production assistants regarding the behavior of one of our actors, who had been called in very early to shoot a small scene, and then would spend the day in his dressing room, waiting around to be called to the stage for the last scene of the day, one in which he had no lines. Situations like this don't happen often on TV shows that move quickly and efficiently. But they do happen and are sometimes unavoidable. There are just times when the work falls in a way that leaves some actors having to work early in the morning and then again at the end of the day. That's what had happened to Jason Frank that day. And while he was trying to be jovial and his usual fun and happy go lucky self, I could tell that he wasn't super stoked that he'd been put in that position. Not only that, but with his karate school a mile up the road, he could have spent several hours attending to business there, instead of sitting around at the stage.

Now, there are those who will leap out of their chairs and scream to the heavens that you NEVER let an actor out of your sight once you have them on the premises. You've paid them for the day, so you "own" them (I always hated this term). Having been an actor, I will tell you that under normal circumstances, I get it, and I accept it. The money is usually good, so for what they are paying, you can sit around for a while and chill the "F" out. This is why SAG has contracts that protect actors and ensure they are paid equitably for all manner of situation. However, when you are paying what equates to $125/day to your actors who happen to be the stars of the biggest kids' show in history, you might need to be a little more reasonable in the way you treat them.

Jason had shot his first scene and spent the rest of the morning playing some harmless practical jokes, cranking his music, and doing whatever he could think of to remind everyone that he was there and thought the whole thing was bogus. Unfortunately, BZ made it a point to warn Jason in advance not to leave without permission or he would be in "deep shit."

> SIDE NOTE: I'd always maintained that threats were never a good plan of attack when it came to Jason. First, what kind of "deep shit" are we talking? There was nothing you could do to this kid that he couldn't undo with a single phone call to Haim or Shuki. Second, who was going to enforce the threat, regardless of what it was? It was ludicrous. But BZ seemed to feel this was an effective strategy, like he was dealing with a juvenile delinquent and not the star of his TV series. This was yet another philosophy in which BZ and I disagreed. Not a big shock.

What had to happen in this moment, what I needed to ensure, was that Jason would stop the music and general mayhem for the rest of the day so the crew could finish and everyone could go home. It's important to note that the music he was playing was by a group called Korn, a band on the forefront of the NuMetal movement, a darker, more intense metal featuring tuned-down seven-string electric guitars, guys screaming and/or rapping the lyrics, and turntables used as instruments. It was a whole new deal, and it was about to completely blow up and become the new Heavy Metal. Unfortunately, it was currently making life impossible for the crew. I had to come up with a distraction for Jason to refocus him on something positive—and quieter. I realize that this was a stupid and enabling tactic. But sometimes on a TV or movie set, you must maneuver the younger stars to get them to behave. The set is a workplace. And within reason, as a producer, you need to do what it takes to make sure the work gets finished.

I had been putting off looking at some casting tapes but had to get it done before the end of the day. It occurred to me that Jason might be interested in this process and would want to go through the tapes with me to see if there were any future "Saban Stars" on them. Turns out he did. So back in my office, we sat down and started watching auditions, looking for actors to fill a guest role on the show. As we watched each one, I asked him questions like why this actor was better than the last one, and who he thought would do best at the role. His opinion was dead-on most times, and as we got to the end of the first tape, Jason was hooked. He was totally dialed in to the technique he had been using and could identify actors who had the goods and those who didn't. I think he had a blast. For the rest of the day, Jason ran between the set where he was perfectly well behaved and my office, where he was doing the very important work of casting the show.

> SIDE NOTE: Just to be clear, having other actors watch auditions is not something I normally do; it just feels weird and kind of unfair to the auditioning actor. HOWEVER, it was a small part in a scene that Jason wasn't going to be in, and in truth, it was helpful for him to be able to see things from the other side.
> AND it chopped down the Korn for the rest of the afternoon. Although this is not to say that it would be the last we would hear from Korn.

As he was watching the casting tapes, Jason told me that

Jonathan, the lead singer from Korn, had invited him to the LA venue the Roxy that night as a guest of the band. As NuMetal was just starting to explode, you could still see bands at smaller venues where it was common to become part of the performance by thrashing around the mosh pit (a human soup of angry young people wearing tattered clothing, doing their best to slam into each other with enough force to cause superficial damage and minor bleeding).

I lay my head down on my desk and started laughing quietly to myself. Jason laughed along and asked what was so funny. I told him he knew exactly what was so funny. He was going to tear up that club and leave it looking like a scene from *Law and Order: Mosh Pit Murders* by the end of the night. We were in the middle of shooting a four-show block, and it would be hard to explain him suddenly showing up battered and bruised.

Jason could not have cut me off any faster. He swore up and down that he was just going there to hear the music. According to him, Jonathan really wanted him to see them live, and Jason really wanted to go. For some reason, this sounded reasonable to me, so I figured why push it. Jason promised that he was going to watch and hang out with the band after the show. That was it. No mosh pit for him. He promised me from the bottom of his heart.

The Roxy Theatre on Sunset Blvd. was big enough to encourage a good-sized mosh pit that would surely get out of control quickly, particularly once word spread that the dude from that kiddie show was in there bashing heads along with everyone else. This probably sounded like a lot of fun to the hordes of Korn fans who would also be in attendance. Fresh celebrity meat! WOO HOO!

Ironically, had the "Korn Holes" done their research, they would have known that Jason Frank was a very well trained, very strong, very unafraid young man who was probably more accustomed to physical contact than anyone else in attendance that night. With actual permission to punish other people with no repercussions of any kind, you might not like what was left of your mosh pit or your face at the end of the night.

But Jason had promised me no fighting, and as the one who always stood up for him when others doubted that he could stay out of trouble, I took him at his word that he would behave. I mean, there wasn't much more I could do but hope he really was going to listen to the music.

CUT TO: It's the following morning, and I'm barely out of my car when a production assistant races across the parking lot towards me, waving a walkie talkie. She hands the radio over and I hear Cynthia, our awesome hair and makeup lead, on the other end. Apparently, she's been looking for me since everyone started arriving at 6:30. She didn't want to talk over the radio, but she asked if she could meet me in my office in five minutes.

"Copy that," I replied and headed to my office. What the "F" was going on? I mean, we'd only been in for seven minutes. Just as I was thinking this, I rounded the corner to my office and discovered the source of everyone's unrest and panic.

Jason David Frank stood in the middle of my office with a goofy, embarrassed smile on his face. Across his cheek was a gash that wasn't enormous, but definitely large enough to be seen on camera. It had, of course, happened the previous night when he was "just listening" to his new buddy Jonathan from Korn and was definitely NOT bashing his face against other fans in the mosh pit. Imagine if he hadn't listened to me and HAD gone into the pit. We could have really been in trouble.

I asked Cynthia what our options were. She basically said a bandage was about it. She didn't want to put makeup on it for fear of infection. They could leave it, but it felt to me like it was distracting enough so that kids would focus on the wound and be taken out of the story. So, a bandage it was. All we needed was a story point to explain why mid-episode, Tommy suddenly showed up to meet Kimberly and the others with a bandage on his face. I'm not sure who came up with it first, but someone suggested that perhaps he'd had a bad dream and fallen out of bed in the middle of the night. This wasn't a terrible thought, a little complicated perhaps, but it could work. The key was don't make a big deal about it and just move on. So, when Tommy walked into the scene, Kimberly asked what had happened and he merely replied that he had fallen out of bed. None of the Rangers overreacted, and in a mere moment, we were beyond the distraction and on to other more important story points.

When Ann arrived that day, she smiled, shook her head, and commented that perhaps our most popular Ranger was starting to take advantage of the benefits of being on a hit TV show a little too far. He was meeting rock stars and getting special treatment when he went out to dinner and clubs. He had opened a new school right up the road in Valencia called Rising Sun Karate that was bursting at the seams with students drawn in by the whole *Power Rangers* thing. The cash had started to pour in for Jason. With the school kicking ass, literally, he decided it would be prudent to purchase a white stretch limousine so that he and his wife and young kids could go out without him having to drive them. All the things that he'd wanted to do growing up were now possible. Skydiving, scuba diving, treating his friends and family to nice dinners and trips—these were just a few of the things Jason's fame earned him.

The Korn incident, we knew, was only a glimpse at how sideways things could go. Ann suggested that we should probably have a CTJ (Come to Jesus) conversation with him sooner rather than later to talk about what it meant to be "Number One on the call sheet"—in other words, the star of the show. There were certain things Jason needed to be aware of, certain places he should probably stay clear of, and behaviors that could become problematic for him. It was all a tradeoff.

The first conversation we had was your typical one: "Dude, you need to chill. Just calm down a little. You can have fun, but don't let it mess up what got you there in the first place." His response, as always, was one of great respect. He apologized profusely and promised he would be cool. It was just a stupid mistake. The thing was, he was so earnest and so contrite, I walked away actually feeling guilty.

Back when I was Jason's acting coach, we spent so much time

together that it was natural for us to discuss his personal issues, feelings, and inner struggles, as they all related to his acting and what he could bring to the screen from his internal life. In this new phase of stardom and emotional struggles, Ann and I became the unofficial Jason wranglers. We were his de facto support system on the set, there to keep him focused and in control. I think we would have been much less successful in that task had Jason not genuinely cared for both of us. He didn't want to let us down. Also, thank God, he took his work very seriously, no matter what was going on personally. He was (mostly) there when needed; he knew his lines and delivered his performance.

As someone who has benefitted immensely from therapy, I had convinced Jason to see a therapist a while back. He went once, and although he found it calming to be able to talk to someone neutral and outside of the PR world, he never went back. Perhaps he was afraid of what he might discover about himself and his upbringing and how he would put the genie back in the bottle once it was uncorked.

Yes, Jason had some shit to deal with, and like many of us, it was freaking dark. Also, like many of us, it had been stuffed down into his inner psyche to fester; anger that had been subdued, the valve periodically released by years of daily martial arts and constant working out and training. Now, becoming one of the most famous people on the planet was only going to make things harder to deal with. The moments where crowds of people gathered around him to espouse his greatness were becoming a much-needed bandage to his soul. It made him feel loved, just as the kids in his karate school did. He was Sensei Jason, the White Ranger. He was a real-life hero to legions of kids who were obsessed with being him. But fame, as we all know, can open a hole that can never be filled. Jason had a mischievous gremlin inside him that he seemed to have less and less control over and it fed off the adoration, pats on the back and "attaboys." We would have to keep an eye out, if only to protect him from himself. Not an easy thing to do when you're dealing with a 10th-degree black belt who could be as unpredictable as a pit bull and had a very good reason for this that no one could have known. We certainly didn't. We just thought Jason was a sweet goofball whose hands were lethal weapons and who had moments of self-doubt that required a pep talk. And unfortunately, our job was not to do a deep dive into his psyche to find the source of his angst and help him through it. Our job was to get him on set and saying his lines. We could only help him as much as he allowed us to. And, somehow, he always seemed to pull himself out of his tailspins and show up on set ready to kick ass as Tommy. It wouldn't be until years later that the depths of Jason's struggles would be truly understood and revealed.

CHAPTER 30

MIGHTY MORPHIN POWER RANGERS: THE MOVIE

As I write this chapter, I think it's important to be crystal clear about my involvement with the first movie. The truth of the matter is, there was none. Zero. Zilch. Unlike the later movie, *Turbo: A Power Rangers Movie*, I merely watched *Mighty Morphin Power Rangers: The Movie* from the sidelines as the studio did its thing. I occasionally got a call from Jason Frank when the frustration would just get to be too much. For a guy with all that energy, sitting around all day doing nothing, away from his family, would occasionally become too much for him to bear. But all in all, everyone, from what I could tell, had fun, and did a great job. The only way the first movie had any effect on me and my job at the time, was praying they kept to their schedule so we could commence shooting the next season of the TV show on time.

The first *Power Rangers* movie was a logistical challenge. Strike that. I can't believe that's how I opened this paragraph. OF COURSE it was a logistical challenge! It was a freaking movie! Every movie is a logistical challenge, and it's never for the same reason. There's always a unique set of problems that go with every movie, and this was no exception. For the first MMPR movie, there was a laundry list of land mines. It was being shot in a foreign country with massive visual effects and effects makeup that saw Paul Freeman (Ivan Ooze) stuck in the chair for five or six hours a day. They had a relatively new director who came from TV and hadn't yet shot a feature film, and six lead actors who had never been in a feature film and had to endure the boredom of waiting all day just to get a single shot. Let's just assume it was always going to be rough going and start with that.

After meeting each of the people who were overseeing the movie, at various times over the following weeks, I came away with the distinct feeling that there was going to be one main issue facing them. These big time Hollywood producers and studio executives in charge of delivering the film made no secret of the fact that they considered the series a ridiculous anomaly and couldn't for the life of them understand how it was such a huge hit. The good news for us was that these amazing, brilliant people, tasked with making this movie regardless of the source material, were going to show us TV weasels how it was done at the adult table, in the big leagues, in the real world. Luck be a lady tonight!

The only exception to this palatable condescension, from what I could tell, was a guy named Chris Meledandri. He was the Fox Studio producer/executive and the suit everyone reported to. From what I remember, the guy was VERY supportive, VERY complimentary, and was really kind in taking Jason Frank under his wing, as I think he may have sensed that the success of the film depended on Jason being okay, both mentally and physically. Jason raved to me about Chris, which made me glad that there weren't only Hollywood types on the movie and that someone had Jason's interests at heart. The movie people were all, on the surface, polite enough and put on a good face when they had to deal with the TV production. If there's one thing I've learned, however, is that people can only keep up a facade for so long. Eventually their true nature will be revealed, and sometimes it can be surprising.

All the dialogue replacement (ADR) for the movie was scheduled to be done at our studio in Valencia. This made a certain amount of sense, as the Rangers would be back at work on the TV show and needed to be close to set. There was one person from the movie who drew the short straw and had to oversee the ADR, and make sure any dialogue that needed to be replaced or added was handled. This woman's behavior was instantly bizarre to me. When she entered the building where the ADR studio was, it was normal that she would encounter members of the crew from *VR Troopers*, as they occupied the same space. What I immediately noticed was that this weirdo literally looked like she was walking down the streets of a third world country as a visitor, staying as far away from any of the crew members, not engaging them, not even making eye contact. It was as if we were the untouchables of the industry, and this person of power and class wanted no part of us in any way shape or form. I admit, we had some interesting looking folks on the team. And guess what? All of them were big-hearted, lovable, hardworking people just trying to do their jobs.

This person's facade cracked a little more when it became obvious that she could not, for the life of her, understand that our ADR stage served several Saban shows and, as a result, was usually booked. This producer became frustrated with the fact that she had to drive to Valencia and was sometimes made to wait while another session finished. She regularly clomped around the office, phone in hand, calling anyone and everyone to step in and clear the studio so she could get the actors in and out and be done with work for the day. There were a couple of times she literally screamed at Scott Page-Pagter, who oversaw ADR, and threatened to call Haim or Shuki and have Scott's job. She even remarked once that no one cared about the quality of the TV show anyway, so why did it take so long to get things done?

Now, if you knew the late, great Scott Page-Pagter, you knew one thing was for certain. He didn't take kindly to threats. In fact, he usually enjoyed seeing loudmouth jerks squirm while trying to throw their weight around and getting nowhere. I won't confirm this, but I believe I remember Scott deciding that he needed to really take his time in the studio as we had been rushing to accommodate the movie and the work for the TV shows was "suffering."

So, he just slowed EVERYTHING down, not enough to be noticeable to the masses, but enough to annoy this person to the point that, once she realized no one was going to step in, finally just gave up. Scott was hilarious that way. I loved to watch him mess with people who deserved it. And this person deserved it! Of course, with an attitude like that, she went on to produce a string of mega hit movies and become insanely wealthy and probably now has a statue outside her alma mater or a street named after her in her hometown. Another show business success story I think we can all feel good about.

Anyway, the intention of 20th Century Fox was to make the movie into a slick, giant, summer blockbuster. They had 20 million dollars to spend, and by golly they were going to lift *Power Rangers* up and give it a whole new shiny, expensive, theatrical look. This sounded intriguing to all of us. In fact, it was exciting to hear that was the plan. I'd always wanted to see the Rangers in cool outfits made of something other than spandex (not that I don't love spandex—I was in an 80s rock band and wore it proudly). But this was the opportunity to create an awesome palette with which to tell the story. The problem was that like most failed creative endeavors in Hollywood, no one bothered to get the story itself right.

This was the result a lot of different factors that no one person could have foreseen. At the end of the day, the TV characters were extreme in the sense that they were who they were and were NOT going to change. They were immovable pieces that each had a very specific place in a series which had to be protected at all costs. There wasn't going to be any real emotional turmoil that allowed them to grow or learn some huge lesson that would change them forever. No one was going to get angry or frustrated. They were the *Mighty Morphin Power Rangers*. On the series, they didn't do that. And they weren't going to do that in the movie either. And I totally get that. How do you develop any character moments for six well-established icons of current-day pop culture? The problem is, if you're developing a movie that will strike any sort of chord with an audience over the age of 10, you've just completely screwed yourself. Entirely. Totally.

> SIDE NOTE: Feature-length motion pictures rely on a set of rules that over the years have been employed repeatedly and are tried and true necessities to the success of a film's dramatic throughline. One of these rules is that your characters must grow. They must go on a PERSONAL journey that changes them in some profound way. Think of your favorite movie. I promise you the lead character has a journey to face and will come out of it a better person for having gone through it. *How to Train Your Dragon*, you say? Why not. In the first film, Hiccup learns how to stand up and be a Viking without giving up the quirky brilliance that makes him Hiccup. Stoick learns to trust his son and is even in awe of him for his bravery. Astrid goes from tough, singular-focused Dragon Killer to respectful, loving Dragon Rider with a side order of butt-kicking bravado. And it goes on. Every character in that movie has a personal journey that changes them in one way or another. This is what the term "character arc" means. Even Toothless, a wild animal who is just learning to communicate with humans, has an arc. That's one of the many reasons the film works. Great characters from the kids to the grown-ups to the dragons are why audiences young AND old went crazy for the movie and still do to this day. Its global box office receipts are just under $500 million. And that's just the first installment. There were two other movies that followed and a 121-episode TV series, taking the total earnings well above the $1 billion mark and possibly closing in on the $2 billion mark with toys and ancillary products tied to the movies. Oh, and they just finished a live-action version of the first movie, which I'm told is a brilliant film, directed by Dean DuBlois, the original director of the animated film and a fantastic human being. Can't wait to see it.

What the first *Power Rangers* movie ended up being, at least for me, was a long, shiny *Power Rangers* TV episode with cool costumes, decent-looking Zords, and a humorous villain with great makeup and even better comic timing. The production seemed to be second guessing itself at every turn but focusing on the wrong things to second guess. Changing actors back and forth several times for the same part after they had already shot thousands of feet of film. Reinventing the helmet visors only to have them not work and delay shooting over and over. Abandoning the fighting foot soldiers (giant overweight rats) they had spent tens of thousands on and replacing them with giant flying crows with black feathers and purple beaks called Tengus. Those are just a few examples, and all of this was happening with the actors waiting in their hotel rooms to work. Days passed, and it quickly became clear that the Rangers would not be home in time to start up the series again and, in fact, no one could seem to pinpoint when they would be home at all.

The TV show had already blown through a two-part miniseries that Shuki and Shell had written in case of emergency. In it, the Rangers as children must fight Rito Revolto (Rita's brother and the newest bad guy) and his band of idiots, then find a way back to their grown-up form. But this was not going to plug the damn that was ready to burst. It was only two episodes. We needed more in a hurry.

While everyone scrambled around as if the world was coming to an end, Shuki, as usual, had figured it out weeks ago. He and Shell, in a matter of a few days, wrote another two-part episode that had the Rangers going back in time to the colonial days of Angel Grove and doing their Ranger best to battle a new foe they had never seen before.

The episodes were shot in Australia with a local crew. Shuki even recruited Paul Schrier and Jason Narvey (Bulk and Skull) to organize and run the shoot! And they did an amazing job! (How could you not love those two? Consummate professionals in every way.) The team ended up using an old-time theme park and several other locations around Sydney that all matched well for Angel

Grove. They also managed to make use of the giant rats that were just too dopey for the movie guys. But for the series? Bring it on! All in all, these two episodes delivered and bought us some time, while keeping the Rangers busy in their off hours.

Those two episodes were the last produced before I started receiving my first onscreen *Power Rangers* credit ever. I thought that was pretty cool back in the day. I mean, who the hell would ever think to put the title of Supervising Producer over my name? I only came to find out later that my credit was lowest on the rung of producer credits, except for "Associate Producer." But who cared? Back then, it was all new and awesome, and we would soon be back to work on the TV series.

CHAPTER 31
BZ BACKS UP

It had only been a month or so since BZ executed his plan to rid the production of one of the nicest people I'd ever had the pleasure of working with. For a while I'm sure he was giddy with the idea that we would all be running the creative together… finally…just as he'd always wanted. Although I'm pretty sure he wasn't counting on Ann Knapp showing up out of the blue and taking her seat at the table. Nope. It was definitely not the switch up he was expecting or looking for. First of all, you had to wonder why he gave me the stamp of approval in the first place. He didn't know me at all. We had barely spoken a few sentences to each other before the drama began. And this, I think, was the key to my hiring. He did NOT know me. On the surface, I probably seemed like a young, inexperienced, affable, clueless oaf who approached everything with humor and tried never to make trouble, treating everyone the same, ignoring the hierarchy that is usually inherent on a TV show and finding interest in speaking with anyone who wanted to hang out, smoke a butt, and talk shit. On the surface, that was me in 1994—on the surface. The truth, however, the below-the-surface Douglas J. Sloan was a little more complicated and lot more fucked up, and that made me an even worse choice than Ellen (in regard to BZ).

The first thing to remember was that inside of me, tucked away, squashed into submission, was a temper that reared its ugly head every four or five years and usually got me into trouble. It was not natural for me to walk around with a big smile on my face, considering that there were still a ton of unresolved issues I had never dealt with (sound familiar?) So as affable as I seemed, deep down I definitely had strong feelings about certain people, and it was all I could do to keep those feelings in check. Ironically, this would be my final downfall, the key to opening the door to BZ's place in the creative process. Because for a good three years, he was not making any headway in that respect. And he was not going to, no matter how hard BZ tried, as long as several things remained fact.

1. BZ had nothing to contribute that was at all interesting or an improvement on anything in any of the scripts.
   a. This didn't stop him from droning on about his ideas, turning meetings into tiresome and annoying marathons with his lame notes and long-winded explanations of why his ideas were so important and HAD to be inserted into the show.
      i. Dude! Your ideas suck! We cannot add them into a script just so you can say you are part of the creative team.
2. His go-to writer, who would write every script if given the chance, was Little BZ, who Ann recognized just as I did was barely passable as a junior freelancer.
   a. His dialogue was stilted and felt young.
   b. His ideas were weird and off brand for the show.
   c. His inability to just accept the notes we gave made him impossible to work with.
3. BZ already had another job! He was supposed to be running the logistics of the show. AND he oversaw a

very busy fledgling trucking company. Why did he need to also be part of our little corner of the PR world?

Eventually, BZ, seemed to get the message, and although he was disappointed that he was not being welcomed in as part of the gang, he said he understood and had enough to keep him busy just running the show. This was the one thing about BZ that you must keep in mind. He was incredibly charming and a perfect gentleman whenever humanly possible. He rarely got rattled or angry in front of people, so it gave you the feeling that you were safe and dealing with a supportive ally. He also had incredible patience and could wait months, even years for a plan to come together. It's what made him so deadly. He was like a honey badger that loved to cuddle up for a belly rub, and then when you were lulled into that false sense of security, he would rip your throat out. Look up honey badger on YouTube and you'll get my meaning, and you'll also probably laugh your ass off.

So, regardless of what was said in public: looking back, although BZ quickly became aware that I was not going to be manipulated, and Ann, who was settling into her new job nicely, SURELY was not going to be pulled to his side of the tug of war, this was merely a stumbling block that would add some time to his ultimate takeover plans. But he could wait. He had an actual job to keep him busy. And he was planning his next directing extravaganza, deciding which classic film he was going to rip off frame by frame.

The good news for BZ was that with Haim growing more focused on his plans for world domination, and Shuki focused less on *Power Rangers*, having reached the limits of his attention span for the show long ago, time was on BZ's side. The longer their interest waned, the easier it would be for BZ to execute his plan to infiltrate the creative on the show, whatever that plan may have been. And, of course, he would have help in the form of his mini me, Little BZ. This dude wore the same clothes, had the same hair, and carried the similar misconception that he too was bound for show biz glory.

However Little BZ considered himself a double threat. He was convinced he could not only write, but direct. And wouldn't the production be lucky to have him around if they were in a pinch? I was going to do everything in my power to make sure we were never in a pinch that required Little BZ to occupy the director's chair.

Over the first two years, *Power Rangers* had been in the capable hands of a group of directors that included Worth Keeter, Terry Winkless, Jon Stewart, Jerry P. Jacobs, Bob Hughes, and Shuki Levy. By the time I arrived, the only two who were left and available to direct on a regular basis were Worth and Terry. For whatever reason, the others had moved on. And then there were two, as they say. Of course, there was always the brilliant and talented BZ, who could sub in as a director on a moment's notice. But he was also busy with his actual job of polishing the plastic throne and overseeing his transportation empire (allegedly).

As it turned out, BZ was the guy who selected and approved the directors (Shuki had the ability to override and usually made the suggestions, so it wasn't as dire as it sounded). I guess they felt that BZ had the unique ability to spot a director able to delicately manage the complex dramatic undertones and subtle relationships that were the hallmark of the show (please, no messages calling me out for this ridiculous statement clearly intended to elicit a groan or a laugh.) OR, more likely, it was originally Shuki's job to find directors for the series, and he no longer had the time to devote to the job, as there are just so many hours in a day. BZ happily stepped in before anyone could protest. And so, as was now protocol, all recommendations went right through the one and only.

He could hardly argue that we needed more director hands on deck. So I immediately suggested two directors I had worked with in the past who I thought would do a great job on the series: John Weil from *Troopers*, who had done such a good job on the "Defending Dark Heart" episode, and wait for it, Armand Garabedian, director of *Silk Degrees*! Yes, that is correct. I loved working with Armand. As completely idiotic as that project was, he did a great job and was always very collaborative and professional. And I knew he could knock I out of the park. It was hard for BZ to argue with either of these two, so we brought them in for the first two blocks of my tenure on the show. It was VERY reassuring to know that the guys out shooting the episodes were guys who had my back, as well as me having theirs. At that point, Worth and Terry both had a long and storied history with the dark lord. I needed to work with people JUST in the beginning, mind you, who I could trust to keep me in the loop and not play any political games. Not that either Worth or Terry would do anything to make my life more difficult. They were both completely professional. But BZ was very powerful in his manipulation of the darkness and seemed to be able to make things go his way more often than not. We simply couldn't allow him to hijack our first shows. There was no way I could let that happen.

CHAPTER 32
R.I.P. SEASON TWO

So off we went. The first group of scripts that were up were the last batch for season two. "Best Man for the Job" was a Tommy/Kimberly story where they both run for president of the school, and in the end, Tommy realizes that the best "person" for the job is Kimberly, so he withdraws from the race. It was a good character story, and all the Rangers got to have a nice moment or two in it.

The script was written by Mark Hoffmeier, who was a "go to" writer for us for many years. He always turned out a very good draft, took notes well, and left me very little work to do on the back end before production. For all you baseball fans, he was like the former utility man from the Dodgers, Mickey Hatcher. Hoff was always ready, always did a good job, and never complained. (Hoff, being a big baseball guy, will appreciate the comparison.) This is a showrunner's dream, truth be told. The closer the initial writer can get you to a script that is ready to shoot, the better off you are, because it leaves you time to attend to the other scripts that need more attention. And speaking of which…

"Storybook Rangers" was a story idea Cheryl Saban had. I was brought in to help get it into shape and producible. The idea was that the school was hosting a book fair for charity. Kimberly finds a book from her past that she adored, a storybook called *Grumble the Elf*, and Tommy buys it for her as a gift. He gets a kiss on the cheek and off they go. Unfortunately, Rita was up to something. Wasn't she always? So, Tommy Kimberly and Rocky get sucked into the storybook and have to make their way out with the help of Grumble the Elf. If this had been a show shot today, it would have been beyond amazing. The stuff we could have done with the computers and software we have available in 2025 would have been awesome. Unfortunately, back in 1994, greenscreen technology was improving but still a bit cheesy, and the results were mixed. Thankfully, the art department did a fantastic job of constructing different pages of the book that really looked great when shot from a high angle looking down. The green screens that wrapped around the sets were filled with mountains, birds, trees, and other denizens of the forest in post-production. What I thought worked best was the section of the script that takes place in the snow. The set looked fantastic. Yuda Ako, the production designer, and his crew knocked it out of the park on that one. The Rangers did a great job selling the feeling of dropping temperatures, and the way it was shot was perfect for what we had and what we needed to accomplish.

In the end, the Rangers figured out how to get out of the book with the help of Aisha's drawing talents and the distribution of a wagon full of toys to the children in the book. Of course, Rita and Zedd figured out how to pull an evil character called Mondo from the book and into the real world, and the Rangers had to hop in their Zords and put an end to the big, bad storybook magician. In the end, it was a fun episode. When I think back on it, there are a couple of things that stand out:

Cheryl Saban: Working with Cheryl on the project was a pleasure. She was an incredibly sweet woman, with a massive intellect and a true talent for storytelling. She could have been a complete nightmare, pushing her ideas through and basically telling me to stay in the corner and look for typos. She was NOT like that at all.

Cheryl was collaborative, kind, and never once used her connection to Haim to muscle anything through. In fact, that year I somehow found my way onto the Saban Christmas list and received a lovely gift from Cheryl and Haim. I was feeling pretty good about myself and, at that point, had nothing but wonderful memories of Cheryl.

The footage/budget: I don't know what it cost us to do "Storybook Rangers," but it certainly could not have been cheap. Not only that, there was also a complete lack of footage. The Turkey Jerk monster was all shot by our own second unit, and the only real footage we used was the Mondo stuff. As far as paying for it all, if I had to guess, BZ figured out a way to piece the money together by taking from little scraps all over the budget for the entire year. And I'm sure it pissed him off that he had to do it, which was a bonus for us.

In truth, it was fun when we saw one of Cheryl's scripts come down the line. We knew that it would most likely be expensive, which would inconvenience BZ. I remember Jabba stomping around and snorting like an angry bison, complaining about the cost of "Storybook Rangers" and how it was unthinkable that Shuki and Haim would allow it. BZ, on the other hand, didn't show emotion. He understood that this was his boss's wife, so it was just how things were going to go. I do remember him saying he didn't like the script and that it was going to look like crap. And I recall distinctly that he did NOT want to spend the money required to produce it. But, as usual, he returned to his office, expressionless, followed by Little BZ, where the two of them got to work on the logistics of it all. Ann, Jackie, and I could only shake our heads and smile on the inside as we watched them run around like two monkeys chasing a single banana. It was kind of awesome.

> SIDE NOTE: If you remember from the beginning of this book, it was while I was working on the rewrite of "Storybook Rangers" that I received my visit from Haim's heavily armed right-hand man Ronnie Hadar. He had shown up with his fierce-looking German Shepherd and literally pulled me into a utility closet for

some strange reason. While we were in there—me, Ronnie, and the dog—he reached into the pocket of his Members Only jacket and fished around for something. I knew that he always carried a loaded sidearm and was praying that it was on the other side of his body. But that still left the question as to what he was grabbing for. As it turns out, it was an envelope. He handed it to me and told me to tell no one. With that, he and his dog left the closet and were gone.

With the coast clear, I went back to my office, closed the door, and looked at the plain white envelope. I thought for a moment, trying to imagine what it could be. Notes? A memo? A pitch for an episode? Thankfully, it was none of those things. It was a bonus check, thanking me for the work I had been doing. And it came directly from the corporate office, not the production. The check was for $1,500, and Haim and Shuki were responsible. Wow, what a swing of the pendulum! Not only was I not going to die, I was $1,500 richer! Man, did that feel good. One of my nicer moments at Saban. It's always great to be appreciated.

CHAPTER 33
BAD, BAD BOY

The final episode of the season was called "Blue Ranger Gone Bad" and was written by Little BZ, who in my opinion, still holds the title of the least talented/most rewarded writer in kids TV history. The sad thing is that Little BZ was given the opportunity to grow and develop as a writer early on and to perhaps one day even be decent at it. The problem was always his resistance to take notes and need to argue about each one of them. This is the sure sign of a writer who believes wholeheartedly that their vision for the script is the best and only vision and that no one else knows what they're talking about. Compounding this was that BZ was there in the corner, cheering Little BZ on, convincing him that he was right and needed to fight for his ideas.

That was always the case with Little BZ. Empowered by his relationship with BZ, they felt like the rules didn't apply to them and that they knew better. And regardless of whether they did or not, they weren't in charge, which made the situation insufferable for everyone. And then to have BZ telling me what a great writer Little BZ was and that I should listen to him more and capitulate to his creative choices made it even more difficult.

The dialogue in that original script was corny and over-explanatory. The action was awful. That script was a freaking train wreck. It needed a lot of work, but that's why I was there. It was my responsibility to make whatever script came across my desk as good as I could possibly make it. This one took some hard work, all of which I remember very clearly. Little BZ was a writer on the show not out of merit, but through his connection with the great and powerful BZ himself. This was the one situation in which BZ could exert some control over the creative. Little BZ was basically there to serve his lord and master, and whatever BZ wanted was what was done.

So, the script we got was a mishmash of BZ's terrible story sense and Little BZ's terrible writing. But, between me, Ann, and Jackie, we were able to rewrite the thing and get it to where we could expect a reasonable result once it was put on film. The one good thing about the episode, at least for me, was that it gave David Yost a chance to shine. I had heard rumblings that he felt underused in the show and wanted more episodes that concentrated on Billy. This was his chance to show off his acting skills and demonstrate the versatility he thought could lead to an expanded role in the show. And I was game. Maybe there was a great artist hidden behind the glasses (those were actually long gone by now—more on that later).

In truth, David did a nice job playing bad Billy on that episode. I was secretly proud of him. For some reason, as the evil version of Billy, he gave a performance that had everything you would want for the storyline and even went a little further than I expected. David was very convincing, and I was happy for the guy. He was still not a lot of fun to be around, but I was pleased to find that when given a more challenging role, he rose to the occasion. I'm not sure if I mentioned it to him, but if I didn't, that was my bad. David, if you're out there, nice work.

Back to our story. The final episodes were shot by my pal from *VR Troopers*, John Weil, and for the most part I think they came out well. Unfortunately, John's style of directing, not the camera moves, but him pacing back and forth and worrying like an expectant father, was a little too frenetic for the locked-down military world of *Power Rangers* production, and BZ requested that he not return. At the time, I was new to the position, so fighting for John to come back would have been a mistake. I needed to keep things civil and not argue about something BZ clearly felt strongly about right off the bat. I felt bad about it, but I was pretty sure that John would be fine. Any job he took from here on out would be a step up from Grumble the Elf. And Bob Hughes had intimated to me that John was welcome next door on whatever show they were doing.

So, the season was "in the can," as they say, and it was time to begin writing season three. While this was going on, there was a very exciting event to which everyone was invited and most of us were looking forward to with great anticipation: the premiere of *Mighty Morphin Power Rangers: The Movie* was right around the corner, and boy was I curious. In fact, I doubt there was a single member of the crew who wasn't wondering how our little show had been represented by the great and powerful studio 20th Century Fox.

CHAPTER 34
LOVE YOU, BUDDY

I had heard mixed things about the completed *Power Rangers* feature leading up to the release. Most of the comments came from Saban folks, who had an agenda that made it impossible for them to give an honest opinion. I figured I would have to see the movie to get the real story.

The production had gone months over schedule (and I'm sure well over budget). I only say this looking back on all the changes and extra days of filming that were added. It would have been impossible to keep a handle on the original numbers. Most movies have a 10% contingency in the budget in case the film goes over. I'm pretty sure they blew through that pool of money like a runaway Megazord. But no one seemed worried. This was the *Power Rangers* movie. It was going to be huge. There was an army of kids who could barely wait until June for this enormous event to come to their town. With this knowledge, the studio kept the show going, paying the overages and assuming they had a mega hit on their hands. What they didn't consider was that there was also a giant fly that would soon be landing in the ointment, derailing the studio's hopes for a truly HUGE opening. Because little did parents know that this would NOT be like sitting through a Disney animated movie. This was a whole different kind of experience, one they would not understand, nor care to repeat.

> SIDE NOTE: One of the keys to a successful kids' movie is repeat business. We all know that children will watch the same TV show or film over and over again until something else comes along to take its place. And in the 1990s, that often meant repeat trips to the movie theater and to make sure they had the full cineplex experience. During the summer, movie studios counted on the idea that parents would take their kids to the theatre day after day or drop them off to see the movie with their older siblings, picking them up when it's finished. In the case of *Mighty Morphin Power Rangers: The Movie*, parents were not so willing to return to the theatre two, three, ten times to sit through a film that made no sense to them. Bottom line? Parents, at the time, could stomach the idea of the *Power Rangers* on a TV screen. The show was a great babysitter; the toys were cheap and kept the little ones busy. It was a tradeoff that Mom and Dad could accept. After all, they didn't have to watch it. It was a zero-effort endeavor that provided time when the kids would be quiet and occupied. However, Rangers on a 60-foot-tall movie screen plucking $50 from Mom and Dad's pockets every time the kids went to the show was another story. For Mom and Dad themselves to go to a cinema complex, pay the money, then be forced to endure the movie again? That was too much to ask. And most parents declined. This, I believe, is partially what lead to the soft box office numbers and ultimate average performance of the film.

News started to trickle in at the production office that there was going to be a premiere of sorts for the movie on the Saturday before the film opened. The screening would be at one of the larger theaters in Westwood, a small town next to the gargantuan UCLA campus. It was a popular hangout for students on the weekends, and the streets were usually flooded with people going to movies, eating at one of the hundreds of restaurants and just enjoying the California weather. It was unclear exactly who would be attending this screening, as most of the crew were local hires in Australia and certainly weren't going to make the trip to Cali just to watch something they'd barely gotten out of their heads months before. So, I assumed it was going to be a screening for all of the Saban, Fox Movie and Fox TV people who had been kept at bay during filming and were excited to see the result of months of headaches and acid reflux. I'm certain that all the filmmakers were very proud of the movie. It was big and shiny and loud and took the characters on a journey across deserts and jungles until they discovered their ninja powers and were ready to fight Ivan Ooze, who had a few tricks up his sleeve that the Rangers were, as of yet, unaware.

The coolest part of the screening (for me) was that we would be able to observe the reactions of the actors. This would be the first time any of the Rangers had seen themselves on a gigantic movie screen. As an actor, I had the opportunity to experience this, and let me tell you, it's a total mind fuck. In that moment, you are forced to watch yourself. There is no getting away from yourself, and it provides a dose of reality for which some actors are just not prepared. Thankfully for Jason Frank, it would be a wonderful experience. His face was made for the movies. His personality shone through. His energy was perfectly dialed in for what the project required. He was fantastic. This is not to say that he wasn't freaking out the week of the screening. Jason came to my office a few days before and wanted to make sure that I was coming and that we could sit together. I told him that was the plan and that I was super excited. I really didn't think much of the fact that he wanted me, in particular, to sit with him. But, looking back, it was quite an honor and spoke to the strength of our bond at the time.

Outside the theater, as you would expect, a crowd had gathered. The screening was in the afternoon, and word had spread that the real live *Power Rangers* were going to show up for the event. So, regardless of whether they had tickets, the throngs of parents out for a nice walk in the village of Westwood suddenly found themselves being dragged by their children to a movie theater. Flashes of the Universal Studios appearance ran through my head, although this screening was thankfully never announced. Who knows what would have happened then?

As for those of us from the show, the feeling I got in the office was one of excitement. Who didn't want to see our actors blown up to the size of Zords, all shiny and flashy on a big movie screen with their new cool suits? But we were all more than a little curious to finally see how these movie geniuses had taken our little show and turned it into the spectacle they'd been bragging about for the past year. Gone was the spandex, the goofy rubber monster du jour, the putties, Rita Repulsa. It was a *Power Rangers* none of us could picture, aside from the glossy trailers that had been playing on Fox Kids, day and night.

At the screening, Jason Frank was wearing a very black suit-type of outfit and looked every bit the movie star. Most of the photos and footage from the premiere that have emerged over the years have him in all white, which was what he normally wore and was for the actual movie opening, which we losers from the TV show were not invited to attend. However, for Jason and I and our years together with him learning his craft, practicing for hours, improving almost on a daily basis, this was a moment that he and I were looking forward to. All the *Cybertron* fuss, back and forth, the worrying, the tears, finally accepting his role on *Power Rangers*, then focusing his energy where it needed to be, on the work. The movie symbolized that accomplishment, and I could not have been prouder of the guy were he my own son or little brother or cousin...whatever. I was beaming for JDF in that moment. And it was hard to hold back my emotions. In fact, I clearly remember turning away at one point before the movie started to wipe away a tear.

When we took our seats, there was the usual chitchat, ribbing one another, talking about the upcoming season, etc. Then, suddenly the lights went down, and the audience began to cheer loudly. As the movie started, I felt Jason reach his hand over and grab mine with a strong, brotherly grip. He whispered to me, "Love you, buddy." I replied with a simple, "Love you too, buddy." This was not unusual for us in those days, but this moment felt a little more special. This was a rite of passage to the next stage of his career. And I think he completely understood the significance of the moment. He released my hand, both of us wiping happy tears away, then we spent the next two hours enjoying the movie and taking pride in his performance. He was really good in that film, and I think for the first time, as an actor, he really felt like he had done some fine work. For me, it was an amazing moment in that it spoke to my early contribution, however small, and my ability to work with someone who came to me with no experience, no training, and through hard work and dedication became very good at something that is not easy to be good at.

I have never shared this story except maybe with my wife Mindy, with Ann, and with Jackie Marchand. Probably because I realize how corny and self-serving it looks, like I deserved any credit for Jason having that amazing day. Whatever my part was, I am, to this very moment, filled with pride and joy that I was there to watch this talented human being flourish as he did. It's nearly 40 years later, and he and I were the only ones who were there for that very private moment. I am talking about it in this book because it speaks to what a kind, thoughtful, giving person Jason was. For him to include me and, in his way, to thank me for something I was paid to do, was exactly him in a nutshell. I believe with all my heart that this was the true essence of the man. This was what lived in his soul. Anyone who's watched him with kids who are *Power Rangers* fans can attest to that. The other side of Jason, the one that's become much more dissected since his passing, that was always there. But I was lucky in that for the most part, I saw the love and the caring and the kindness. I truly hoped that including this story would shine a light on the part of him that the public rarely got to see.

In terms of why Jason was able to achieve what he did, a lot of stars had to align for this to have happened. You had a kid who wanted to succeed, big time. A gifted athlete who was not afraid of hard work and who busted his butt, focusing on a basic acting technique that happened to work for him and allowed him to get through those early shows. And he possessed the desire to get better, go deeper, challenge himself. Jason was the perfect student, really. He worked and worked and got to the point where he could be on stage with just about anyone and hold his own.

The darker side of his motivation spoke to the mental baggage he carried around until his death. For most actors, part of what draws them to the stage is the desire to show love to millions of people at the same time, and in return, receive that love back tenfold. That's the payoff. Jason was absolutely one of those actors. He wanted those feelings of validation, that what he was doing was important, that it meant something to the legions of fans we never could have dreamed would stay loyal to him for his entire career.

CHAPTER 35
WHAT A STRANGE, STRANGE YEAR IT WAS

When all the dust settled, it was determined that the movie had performed decently but certainly was not the blockbuster Haim or the studios hoped it would be. As I said earlier, in those days you had to get the parents to come back with the kids. That didn't happen. And truthfully, there was nothing that could have been done to change that. The property is what it is, whether on a movie screen or a TV screen. Parents back then didn't get it and didn't want to see it or know anything about it.

Back at Ranger Control (the writing office), we were gearing up for season three. This would be my first full year on the series, and it immediately became apparent that it was going to have its challenges, some unique and some familiar. This started right up with the first three episodes. The three-part miniseries was called "Friend in Need." Clearly it was not a true Ranger affair. It was the pilot, or introduction of, Saban's new Masked Rider series that would begin running on the Fox Kids Network later that year. The idea of setting the show up on *Power Rangers* made a lot of sense. But as a Rangers' Episode, it was dull and just weird. There was an excessive amount of standing around talking and setting up the history of the Masked Rider franchise. The Rangers and the Masked Rider hero, Dex, and his pals stood in Bronson Caves for what seemed like for days, lamenting how crappy things were in the galaxy and how the Rangers were going to help Dex in the upcoming battle he was sure to face.

For some reason (for the life of me I cannot remember what that reason was), Amy Jo didn't appear in the *Masked Rider* episodes, except for a few scenes that were shot later where she showed up in her pink bedroom clutching a tissue box, distressed by the fact that she had the flu and couldn't fulfill her Ranger duties. Whenever they needed a cutaway to make the show fit together more smoothly, they would just check in on Kimberly, who would be checking in with Aisha to see how the Rangers were doing. All of this was accomplished by Kim calling the Juice Bar and Ernie passing the phone along to Aisha. Now, I get that all of the kids didn't have cell phones back then. But the Rangers DID have communicators. It always seemed strange that Kim and Aisha wouldn't just use those devices to talk to one another. Maybe there was a "no personal calls" mandate in effect after Zordon saw the power bill for the morphing grid or something. I guess we'll never know. Anyway, let's move on. (Please, no letters informing me that there is no charge for the Morphing Grid. I was just being stupid and shame on you for not recognizing that this many pages into the book.)

The next four episodes were called "Ninja Quest," and they existed for one reason and one reason only—to completely undo the mythology that the feature film had established and rebuild it for the TV show. There were a couple of issues that led to this decision, not the least of which was the presence of a big blue dude in a rubber suit, sort of a cross between Iron Man and the Michelin Man, who was impossible to cut around in the Japanese footage that we were scheduled to be using. Ninjor, as he became known, was chosen to bestow the ninja powers upon the Rangers once their latest quest led them to the big blue dude.

Then there was the fact that there may have been a decent

chunk of our audience who (perish the thought) had not seen the feature and would be confused by the ninja costumes and new spirit animals. Adam being a frog would need to be explained again. The audience was not just going to let that one slide. Then there were merchandising issues. As an example, when we were going through the scripts for the four-part mini-series, we were told that "Tengu" warriors, the big black birds from the feature that we were using for the show, could not be called Tengu warriors because the name didn't clear with the legal department.

Legal checked every new name in a script, from people to companies to products that we made up for use in the show, to ensure that we weren't infringing on anyone's actual name and didn't open the company up to a lawsuit. It wasn't usually a big deal, and if a name didn't get through, we submitted a list of replacements, then picked one that passed.

My question here was, "How in the 'F' did 'Tengu' not clear?" Tengu warriors are mythical demons taken from the Buddhist faith that are thousands of years old. No one can own that name. Not to mention the fact that they used the "Tengu" Warriors in the movie. So why did we have to change it in the series? Here's what seems to be the likely answer to that age-old question that has been burning in the minds of *Power Rangers* fans young and old:

Bandai America owned the primary toy license for the *Power Rangers* TV series. For some reason, when it came to the movie, another company called Gordy Toys got in on the act and created a line of movie-specific figures, I'm sure as a way to give Saban and the Fox movie Studio a bigger cut of the merch than they would have gotten with Bandai. The Tengu Warriors were part of the Gordy Toys line. So, if I'm Gordy, a relatively small company, and I just signed this awesome deal that got me in on *Power Rangers*, the crown jewel of toys, why would I allow Bandai to make their own Tengu Warriors? Wouldn't that completely cut off Gordy's exclusivity at the knees and ensure the kids would just buy them from Bandai, who had an entire wall at toy retailers? There had to be a way to prevent the Gordy birds from sitting in a bargain bin somewhere while Bandai reaped the rewards for a product they had nothing to do with.

But the birds WERE going to be in the series, giving Bandai the right to make their version of them. So, if Bandai was going to sell these big birds as toys in the series, we had to call them something else. I offered up Tenga Warriors, kind of as a joke, never imagining a one letter swap would do the trick. It was approved, and off we went. Tenga for the show, Tengu for the movie. Clearly this cross contamination of merchandising also contributed to the story for Ninja Quest. It kept it cleaner, no overlap (well, not exactly, sort of, eh, never mind), and it allowed for the introduction of everyone's favorite Dudley Do-Right in blue—Ninjor.

As I am writing this, it occurs to me that re-shooting the Ninja Rangers and their new mentor, Ninjor, was probably a gift from the Ranger Universe that was bestowed upon us without anyone even realizing it. The location where we shot the actual Ninja power-up scene was a nice garden, with water elements and rock formations. Of course, it wasn't as nice as the location in Australia, but this was the TV show. That's not what we were about. The fact that we shot it in kind of a corny version of the movie set and that the Rangers were now being mentored by a guy in a blue foam suit and not a beautiful woman in a copper-colored battle bikini was kind of perfect. It brought the viewers back down to Earth and back to the look and the feel of the series, letting them know they were NOT going to be seeing what the movie had given them. We were going to be using the same old Zords from Japan, the same spandex suits. We were back to the formula that had made us a smash with the kids. We were re-establishing our "cheap and cheerful" (as my Kiwi friends like to say) world and owning it like we always had. To no one's surprise, it seemed to work just fine. The kids went back to the series in droves, the ratings stayed up, and all was well in Angel Grove. At least for the next couple of years.

And what about Bulk and Skull? As with every season, there needed to be some sort of dramatic motor to drive the comic relief and provide a reason for their zany antics. In season three, it was decided that they would join the Junior Police Academy. It was set up that this would be their way to meet girls, figuring the uniforms alone would do the trick. So, it was off to Junior Police boot camp, where they received some serious "high and tight" military haircuts. Terry Winkless decided that it would be a great idea to bring in two actual barbers to do the honors right then and there, on camera. It was a fantastic start to their Junior Police journey.

> SIDE NOTE: It's amazing to me that regardless of the measly wages Bulk and Skull were paid, those two loved the work so much, they would do just about anything to keep the show as funny as they could, even if the script didn't really allow for it. For some reason I got it in my stupid head that they didn't just deserve a raise, they *needed* a raise, and I was going to be the one to facilitate it. Huge mistake. I was scheduled for a meeting at the new Saban building on Wilshire Blvd. in Westwood, which now housed the entire company, from music to TV to movies and merchandising. I had not been to the new location yet, but I was told it was massive. The first indication that this was true was the huge sign on the top of the building that just read, "Saban," with the logo in gold next to the letters. Impressive. The offices followed suit, decorated beautifully—a seriously cool place to work. After the meeting, I asked Haim if he had a minute to talk. He did and walked me back to his office, where I sat down in the chair in front of his massive desk. Haim and I, at the time, seemed to have a pretty good relationship. I think he appreciated the work I was doing, and although I'm pretty sure he thought it was weird that I was dating/not dating Shuki's ex, he was always cordial with me and even joked around about the show, politics, whatever, depending on his mood.
>
> I knew Haim was busy, so I got right to it. I told him that in my opinion, a huge part of the show's success could be attributed to Paul Shrier and Jason Narvey and the substantial comedic

skills they possessed. Not only that, but these two worked their asses off and never complained, always had smiles on their faces and were always trying to find a way to make the scene funnier. I went on to say that any attempt at humor with the Rangers themselves usually fell flat for a variety of reasons, ranging from bad acting to bad directing to bad writing (had to be honest).

So, there it was, a completely logical request, a small bump that would have basically zero effect on the bottom line. A request, that if granted, would raise their pay up just a little, but would mean the world to the two actors. Just a few hundred bucks a week would go a long way to keeping them happy and in groceries. In the grand scheme, it didn't seem like a big ask. Haim sat there for a moment or two, still smiling, then said the words to me that I will remember as long as I live. "Mr. Sloan, the sign on the front of the building. What does it say? Does it say, 'Social Security'? No. It says Saban." (Keep in mind he's still smiling.) Haim went on to remind me that Paul Shrier and Jason Narvey had contracts, and that Haim planned on sticking to those contracts, as should the actors who signed them. And that was that. No drama, no ill feelings, just flat, polite business.

I knew better than to push. Haim had always felt strongly about actors, or anyone for that matter, adhering to the terms of their agreement. This was a no-brainer, since the contracts were all well weighted heavily in Saban's favor. None of the actors should have signed them in the first place. But they were kids. They were dying to be working actors. How could they have predicted what would happen once the series took off, or that it even WOULD take off? This is a great lesson for anyone starting out in the entertainment industry, or any industry. Your first contract will most likely be one that favors the production company or studio, HEAVILY. You have no leverage at this stage of your career. So, you take what they give you. If the show's a success, then you try to renegotiate, with the understanding that you still have little power as you are bound by the original agreement.

So, despite my best efforts, Bulk and Skull were not getting a raise. This bummed me out as I know it was something they would have greatly appreciated, which is why I never mentioned that I was even going to try. But they freaking deserved it. They just had the misfortune of being paid out of the SABAN BUILDING and not the SOCIAL SECURITY BUILDING.

Once the Ninja miniseries was finished and we had the TV show back on track, the setup with Rita and Zed back in place, and the Tenga Warriors as the dirty bird henchmen, I was excited to get back to good old stand-alone episodes. We had been banking scripts, so we had probably eight shows from which to choose in terms of the next block we were going to shoot.

What we didn't realize at the time was that this season was going to present a higher degree of difficulty than past seasons. There were many reasons for this, but high on the list was the departure of Kimberly and Aisha from the show. Both actors wanted out for whatever reason. At least this time it was going to be amicable, and we could write them off gracefully instead of that BS with the stock footage and body doubles they did when the Jason, Trini, and Zack characters left. More importantly, the ratings were still very strong. This gave Haim the upper hand in that no one actor (aside from Jason Frank if he chose to) could argue that their presence on the series was so important he could be held for ransom over their salary. And he never was. Rangers became an ever-rotating repertoire company, where new talent got to work on a real TV series for a single year. Whatever they made of that experience was up to them. Sometimes they would come back for a bit and then leave again. You never knew. In the Disney years, starting with *Ninja Storm*, the pay went up. It was still nonunion, but the actors seemed happy with what they were given for the year they were on the show. They were treated well, given respect, and rarely found reason to complain. (But that's in book two: available on Amazon and in bookstores everywhere sometime in the future if bookstores happen to make a comeback.) I even saw on a documentary that the Rangers, at some point during the New Zealand years, became union and were given all the treatment and luxuries that go along with being a union actor. This was a far cry from those early days when the actors were doing their own stunts and working 14-hour days.

CHAPTER 36
ANN AND I GET OUR WINGS!

One morning, I pulled into the parking lot at work and noticed that there was a bright orange windsock on the top of the studio, hanging limp because there was no wind blowing at that moment. Once inside, after setting my things down, I asked Jackie if she had noticed the windsock and if so, what was it for. Jackie reported that it was for Shuki.

Unbeknownst to me, Shuki had completely immersed himself in becoming a licensed helicopter pilot. He had his own instructor and would periodically fly from Burbank Airport to the stages when there was work to be done and he wanted to get in some flying time. The sock was so that Shuki could judge the wind direction and speed to land safely in the empty parking lot across the street.

For those who don't follow the world of aeronautics, the helicopter is arguably the most difficult flying machine to master. It takes coordination, patience, brains and I'm sure a plethora of other qualities which most of us are missing. The good news was that Shuki was always very good at anything he attempted. Had he not been above average at flying and on the fast track to his license, we never would have heard a word about it. He would never allow himself to suffer the embarrassment of failing at this new endeavor, or worse, crashing into the side of the stages and putting us behind schedule.

The following day, we had heard that Shuki was coming up in the helicopter for a group of meetings and was going to be there for most of the day. As the hour of his arrival neared, Jackie, Ann, and I gathered at my window, where we had a great view of what seemed like a perfect touchdown across the street. Shuki hopped out moments later, looking even cooler than usual, something I would never have believed possible. Before she went back down to her office, Ann commented that as long as she didn't have to go up in it, she was fine. Jackie and I both looked at her, knowing she had just initiated a cosmic tailspin that would put us both in that two-rotor spiraling coffin before day's end.

I was walking down the hall to check on the Rangers, and there was Shuki with a big smile on his face. The first words out of his mouth were, "We're gonna go for a ride later." Before I could think of an excuse not to, I was nodding my head and happily accepting the offer. I mean, there was an instructor with him, so I figured we would be fine. He said he would come find me.

The moment Shuki left to go into his meeting, I raced down to Ann's office and filled her in on what had transpired. I could see her face flush and her heart nearly pound out of her chest. She asked what I thought we should do. I told her the best option was to disappear. Go anywhere. Hide ourselves in a corner of the stage. They're shooting. It's dark. He'll never see us through his sunglasses which, by the way, he never took off.

Unfortunately, as we were discussing the plan, Shuki appeared in the doorway and asked me if I was ready to go. He then turned to Ann and asked if she was ready. "For what?" she asked. Shuki looked at me surprised that I hadn't told Ann the good news: We were the lucky recipients of a helicopter spin around the neighborhood. I insisted I hadn't told Ann because I wanted it to be a surprise. Before I could even finish the sentence, Shuki was at the end of the hall, motioning for us to follow.

As we crossed the street towards the chopper, I had to look

straight down and avoid Ann's gaze. I knew she was shooting me a look designed to kill me before the helicopter had a chance to. I just stared at my shoes until we arrived at the flying machine.

As we strapped in, belts clicked and pulled tight, Ann was trying to smile and make the best of what to her was a terrifying situation. After all, she had a family to go home to, a new baby, people who would miss her.

As the instructor guided Shuki through the preflight checklist, and the powerful engine started gaining RPMs, Ann's face and neck began transforming into a bright red manifestation of her inner discomfort (a reaction she's had since the day I met her). It was clear that there was no turning back. Shuki was concentrating like I'd never seen him before. Ann was silently praying (or at least that would be my guess, having never really gotten into the whole faith/religion thing with her). I closed my eyes and turned to logic to assuage my fear. It didn't take long before it came to me—the reason I wasn't going to die in that helicopter that day.

It was so obvious.

I had been watching Shuki go through his checklists, and I started to think about his life, and the fortune, both monetary and personal, that his hard work had yielded. Let's face it, things were all good in the land of Shuki Levy. He had a lovely girlfriend, an amazing career, money he could never spend. This was a guy who literally had it all. Why would he ever want to put his glorious existence at risk for a joyride around the suburbs of L.A. with two mid-level producers along for the thrill of it? The simple answer was: he wouldn't. He would never put himself in that position! Shuki Levy loved his life, his kid, his job. Shuki was right in the middle of the dreamy chapter of Hollywood success where nothing seems like it can go wrong. Every day is another adventure. He would NEVER take a chance of losing all this. He had to feel pretty freaking strongly that nothing was going to happen to us on our little journey. I let out a deep breath, gave Ann the thumbs up, then off we rose into the blue California sky.

Of course, there was absolutely ZERO logic in my "Shuki loves life theory." In fact, it was idiotic. Many successful people who loved their lives have died in helicopter crashes. But back then, I didn't possess the ability to prove or disprove my own hypotheses, so up we went.

As the chopper rose above the studio and flew off towards the hills, it became obvious that Shuki was pretty good at this. He was smooth, confident, and enjoying it. And his instructor seemed equally calm. I took this as a good sign. And I think Ann did as well. I could see the red leaving her face and her heart slowing enough to fit it back in her chest. In fact, after a few minutes, we even started to have a good time. Helicopters are quite enjoyable if you can manage to relax and take in the moment. For some people, that is a big "if," however. So don't feel bad if you find yourself in a similar situation and walk away to the safety of the nearest Starbucks to wait for your friends to return.

CHAPTER 37
THE ELEVATOR GOES UP, THE ELEVATOR GOES DOWN

"The elevator goes up, the elevator goes down."

The first time I heard someone utter this simple yet brilliant axiom was on a weekend news show where they were interviewing a film director by the name of Shawn Levy. He was commenting on the fact that it's best to not burn bridges in our town, and smart not to have too many people out there with hard feelings towards you. The idea was that you may be very successful now, on top of the world, elevator to the penthouse. But all elevators descend. And when yours does, you might need the person you threw shade at on the way up to be the better person, grab your hand, and help you back up into the cool kids' club again. Some would even broaden the whole idea and add the concept that the better you have it before you fall, the better chance you have of hitting terminal velocity on the way down and disintegrating upon impact.

For his part, Levy was basically saying, "Don't be a jerk or screw people over. It will come back to bite you." I'm going to leave it at that for the time being. The good news is, of course, that I have an entire story that includes Ann and I, the Disney Channel, a pilot we wrote, and the famous Shawn Levy before he was the famous

Shawn Levy and landed on a gilded throne in what appears to be a very secure top floor of our metaphorical penthouse. You'll have to wait until the second book, unfortunately, as we are really pressed for time in this one. But I promise it will be worth the wait. The point here is, we shouldn't burn bridges. For me, it's probably too late. But save yourself if you still can.

At *Power Rangers*, we were getting ready for a new episode called "I'm Dreaming of a White Ranger." The script had been written by two freelancers named Ron Milbauer and Terri Hughes. Ron, at the time, had super long hair that he wore in a baseball cap turned backwards. He was never without his flannel shirt, baggy pants, and Chuck Taylors, a look that worked for him in a strange but cool way. He was a smart, personable guy, but for some reason he weirded the living crap out of me back then. I could never figure out why. Just know that it had absolutely nothing to do with him—that was a "me" issue. I tried being extra friendly, hanging out when they came by to go over notes on a script, but he and Terri just were impossible to connect with on a human level. At least (I believe) I finally figured out why.

You see, the thing about Ron and Terri was that their ideas were brilliant. Their dialogue was great. They just knew their way around a story and as a team were better than I could ever hope to be if I did this for another hundred and fifty years. This is what probably had me on edge. The two of them were constantly coming up with ideas that were fantastic. Ron and Terri had written a feature script called *Idle Hands* that was actually going to be in theatres. Here was this young kid, with a backwards baseball hat, long hair, pushing his way past me, and past kids TV, into a part of the business to which I could hopefully transition someday. And he and Terri were both always SUPER polite and SUPER nice. And I guess I just didn't know what to do with that.

Today, Ron is a very successful writer/producer who hasn't stopped working for years. Elevator up and staying up for the foreseeable future. It would have been nice if I hadn't been such a dick to the guy back then when maybe there was a collaboration to be had. But it was a good lesson that anyone can go from being your employee to being someone who can employ you. And once again, you WILL need that at some point. Trust me.

So, you might be asking yourself (or you might not): "How did the episode come out?" "What ever happened to 'I'm Dreaming of a White Ranger'?" "Was it super fun to shoot?" "Was it sooo awesome working with all those amazing young actors?" These are questions I hadn't even considered until I rewatched the episode before I wrote about it. So, in an attempt to answer the questions you probably weren't really thinking about asking, but I suddenly wondered about myself, here's what I remember most about that particular show:

Holiday specials are a staple of kids and family TV, and have been, as long for as I can remember. Kids love seeing their heroes experiencing the joys and sometimes the heartbreaks of the holidays. Plus, it's just cool and festive and a different vibe than what you get the rest of the year. The thing about holiday movies and specials is that they have their own unique set of issues to deal with. Halloween is all about tons of extras wearing costumes you have to rent, traipsing around a neighborhood whose residents you had to pay for the inconvenience of having a noisy movie crew take over and light up their whole street. A production manager with a big wad of cash stands by ready to pay off the really cranky neighbors who decide they aren't satisfied with their initial payment and threaten to hold the production hostage. (Because the truth is, it's all fun and games for the first hour of a film shoot, but then the neighbors resent the crew and just want their lives back so that they can go to bed without a giant film light blasting through their upstairs window.) We weren't doing a Halloween special, thankfully, but we were in trouble in our own way, the Christmas show way, which can be just as painful and just as hard to deal with.

With Christmas shows, the problems start with the elves. I get that there's no such thing as elves. And, if there were, I would love them and would never see them as a problem. Elves are a staple of any movie that involves Santa Claus, especially when it's one where Christmas is being stolen or ruined by bad guys, which is exactly what our story was about. Rito and Goldar are sent to Earth by Lord Zedd to ruin Christmas and lure the Rangers to the North Pole, where their powers don't work for some reason. From there, it's like shooting fish in a barrel and the Rangers are finished. Of course, none of this ended up happening. Not important. But we needed about 10 non-union little people with serious acting chops to pull this thing off. And that was NEVER, EVER going to happen in the summer in LA. Christmas shows and movies, like ours, get shot in the summer. That means any talented, in demand, little person is going to be, well, in demand, most likely working on a higher paying, more prestigious production than ours. It was going to be almost impossible to cast the parts. Notice I went from "never, ever," to "almost impossible" in less than a paragraph. I'm not sure why I was even worried, now that I look back on it. Katy and Thom, once again, pulled it off and delivered a great group of actors to play the elves, and a fantastic young woman to be the lead elf who had most of the lines. Unfortunately, she's one of the people whose name I tried to find when researching this book and couldn't. If you're reading this: You were terrific in the episode, and we were lucky to have you.

The next challenge was the heat. Southern California in July can be brutal. That summer, the temperature rarely dipped below 100, and there was actually a bit of humidity in the air, which robbed us of the "At least it's a dry heat," excuse that for some reason seemed to make folks feel better about working in the same zip code as the surface of the sun. I never understood that hopeful little adage. Hot is hot. If you're into the 100s, you are miserable and praying for it to end, regardless of how dry or wet the heat is.

Okay, so we've established that it was hot, which meant that creating any semblance of a North Pole exterior was going to prove insanely difficult. Nowadays, you would just slap a green screen around the borders of the set and shoot away, knowing that the Visual FX department would build an insane-looking Santa's castle in the computer and it would be awesome. Just our luck, we were about 15 years too early. Plus, we had our usual crap budget, so we weren't going to be renting any giant sound stages with snow machines to create our winter wonderland. We were going to be shooting Santa's workshop exterior at a busted down Beer Garden restaurant off the 5 freeway in a very questionable part of town. And we had to start as early in the morning as possible so the fake snow wouldn't melt into a dirty disgusting soup and wash away before we got anything on film that even slightly resembled the North Pole.

As usual, our art department had worked miracles, and the place looked like a fair imagining of the outside of Santa's workshop. Also, as usual, they were very honest about our limitations. We really needed to hurry up and shoot before it got too hot.

If you watch the episode, you can see that as the day goes on, the walkway slowly turns into a water way, and as the snow broke down, we substituted white blankets made of cotton balls and fake snow in a can to touch up areas that needed it. Finally, we came to our last shot of the day. It felt like we were playing beat the clock with a bag of ice cubes sitting in a microwave set on defrost. By the end, the fake snow formed a small river leading away from Santa's Workshop. The Rangers had given up trying to look like they were freezing. No one was buying it. They were all sweating profusely. As I've said a thousand times in this book, we did the best we could with what we had, and surprisingly, it didn't look awful. I mean, it was no *Santa Claus III* or *Elf II*. But it was the economy small screen version of something vaguely related to Christmas. And it kinda worked. Now all we had to do was start all over again INSIDE Santa's workshop, which had issues that made the exterior seem like we were working with Harry Potter money.

Inside Santa's workshop was going to be a complete ball breaker. For some reason we had chosen to build it in an old barn that was, of course, not air conditioned. Thanks, BZ. So right off the bat, it was going to be a challenge. The art department had to build this giant set that was every kid's fantasy of where Santa preps his toys, which meant it had to be busy and full of eye candy and just stuffed to the gills with anything related to Santa and Christmas. They did a great job, and when we arrived on set, I was blown away. It looked amazing. The fans they set up to keep the temperature at least livable were doing their job, and I felt like we had a shot at making it work and getting some really good stuff. Of course, there were some variables that had to fall into place in our favor for it all to come together. First, the actors playing the elves had to deliver on the performances they gave in their auditions. This was a BIG no problem. They were great. They all nailed their parts, and in spite of the fact that our lead actress had a slightly gruff voice that I hadn't remembered from the audition tapes, she was excellent. And Scott Page-Pagter could work his magic in ADR, tweak her voice, and have it sounding more elf-like in no time.

There was one great thing about her natural voice. She was a little bit bossy and used her intimidating tenor to keep the other actors in line. She also took the thespian thing very seriously. In the scene she did with Rito, she didn't have many lines. But she listened very carefully to every word he said and followed his eyes perfectly. She was a well-trained pro, which was great for us. Plus, she obviously loved ordering the guys in the group around, which was kind of funny and also greatly appreciated. At one point, I caught her look over at me and smile as though she knew she was being bossy and was having as much fun doing it as we were watching it.

That day in the workshop turned into what you might expect. The heat rose. The lights and thick costumes made it more and more difficult for the actors. The Tengas started to need longer breaks, Santa was a mess, and the elves were dropping like flies. We cranked up the fans and did the best that we could, but you just cannot fight that kind of heat without a serious air conditioner pumping in cold air from a massive unit stationed outside the set. For the life of me I can't remember if we ended up getting one and solving the problem, but if you want to talk about miserable working conditions, this was as bad as any.

SIDE NOTE: There has always been a lot of talk in the press about the torturous working conditions on Rangers. I would have to say that although it wasn't a first-class operation by any stretch of the imagination, there was care taken in making sure the actors and crew were safe and had at least the minimum creature comforts they needed. There was always food and water around, a medic on set, and safety issues were handled quickly and taken seriously. I don't know what it was like before I arrived and was on set consistently, but I always thought we were treated decently for what the show was and how little the production had to make it. I also always felt like the company could have upped their game a little when the money started rolling in. But that was naive optimism and was never going to happen.

Thankfully, no one perished in Santa's workshop. That would have been a tragic way to go out. I can imagine the headlines in the trades: "Rangers Ruin Christmas!" "Santa's Got Heat Stroke!" "Heat Wave Melts the North Pole!"

The last part of the special that needed to be shot was the children's Christmas pageant. Here we were again, looking for a room full of non-union kids to play roles that experienced child actors would have struggled with. And this time Katy and Thom ran into a dry spell. The kids we were seeing were okay...but just okay. With the clock ticking, we finally cast the parts, settling on an adorable 12-year-old girl for our lead guest star, a girl who didn't have an ounce of acting ability in her, but she was the best we could find. You can't have everything, and thankfully most of that show took place in the North Pole

As the season rolled on, we were starting to feel the pinch of changing out two of the Rangers once again. The fans seemed to have gotten over the exit of the previous OG Rangers with little lasting effect. The ratings remained about the same as they had since the show exploded into the stratosphere. I'm sure in Haim's mind this was more proof that it was the *Power Rangers* suits, not the actors in them, that kids tuned in to watch every day. So, when Amy Jo Johnson decided she wanted to leave, no one seemed too worried. I will admit that I worried...a lot. AJ was, without question, the most gifted actor in the cast. We relied on her a lot in the writing room, knowing that she could handle whatever we threw her way. I knew there would be a void when she left. I didn't say anything of course, as there was nothing to be done about it. Shuki had already given me the sales pitch on the new Pink Ranger, telling me how fantastic she was and that she was going to blow my mind, etc. I had learned by this time that if Shuki felt that strongly, then he was usually in the ballpark. The first time I'd heard him use superlatives like that when speaking of an actor was when he called me about Jason. So, I was excited to meet this new wonder girl and start writing for her.

CHAPTER 38
THE SLOW BOAT TO MAYHEM

We were heavily into Season 3 and the white board in my office, listing the episodes, completion dates, and script progress was starting to get filled in. It was also beginning to look like a complete mess. Ann, Jackie, and I knew there were a ton of rewrites to do, enough to make us want to pull out our hair and run into the California desert screaming. Season three, to me, is always interesting to look back on for many reasons. The complete mishmash of directors and writers we hired to stir things up yielded us a strange string of episodes written by some freelancers and directed by some new directors, one of whom turned out to be totally bizarre and almost had to be replaced while shooting. The three-parter we planned to start the season with was written by Shuki and Shell. Their scripts were always wildcards in terms of making sense dramatically, but at least any budgetary concerns would be fought out between BZ and Shuki and I didn't have to get involved. Also, since Shuki was the one who decided where the overall story arc was going, we didn't have to worry about the episode going off the rails and ruining plans for what was to come.

The next set of scripts was a four-part affair called "Ninja

Quest," written by, you guessed it, Shuki and Shell. If you're keeping score at home, that's seven episodes in a row written by them to begin the season. And honestly, that was fine by me. "Ninja Quest" was basically the TV show undoing everything that had been established in the feature film and conforming things to the new footage that was arriving from Japan. Gone was Dulcea, the girl in the brass bikini with the big stick, and in came Ninjor, a big blue goofy mentor the Rangers had to find to get their Ninja Powers since their MMPR powers were destroyed at the fiery end of season two.

Ninjor gave them their Ninja Coins and Zords and the rest of the Power Ranger gear they would need to battle their enemies. To me, what stood out about Ninjor was his voice. Somewhere along the line the decision was made to turn Ninjor into a giant blue Dudley Do Right impersonator. I was certain that one day while giving instructions to the Rangers, Ninjor would finish, call out, "Nellll!" (for his horse) and ride off into the sunset. It was bizarre, but in the grand scheme of things, any little bit of comedy we could find was welcomed with open arms. And Scott Page-Pagter, who hired the voice actors and directed them, felt the same. He was usually spot on with his choices and always brought the funny. So, who was I to shut down Ninjor's Dudley voice when it ended up working so well? Can you imagine Ninjor having a commanding, in-charge voice like Zordon? That would have been so freaking boring. And Scott knew it. Wherever you are up there, buddy, thank you a million times for all that you did in our years together.

We also both knew we were on the right track when we heard that BZ hated the voice. He thought it needed to be serious and powerful, to which I replied, "Just look at the guy!"

So that was the first flurry of episodes done. We were now going to move into a nice long stretch of shows that had little overarching material to worry about and could just be fun episodes we could enjoy making and, hopefully, the fans would enjoy watching.

The first script in the next batch of shows to be produced was "Passing the Lantern" from a writer named Kati Rocky. I had never actually met Kati (and never did), but she was someone Ann trusted, and that was good enough for me. Her script was a story about Adam being given a paper lantern by his family and it turns out to have special powers, then gets turned into a lantern monster. The rest is as you would expect. To me, this episode never stood a chance at being anything more than a typical cookie-cutter MMPR episode. When the footage has a lantern monster in it, you are pretty much doomed to tell that story with very little room for offbeat innovative dramatic license. It's just going to be what it's going to be. Boy finds lantern. Boy loses lantern. Boy fights 50-foot-tall lantern. Boy gains perspective upon learning valuable lantern lesson.

What really bummed me out about that episode, and I know this sounds ridiculous, was the actual lanterns. Now, let me start off by saying we had amazing art and props departments. Those guys worked miracles with a budget that was barely equal to that of a Roger Corman film. On this episode, I feel like communication wires got crossed, or maybe BZ stuck his mullet head in the middle of it. But the lanterns the art department came up with, the ones that were supposed to be so significant, and Adam's, which was infused with all sorts of powers, they all looked like souvenirs you would find in downtown L.A. The lanterns looked ridiculous. I never asked why they were such crap. I was still new as a producer and didn't want to make waves. I think I probably did the right thing. In the grand scheme of things, Adam's little paper lantern didn't really mean squat. It just would have been nice.

Then Rocky had a nice episode where he switched places with his teacher on a special day when students and instructors swap roles to see what it's like to walk in each other's shoes for a day. Unfortunately for Rocky, the special teacher-edition books he needed to teach the class were stolen and the whole thing goes to the dogs.

The next episode once again featured Steve Cardenas as Rocky front and center. I would like to think that this was our attempt to allow Steve to stretch his muscles and tackle some juicy drama, but it probably had something to do with the fact that we had plenty of Japanese footage of the Red Ranger to work with. Anyway, the episode was about Rocky's uncle, a star quarterback who comes to the school to give a talk. Rocky is helping a friend study for chemistry class. The friend is having trouble despite the fact that he is super smart and should be doing fine. In the end, we discover that the kid has dyslexia, and what do you know, so does Rocky's uncle, who helps the kid (also a football player) get hooked up with people who can work with him to get through it (and who we hope are better qualified than Rocky to do so). I mean, jeez, you know what would have been great? Why not throw Billy in there for a little brainpower and have him help figure out the issue? Unfortunately, Billy wasn't into being stereotyped as smart anymore, and he wanted to be cool and wear Tommy's wardrobe. So that was off the table.

When the Rangers got back from Australia, they went right into their characters as if they had never left. Well, five of them did. David, it seems, had been given the green light on the feature to ditch the glasses and lose the standard issue Billy wardrobe. He was now wearing fashionable tees and jeans along with Doc Martins, the cool kids' shoes of the day. He looked nothing like the lovable nerd we started the show with and who had become so popular. Billy looked older, had clearly spent a lot of time at the gym, and it seemed like he was trying to cultivate his own Tommy Oliver look. I have to hand it to David. He was like a dog with a chew toy when it came to his character. If he wanted something done about Billy, David would make his way up and down the hierarchy of producers until he could find someone to tell him that he could do the thing he wanted to do. This time it was ditching the dorky Billy gear.

It was kind of weird to me that this had just sort of happened and no one had said anything to any of us. So I went to the costume designer and asked where the miscommunication was. She pointed me in the direction of Shuki (of course she did). Shuki, in his typically charming way, informed me that this was going to be the season that David Yost hung up his overalls, glasses, and pencil protector and became the cool, buff "nonstereotyped" Billy. I guess David had convinced Shuki that this was better for the character and, as Shuki sometimes did, he got tired of talking about it and just let David do what he wanted to do. I'm certain that Shuki figured Billy's wardrobe was not the thing that would ever sink *Power Rangers*. Now if Tommy suddenly became say, a nerd, there would have been a stop put to that in short order.

What sucked about the whole thing, for me at least, is that the writers were never given any warning. And this was a pretty big change, one that didn't necessarily have to reflect negatively on Billy's character. In fact, I remember commenting to Jackie that it was a missed opportunity. We could have done something with his transformation on screen instead of him just showing up one day looking like a 40-year-old Benetton model. We could have shopped for a new look that was not geeky, but cool, intellectual, and quirky. Something that set him apart from Tommy, something that would allow his fans to stay his fans because he was still smart, and a little shy and all that, AND still had a look that was all his. But I guess everyone back then wanted to be like Tommy, and that included Billy. So that was the end of Billy as we knew him. Poor David was getting grumpier every day and most of us didn't want to deal with it, so we just capitulated when he demanded something. It was a bad dynamic and as much our fault as his. Why would he stop demanding stuff if we kept giving it to him? Well, the answer is, he wouldn't. If you don't take the chew toy away, the dog will continue to chew it until it's been chewed up.

When the new batch of scripts came out, David was the first to line up at Jackie's desk in his new GQ Billy gear, his tanned muscular arms outstretched for the still warm teleplays hot off the copier. He was a man on a mission.

As was his routine, David would take the new scripts and run off like Newman from *Seinfeld* clutching his "Jambalaya." He'd take the scripts somewhere to read through and digest them, oh, and to "count."

MORPHERS, MONSTERS & MAYHEM   223

Right now, you're thinking, "Count?"

I had the same reaction when David poked his head into my office and asked to talk to me. Of course, I obliged, and in he walked with his scripts under his arm. I could tell he was seething about something but had no clue what the source of his discontent might be. I asked how I could help, trying to be as pleasant and accommodating as possible. The first words out of David's mouth were, "Have you counted?"

I truly was perplexed by the question and asked him to repeat it.

"Have you counted them?"

I took a moment and a deep breath. "Counted what?" I asked.

"The lines," he said. "Have you counted the lines?"

I thought, *Where the hell is this crazy conversation going? What is he asking me?*

I didn't have to wait long for an answer. He said, "In this script, Tommy has 60 lines, Kimberly has 54, Billy has 19. Did you know that?"

I went on to ask David why he was counting the lines, and whether this was something new, or had he been doing it all along. I'd never been on a series or movie where an actor counted their lines—surprising, as it seems like something certain actors would definitely do. But what they wouldn't do is bring it to the attention of the head writer/producer for fear of being ridiculed or shown the door. But idiot me, I did neither. I could tell this was a genuine concern of David's, however wacky it seemed to me at that time, and I wanted to address it. I couldn't help but think he had just had his own episode where he got to turn bad and had most of the lines. But I didn't bother to mention it.

I explained to David that on our show, since the beginning, we have tried to dole out character specific episodes as evenly as possible. There had been tons of Billy scripts over the years where David had surely been blessed with the same, if not more, lines than the other Rangers. The script he was holding happened to be a Tommy/Kimberly script. As such, it was going to feature more lines from the two of them. When the next Billy script came along, things would be different.

"When is that going to be?" David asked.

I looked at the board with all the episodes listed and told him that in the next batch of four, there was a Billy script. He demanded to know which one. I said that I wasn't allowed to discuss future episodes, so I was sorry I couldn't tell him.

"You talk about them all the time with Jason," was his reply.

In my mind, I was desperate to answer with, "Yes, I do. Because Jason is nice. I love the guy, and oh yeah, he is the star of the show. You get your name up to number one on the call sheet and we'll talk."

But that is NOT what I said. I didn't have to say anything. One of the production assistants came in at that moment and told David he was needed on set. David answered the PA, without turning around, promising that he'd be right there. The PA almost pleaded with David that he had to go now. David didn't budge. He stared at me for a long time, waiting for me to say something.

"You better get down there," was all I said. Then I picked up a script, pretending to read. Within a few moments, David was gone.

After David had left, Jackie came bounding in and we just stared at each other in shock, not wanting to laugh, but having no idea exactly how to react. I'm pretty sure we called Ann to come up. She was in disbelief. But as is the norm with Ann, she instantly wanted to make sure that Billy was going to be taken care of down the line and that David's feelings weren't too badly hurt. Jackie assured her that David was fine. She knew because she had been listening to the whole convo from her desk outside my office. The moral of the story? Actors, don't count the lines! You have no control over how many you have. Just say them and be happy you have any. It's a brutal business, and working as an actor is a blessing, no matter how many scenes you're in or lines you have.

That whole thing probably should have been its own chapter, but back to Steve Cardenas. To my surprise, as I said earlier, his work in those shows was very respectable. I think the time on the movie was very well spent for most of the actors and helped them get more comfortable in their roles. When you stand on a huge film set and act in front of a large crew for any length of time, the return to a TV show seems much less menacing. Steve was relaxed and easy to direct. He also had a lot less of that nervous energy. When I think about it, coming into this show must have been freaking terrifying for him. No wonder he couldn't get a word out in the beginning. It was a great lesson for me, which is one I've been reminded of many times since. Actors are a funny bunch. They all have different insecurities, and all need different handling and different kinds of attention, from the beginners to the seasoned pros. They are all worried about something and all, deep in their hearts, are terrified. As must poor Catherine Sutherland have been when she arrived to start her journey.

> SIDE NOTE: The Power Morphicon is held usually every summer in Pasadena, California and is the biggest gathering of fans who follow the Saban shows. But mostly, it's about *Power Rangers*. Every year for the past couple of decades, actors from various seasons show up to autograph memorabilia or photos and take pictures with fans. The actors seem truly grateful to have this renaissance in their careers, and not just for the money they make. That is, of course, part of it. But *Power Rangers* fans are the best out there—enthusiastic, fun, respectful, and supportive. The actors appreciate the fans and treat them like gold, which is really wonderful to see. Our fans are also an incredibly diverse group, ranging in age from 9 or 10 all the way up to adults sporting gray hair. The show was on the air for 30 years. Over those years, we've picked up more and more lovers of the show so that every year the fan base grows.

At the 2015 Power Morphicon, I was working on the *DreamWorks Dragons* TV series at, you guessed it, DreamWorks. I was feeling like things were going well. Money was coming in. I really wasn't stressing about anything. So when my wife Mindy announced that she would like to attend the con just to see what this strange, off the main highway world was all about, I was happy to oblige.

When we arrived at the con, we were met with the usual assortment of oddly dressed superfans. One guy, wearing only a red sparkling Speedo, wanted to take selfies with us. After a few minutes of this, Scott Page-Pagter spotted us and whisked us away to a hidden staging area, where we found Catherine Sutherland, Karan Ashley, and Nakia Burrise, among others. We chatted for a few moments. Catherine and Nakia even invited me to join them and Scott Page-Pagter on a panel. I agreed, because why not? Then Mindy and I decided to head out to the main floor and see what was cooking. The line for autographs was mobbed, especially since Jason Frank was there. People were waiting for hours just to get a shot or have a brief conversation with him. Walter Jones, Austin St. John, and David Yost were also there, sharing the main booth with Jason. When I approached them, it was like old home week. I hadn't seen Austin or Walter since they left the show. I couldn't remember the last time I'd seen David, but I assume there was no tearful goodbye, much like there was no tearful reunion between us at the con on that day. Jason, of course came in for the big hug and was super excited to see me, as we hadn't seen each other in person since we'd worked together in New Zealand. So much had happened in his life and mine as well. We talked about cars and shows we were working on, and it was just a really nice time. It was much the same with Walter and Austin. I really liked both of those guys, and they could not have been nicer to both me and my wife Mindy, who was experiencing this lunacy for the first time.

It's worth mentioning that my wife is way cooler than I could ever hope to be. She has done some amazing things in her life, not the least of which was being a backup singer for Marilyn Manson on his "Golden Age of Grotesque" album and nearly the tour which she decided was not for her. It was wild to watch her amongst all these *Power Rangers* fans and former cast members. She was fascinated and wanted to know everything about everyone, who played what part or did what on the crew. I was so glad I brought her. She was loving it. One of the reasons she really wanted to go was to meet David Yost, who I told her didn't like me and would most likely still be carrying a grudge after all these years. Mindy thought that sounded ridiculous. Why would he be carrying a grudge in the first place? I told her I wasn't really sure. Since we didn't know that, she countered, how could we assume he was still holding on to negative feelings? My wife always gives everyone the benefit of the doubt and forces me to look at the situation from the other person's point of view. She realizes that I tend to be a bit of a bridge burner and has given me the gift of self-reflection which has served me well.

On this day, however, I was proven right. David ignored us most of the time we were there, and when he finally did look our way, he scowled at us like a school bully waiting for the lunch bell to ring so he could start the ass kicking. I love my wife dearly and try to make sure she is treated with respect and dignity by people I know and strangers alike. This was neither respectful nor dignified and kind of pissed me off. Mindy, of course, shrugged it off and merely said, "You were right. You should tell the 'line counting' story on your panel with Scott." Great idea, I thought. And so I did tell the line counting story. And I didn't even give him a stupid phony name. The fans at the panel enjoyed the story. I told them there would be much more like it in the new book I was writing. They applauded loudly and that was that.

To this day, I will never understand why David and I couldn't make a connection. On paper we seemed like we should have been fast friends. In retrospect, I now know that he was hiding his sexuality during his time on the *Power Rangers*, something he's talked openly about. I hope I didn't contribute in any way to him feeling like that was necessary. I'm truly sorry if I did. What I do know is that for some reason he just didn't like me. I don't know if it was Jason-related or what. But we all have our issues to work out. Unfortunately, my need to be liked, which was at an all-time high back then, made me dislike David right back rather than be the better person and try to get to the bottom of it. It still bums me out to this day.

BONUS RANGERCON NOTE!: Back when I was working on *Ninja Storm*, the dude who runs Ranger Con would hit me up months in advance to show up and be a part of the festivities. He wanted to make sure I was well taken care of, knew where to go, etc. I guess because I was the showrunner at the time, it made sense for him to take special care to ensure I was there. When I went to the con with my wife, we had to purchase tickets to get in, and it was as if I had never been a part of the show. The only way I ended up on any of the panels was that Cat and Nakia were there and asked me to go up with them, along with Scott. Turns out it was casual enough that I could just show up at whatever panel sounded good and sit on stage to answer questions.

Before I left, I ran into the dreaded Little BZ, who had scabbed his way into running the current series and was there to be drooled on by the convention organizer. I was talking with Little BZ when the guy approached and greeted him like a conquering hero. He then placed what he claimed was a limited-edition Showrunner coin or some shit into BZ's hand and the two of them chatted away. I was a little miffed, I will admit. This guy had begged me for years to show up, and either didn't recognize me and didn't bother to introduce himself or was so all over Little BZ that he couldn't be bothered. Either way, I left and vowed never to go to another of his events again. What would be the perfect ending to that story is if the book I am writing at this very moment becomes super popular with the fans, they want a signing event, and I just can't make time to show up at that particular event. Instead I do one at a nearby bookstore. That would be sweet. But that's just petty and small and I'm trying to be better than that. It would be a good lesson for him about how elevators work.

CHAPTER 39
HELLO KITTY!

As I mentioned, when Amy Jo Johnson decided to leave the show, I was worried. But Shuki was confident he'd found the perfect replacement. While he was down under working on *Mighty Morphin Power Rangers: The Movie,* his eagle eye for talent fell upon a young Australian woman by the name of Catherine Sutherland. Cat was the opposite of Amy Jo in every way. Where Amy Jo was full of bouncy high School girl energy, Catherine was grounded and very calm. Where Amy Jo was tiny and athletic in a very intense way, Catherine was tall, lithe, and graceful. Cat was shy emotionally, where AJ was an open book. The way I've always described it was that Amy Jo would have been the perfect Disney kid, where Cat would have been great on a daytime drama (soap opera). They were just different. Both brought something to the table, but in very unique ways.

We were now tasked with figuring out the best way to incorporate Catherine's character into the show. We had to find a way to make this transition and hopefully do Amy's character justice, as Jackie, Ann, and I felt like she deserved a nice send-off after the dopey fainting thing back when the White Ranger was revealed. But first it was Cat's turn to make her appearance in Angel Grove.

When Catherine arrived in L.A., I was blown away by how calm and professional she was. Clearly, she had been through it before, and this was in no way beyond her capabilities. The first thing that Shuki wanted to do was a screen test. I'm not sure why. She had already moved halfway across the globe. She had a place to live, a car, the whole nine yards. Was there really ever a chance that Shuki would see the test and send her back to Australia? Of course there was. There was always a chance that just about anything could happen on the show. But Shuki hated dragging things out, so it was clear to me that Catherine Sutherland was going to be our new Pink Ranger. Not only that, but she was going to enter the series as a new girl at school under Rita's spell and could transform into, you guessed it, a cat. How clever was that idea? Well, I suppose it worked for Tommy, so why not for our new Pink Ranger as well? Redemption stories of bad guys who come out of it and join the team are pretty much standard comic book fare, and it is one of the only times we get to see our main characters as anything but the bright, shiny positive role models they are. Also, we were going to be using the very latest in visual effects to transform her into a cat, and that was super exciting. Of course, the very latest in 1995 is not quite as spectacular as we are used to these days. But I was looking forward to it.

I directed the screen test up at the park by Lake Castaic, a location where the company shot just about everything that required an outdoor grassy location. After a couple of takes to shake off the nerves and the jet lag, our new Pink Ranger dove right in and made the role hers. I was hopeful that this was going to be it and that we were moving forward. There would be some great opportunities with this new character, which is always a fantastic way to reinvigorate the writers. As we drove home from work at the end of the day, I spotted a little blue hatchback heading down the freeway towards the valley. At the wheel was Catherine, concentrating hard, but smiling as well. I wondered to myself how she was feeling about this new adventure, if she missed her family. But most of all I wondered about the fact that suddenly, she was driving a car on the complete other side of the road from what she was used to, with the steering wheel on the other side of the car as well. She seemed to be working it out, but it was impressive to me at the time, and I prayed I never had to do the same thing in reverse in a British country. That prayer of course fell on deaf ears. More on that in book two!

> SIDE NOTE: Catherine was one of a few Rangers, other than Jason, that I became close enough friends with to spent time with outside of work. When her family visited, I was invited to lunch with her lovely mother and good old Scottish bloke of a father. We sat outside a cafe in Encino, CA and I remember how incredibly warm and loving these two people were. Catherine's mom was very polite and was full of questions about what my job was and anything else I cared to share with them. Her dad was a loveable bull of a man who I could tell was missing his daughter terribly. And I think that he was more than a little worried about their little girl being halfway across the world acting on some weird TV show. Our conversation was a combination of chatting about various things that were going on in the world and him making me promise that I would look after Catherine. I think the idea of an older person in a position of power on the show keeping an eye on Cat was a big relief to him. So, of course I promised him that I would. (I only messed that up once, which I will always regret. More on that later.)
>
> From then on, whenever I spoke to Cat, the first thing I asked about was her parents. She would tell me they were fine and had asked about me, which I always thought was very special. Years later, when I heard the news that her dad had passed, I was surprisingly emotional. I knew how much he meant to Cat and knew that she was going through an excruciatingly difficult time. But to this day, I will always remember that wonderful lunch we all had.

As introductory episodes go, the "Ranger Catastrophe" two-parter, directed by yours truly, was just okay. Looking back, it's pretty obvious that my directing skills when it came to moving the camera at the right time and for the right reason were barely passable and I had a lot to learn. The acting was actually good, as it was working with actors that got me this job in the first place. There was just nothing special about this show, at least on my part. All the cool stuff was, of course, done by the second unit who always came up with at least a couple of really great shots during the action scenes. As I looked at the final edits, I vowed to go back to the drawing board, study my favorite films, and try to come up with something more interesting next time. I think I let my insecurities about making my day (finishing on time) and not missing anything, dictate my shot list and how much time I spent on each setup rule me. This was great for the crew, as they always got out on time or even early. But it just meant boring material in a show where boring equals failure. As I said, I would never let that happen again.

As we discussed Kimberly's exit, Ann and I wanted to be absolutely sure that we gave AJ a sendoff that would not only satisfy the fans but would give her some scenes and moments that she could be proud of. I never worried about AJ's ability as an actor. Over the years, I'd seen her cruise through material that many other actors would have struggled with. Her character had started as a bubble-headed valley girl with little concern for anything that was not directly adjacent to the local mall. Over time, Amy Jo had managed to find a humanity, a heart, and just the right amount of humor in the character. This was the reason Kimberly became so beloved, and why it was going to be so difficult to see her go.

The issue we were facing with Kimberly's departure (which we were determined NOT to be a sad story in which she was forced to leave the team) was that we needed to figure out a way to sell the audience on the idea that there would be something in this character's life that had become more important to her than saving the world every day. We had to figure out what possible justification there could be for leaving the *Power Rangers*, and it couldn't be that her mom was moving to France with her artist boyfriend, or that she was helping Ernie haul rebar across the Amazon or something equally as ridiculous. Kimberly needed a meaningful reason to leave the Rangers, like the peace conference we'd sent Jason, Trini and Zack off to join.

We had kept up the idea that Kimberly was a gymnast and that it was something she took very seriously throughout the show, so we decided to launch into a story about a world-famous gymnastics coach who takes an interest in Kimberly and agrees to work with her as long as she promises to dedicate herself to the plan of going to the "Pan Global Games" and not let anything interfere. Easier said than done. There was no indication that Rita was a big fan of gymnastics, and she sure wasn't a fan of Kimberly having any happiness in her life, so this was going to be tricky.

I won't go into too many specifics of the episodes in terms of the story points and all of that, as I'm not sure retelling it is all that interesting. To my mind, we were able to put together a halfway decent, touching sendoff. The one thing that I think is important when writing an actor off a show is not to be too obvious or weepy about it on the page. The conversations they have can be about anything—their future, their past, what they'll miss about the place they are leaving, a funny story. You have to put in moments you would not normally expect from a farewell scene. To me, this helps the actor when they have to say goodbye to that one particular person who means the most to them, who they will find that without this person they can barely breathe.

At first, this can seem like a daunting, impossible task for an actor, getting one's emotions to such a turbulent place. And it is. But what most actors don't realize is that they are already in that place. There is a secret weapon available to them that works pretty much every time. They just have to acknowledge it, and once they do, BOOM. What needs to come out is how the actor feels about leaving the show. They will have those feelings in check on the day so as not to make their work any harder, not realizing that these feelings are what could make their performance brilliant. Throughout their last day, actors think about the people they will miss, the joy of being able to do something they love every day, leaving the familiar safe environs of a show they know so well. This feeling is often the one that takes over when the camera is rolling. I know it did for me in my last days on *The Young and the Restless*.

Amy and all the others did a really nice job of saying goodbye, which was a big relief to all involved. And in terms of it being okay that Kimberly was forsaking being a Power Ranger for gymnastics, there was an especially nice speech by the last person you'd expect, Zordon, in which he told her that he never meant for their duties as Rangers to interfere with their dreams and that this new adventure she was going on would serve her well if she ever decided to return. Finally, we created a bond between the two characters, Kimberly and Katherine. (Yes, you read that right. If you didn't know already, the new Pink Ranger, played by Catherine/Cat was named Katherine/Kat.) Anyway...Katherine finds Kimberly passed out at the Juice Bar and rushes to her aid. Kat admits that she was working for Rita and her regret about all of it. This was designed to help the audience feel comfortable with Katherine stepping in, knowing that she and Kimberly were now friends and Kimberly herself was okay with someone else donning the pink suit. If they only knew how "okay" with it Amy Jo was. She was sick and tired of the grind, the crappy pay and the missed opportunities that were out there for her. The last thing I remember from that whole thing was AJ hopping into her little pink Honda with the sticker of the Pink Ranger helmet in the back window and tearing away from the stages in Valencia for the last time.

CHAPTER 40
WINDING DOWN MMPR

As we continued with season three, it became obvious that there was going to be a big change coming, one that we could no longer avoid. There was footage coming from Japan that had zero (or "Zeo" if you like stupid dad jokes) to do with Ninjas or spirit animals or anything remotely similar to what we had done before. Additionally, the villains were completely different. They were machines. The Machine Empire was an homage to the early sci-fi movies from the 1920s and '30s, specifically Fritz Lang's *Metropolis*. And there was a ton of footage we could use with easy matching on the lip sync as they were machines, many of whom didn't have mouths at all. We were going all in on this new footage and series, which we were calling *Zeo Rangers*. We had to find a way to transition slowly and smoothly.

Towards the end of the season, we introduced the Zeo crystals, which were said to be so powerful they could destroy an entire planet. And what do you know? Master Vile was jonesing to get his hands on those bad boys. Unfortunately, in the last episode of the season, Master Vile manages to reverse the rotation of the Earth, as a result turning the entire planet into children. Not sure how this worked scientifically speaking, but who says it couldn't? At least that was the thinking back then. This all happened while the Rangers were at a carnival that they brought Katherine to as a birthday celebration. After all, every Ranger gets at least one surprise party (or at least that's what was in the script).

What I remember about this season ending is that Shuki had brought in a new director, one who had never actually done that particular job before and one who was completely enamored with his own voice and his own ideas to the point that he was going to show us all how it was done. He was going to show us the artistic way to shoot a *Power Rangers* episode. Which was lucky for us that he came along when he did. After all, his was one of the most important episodes in the history of the show.

Marco Girabaldi was the live-in boyfriend of Priscilla Presley at the time and was everything you would expect of a Brazilian-born, Italian-raised, '90s boy toy, who had spent the last decade living with Elvis's ex. His confidence was through the roof, and he approached the job as though he was James Cameron preparing to shoot the next *Terminator* movie. Marco seemed completely nonplussed by the fact that *Power Rangers* operated on a low budget and was financially viable as the result of a specific proven production paradigm.

Upon his arrival, Marco made it clear that there was a lot of equipment he would need if he were to achieve his vision for the show. BZ, of course, pushed back, explaining the rules that directors had to follow in terms of how many days they could have with a Steadicam, how many days with a crane, how many extras they could have, whether they had video assist or video record to see what the camera was seeing, etc. All these rules were in place to keep the costs to a bare minimum. When working on *Rangers*, a director had to carefully choose the things he really needed and be prepared to sacrifice the ones he could live without. Marco was not interested in any of these rules. He wanted it all. And, somehow, miraculously, he got most of what he'd asked for. This was a real headscratcher for most of us who had been there a while. How had this new guy come in and just ripped open BZ's fist, the one that so firmly clenched the checkbook?

I didn't make this connection at the time, but I later recalled that Deborah and Priscilla had starred on the TV show *Dallas* together for several years and had become good friends. Deborah could be best friends with just about anyone. She just had that magical thing about her where people adored her instantly. I'm sure that at the time of the series, Shuki was introduced to a plethora of actors on *Dallas* and through meeting Priscilla, he would have met Marco. Now, who made the call that resulted in Marco receiving the keys to the *Power Rangers* war chest, I couldn't say. But it was clear that Shuki wanted him to have a great experience with no interference from such trivial things as budgets and time limitations.

So, in one of the few times I saw Shuki get involved with the money aspect of the show, he somehow got BZ to stand aside and give Marco the extra toys he absolutely had to have…within reason. Being that it was the end of the season, I can pretty much guarantee that this was no skin off BZ's nose anyway. He had most assuredly been stashing money away across the budget, in every department, and was probably already preparing to march into Haim's office and declare proudly that he had come in under budget for the season. So, this minimal amount of money, what probably amounted to less than a couple of thousand dollars, was meaningless in the grand scheme of things. It was just so freaking distasteful to all of us that this guy was the one who was getting carte blanche out there, when it would have been so much more impactful to see what Terry or Worth could have done with that kind of freedom.

So, for those last episodes we had a large Chapman crane parked on standby and a Steadicam with its operator next to it doing crossword puzzles as he waited to be called into action. What we all found hilarious was that Marco, for some reason, planted himself in the chair on the crane for every shot in which it was used. And he used it in quite a few shots. I remember thinking that he looked like someone playing a director in a bad movie instead of an actual director doing his job. This was especially amusing when you consider that on the crane, he wasn't seeing what the camera was seeing at all. The video screen that was wired up to the camera on the crane, was in the Video Village tent off to the side of the set. This was the place all of the other directors watched the scene unfold because it showed exactly what was being seen by the camera in real time. I think that maybe Marco liked riding up and down on the giant arm and calling action from high over the set. He didn't want to be cooped up down on the ground with us peasants who made up the crew. Not a chance.

I'll never forget our script supervisor Janie Hull Page and I absolutely falling off our chairs at the sight of Mr. Girabaldi going up and down, up and down, take after take, us knowing he had zero idea what he was getting on film. Thankfully, we had our director of photography Ilan Rosenberg there to make sure things didn't go too far off the rails.

> SIDE NOTE: Janie Hull Page was with the show the entire time that I was there. She later worked at the Disney Channel in the production department. She is smart, funny, observant, and a pleasure to work with. The two of us sat side by side many times when I directed the series, as her job as script supervisor required her to have access to the director at all times. If I saw something that was just ridiculous and made me laugh, I would inevitably look over to find Janie already cracking up at the same thing. She totally got the joke. However, Janie's finest quality, to me at least, was that she was an amazing mother, a single mother at that. Her daughter Sam was a wonderful, polite, brilliant kid, and I always was impressed that Janie worked so hard all day from 6 a.m. and managed to get home and do an incredible job at mothering. But she did. She was truly one of my all-time favorite crew members.

CHAPTER 41
THE ALIEN RANGERS OF AQUITAR

At the end of season 3, we had run out of footage, again, and were digging deep into the vault for anything that remained of the Ninja season sent from Japan. The Zord situation was getting out of control, with so many different iterations of the battle vehicles that the callouts by the Rangers had become more like Shakespearean Sonnets. It was time for a reset. Shuki and Shell had a plan for this that, to this day, remains an incredibly important moment in *Rangers* history and gave the series time to breathe before the switch over to *Power Rangers Zeo*, which as I said was based on an entirely new Japanese show with a new villain, new suits, and new Zords.

At the time, I'm not sure many of us realized the enormous step we were about to take and the great risk that it would bring to the franchise. After all, who *really* knew why the kids liked the show so much? I mean, Jason Frank was a big draw. But would the changing of the bad guys have any effect on the success of the series? Would having no animal tie-ins for the Rangers be an issue? Would calling the Zords by numbers instead of names screw things up? For me, it was just exciting to be getting a clean slate.

The connective tissue from MMPR to Zeo was this weird quirky little miniseries called "Alien Rangers." In it, the Rangers are back as children. They have full recall of their grown-up identities but are unable to use their powers. As a result, something has to be done to ensure the safety of the world. Apparently, on a far-off planet that is mostly comprised of extremely pure water, there lived an alien race, who by chance also happened to be blessed with Ranger Powers. "How could this possibly be," you ask? As with any big change or event in *Power Rangers*, let's go to the footage.

In the tape vault at Saban, there existed a series from Japan called *Super Sentai Kaku Ranger*. There were 53 episodes of the show that were available to the American production, and although it was decided that these shows would NOT be used in a full *Power Rangers* season, they were perfect for "Alien Rangers."

What I remember about the "Alien Rangers" episodes over anything else was that the actors who played the Aquitians had such reverence for the series and for the characters they were creating. A lot of the moves and salutations that they are known for were created by the actors themselves. Leading the charge of this new group of thespians was an incredibly smart, very beautiful, and a bit mysterious woman called Rajia Baroudi. Rajia was Lebanese, Scottish, and Spanish, if I remember correctly, and spoke with a very proper, high society English accent. To this day, I don't believe "Alien Rangers" would have been near the success it was without Rajia. This is not to take anything away from the others. They were all fantastic in their own way. She was and is just one of those magical, warm, charismatic people you meet who knocks your socks off. One thing that always blows my mind about Rajia is that every year since it has been around, Rajia is the very first person to wish me happy birthday on Facebook. And she always includes a sweet personal message with it. This is something I can't even say about some of my family. To this day we have stayed in contact. Mindy and I were invited to a party at her home and Rajia went above and beyond to welcome my wife, whom Rajia had never met, into her world. The two became fast friends and still communicate through social media. If anyone who reads this happens to have a chance to go to a Ranger Con where Rajia is appearing, I strongly recommend that you spend some time talking with her. She is simply brilliant and a complete hoot.

The other thing about "Alien Rangers" was the fact that all the costumes and masks were designed by our costume and prop departments. This was a first, as we never needed any sort of masks or fighting suits before since they were drawn from the Japanese footage. I think that our people did a remarkable job with what I'm certain was an incredibly limited budget. By today's standards, of course, the costuming is a bit crude, but back in 1996, it was awesome, and I think a great source of pride for our hometown design crew, led by production designer Yuda Ako.

> SIDE NOTE: Yuda was a funny little guy who was an amazing ally to me, Ann, and Jackie during our time there. He felt the same way we all did about BZ and Little BZ, that they were corrupt, egomaniacal, and basically devoid of creative talent. Yuda would often shut himself in my office and we would commiserate as to the BS we had to put up with daily with BZ being all over us about our creative choices, which he was never meant to be a part of (according to Shuki). In fact, it was after speaking to Yuda one day that I decided that something needed to be done about the meddling. Not only was BZ telling me and Ann how much he disliked the scripts, but apparently, he was not shy about sharing the fact that he thought the scripts sucked with his group of flunkies or anyone else who would listen. Now, I know you're thinking that this is America, and we are guaranteed freedom of speech. So BZ had every right to say whatever he wanted about the scripts. BUT, and this is a big BUT, a cardinal rule of production is that if you think the material sucks, keep it to yourself. It's a very bad look around the set. It can lead to the entire crew not caring about the show and that can lead to the quality suffering (insert "Quality?" joke here). We needed everyone on board with the scripts, at least in principle, so that we could get the best from

them. And the worst thing that could happen would be if the actors got wind of it. We couldn't afford that.

Fortunately for me, as was Haim's gift, he knew all about the struggles we were having and decided to call me into his office. I wasn't overly concerned about the meeting. This friction clearly needed to be resolved. It would not end poorly for me or Ann. We were just trying to make the best show we could, and BZ wasn't helping, at least in the morale department. Haim and I discussed the fact that Ann and I needed to have creative control of the show under Shuki's guidance. But we couldn't do it with BZ always looming, trying to change things that he didn't care for in the scripts, complaining about the shortcomings of the writing. In my meeting (Ann wasn't there for some reason), Haim literally asked me if I wanted to have BZ fired. He said he would pick up the phone and do it if that's what we needed to keep the show on track.

Holy shit! Here was my chance to rid the show of the plague that had been seeping into every area of the production once and for all. Unfortunately, back then, I had an incredibly strong belief, as I still do, that karma is a royal bitch. I tried not to screw anyone over when at all possible. Looking back, I was a bit naive. BZ would not have extended the same courtesy if things were flipped the other way. Nevertheless, I told Haim that I didn't want to see anyone lose their job (or their trucking empire) at my recommendation and if someone could just make sure BZ knew that we didn't require his two cents on every single script and to keep his "Spielbergian" thoughts to himself, that would be enough. But would it? Really? Would it ever be enough for BZ?

The "Alien Rangers" episodes were leading us to the transition over to *Zeo Rangers*. It was nice that the Zeo crystals were already introduced in the "Alien Rangers" episodes, as it gave us some continuity. It was also the first time we blew up the command center, something that would become a season-ending tradition until the show was finally put to rest just a couple of years ago. Koichi Sakamoto, our expert in all things martial arts and demolition, loved those final scenes, as he got to destroy everything in sight and set off powerful explosives (under the guidance of our special effects experts, of course). This was before we had CG to do that for us, so it was always quite thrilling for everyone to watch the command center set of that particular year demolished. Even after the show moved to New Zealand, the Kiwi crew seemed to really look forward to it. Perhaps it was because it signaled the end of one season and the clearing of a path to the next. But probably it was just the fact that they got to blow shit up. Who knows?

At the end of "Alien Rangers," we also said goodbye to Yellow Ranger Karan Ashley and hello to her replacement Nakia Burrise, an actress who made sassy Karan seem mild-mannered. Nakia was a bold, strong, no-nonsense actress who jumped right in with zero hesitation. We ended up calling her character Tanya Sloan, I will admit, a weird name for a girl living on the plains of Africa, but everyone thought it would be funny to give her my last name and so that's what happened. Plus, it was easy getting clearance as there was no Tanya Sloan of note out there in the world to object. Nakia fit right into the group and immediately passed what I liked to call the "JDF test."

The JDF test was Jason David Frank's way of initiating a new actor into the very private club of which he considered himself the president. As kind and as loving as Jason was, as I've said in the past, he had that devilish side to him. Back then it mostly presented itself as a desire to mess with people and nothing more destructive, as it would in later years. New cast members were usually subjected to Jason's practical jokes and ribbing, at least until they gave it back to him, which he LOVED.

Nakia never let Jason even get started, as I remember it. She had this look she would give that was priceless if she thought you were being a jack ass. I remember Jason coming up to my office and asking if I thought Nakia was cool. He wasn't sure and just wanted to get my take on it (like the opinions of either of us mattered two weeks into filming with her). I told him that she was incredibly cool and very smart, and more importantly, that I wouldn't mess with her. Thankfully he didn't take this as a challenge to really mess with her. From what I can recall, they were all good from there on out. Nakia was a good sport about Jason's hijinks, and Jason realized he wasn't going to get a rise out of her and moved on. In the end, she was a great replacement, which is not something that can always be said when one actor leaves and another actor takes their place. I wanted her to enjoy her time on *Rangers* and the biggest hurdle to that had just been crossed. She had the JDF seal of approval, and life on the set would be a lot easier.

Sadly, the time had come to say goodbye to the Alien Rangers and get going with *Power Rangers Zeo*, which I still feel was one of our more adventurous and well-told seasons of the show to this day. Many of the fans I've talked to feel the same and look back on it fondly. I feel like as time goes by, it will only increase in popularity. At least that's what I hope. Now, let's turn a page and get on with the biggest change in *Rangers* up to that point. But before we go into that I want to backtrack a little, just briefly, and talk about something that was and is a MAJOR part of the history of *Power Rangers*.

CHAPTER 42
SAKAMOTO-SAN AND THE BATTLE GRID

Back in the early days of *VR Troopers*, there was a lot of uncertainty as to how closely the show needed to follow the *Power Rangers* format for it to be successful. One issue was that there was no fighting action in the first act. In *Rangers*, there was always a fight with the Putty Patrollers to kick things off. Regardless of how well it fit into the story, there it was, a scene with the Rangers battling these gray-colored foot soldiers and usually defeating them pretty handily. *VR Troopers* didn't have that type of built-in fight convention and relied on a Percy or Dog humor or some other sight gag as the thing that the kids would stay tuned for. As funny as they were, we were just not getting the job done in terms of providing an entertaining first act to keep the audience engaged. We needed action of some kind.

Enter the Battle Grid.

The Battle Grid was another dimension the VR Troopers could teleport to through a strange 90s VFX tunnel Dr. Hart created. Once in the Battle Grid, the Troopers could fight whatever terrible threat had shown up there. The set was a nice creepy space, with boulders, smoke, dead trees and whatever the threat of the day was, usually a Skugg platoon or something equally as dangerous the

Troopers would have to defeat, hence satisfying the need for more action. And to give the Battle Grid the intensity and bang-up action it needed, Bob, Shuki, and the *VR Troopers* higher-ups decided that it was time to call in some big guns to stage and perform the scenes that would be needed to make the whole thing work. Now, I'm not going to get into the success or failure of the Battle Grid and whether it was even needed. The point of this whole protracted introduction is that it brought us, ta da! Kochi Sakamoto and his Alpha Stunts team. Koichi was a diminutive Japanese man with a huge smile and a huge heart. His group of dedicated performers, known as Alpha Stunts, were like a precision acrobatic team that also happened to kick ass, creating amazing action footage that was exactly like what was seen on the tapes we received from Japan, because that's exactly what it was. In fact, some of the same guys who were now working in the Battle Grid had worked on the most recent Japanese *Sentai* show that had completed filming a year earlier and would eventually be used in an iteration of *Power Rangers*.

Meanwhile, BZ and his confederacy of dunces next door at *Rangers* had started to figure out that using the Rangers in fight scenes after they had been shooting dialogue scenes all day was ludicrous. It was also unfair to the actors and a bit unsafe, if I'm being honest. This was probably where all the talk of working conditions started. It was tough on those guys and completely unnecessary. The other issue was that the action footage that was being shot, as close it got, was not an exact match for the Japanese shot material. The stances and poses were just a bit off, as were the basic moves and styles. So, when the footage was cut together, it felt a little odd. There was now a chance to fix this. And so, they did. Sakomoto-san and the rest of his high-flying Alpha Stunts fighting team were installed as the newest members of the Rangers family.

The day they started, a white van pulled up, then out came about twenty Japanese men in tight training suits, all smiles as if they had won the lottery. They were all in fantastic shape, as you would expect athletes to be, and were brimming with enthusiasm. Sakamoto-san, who had been a part of the *Sentai* series in Japan for years, was in charge, and he ran his team with military precision. Not like a barking field general necessarily, but they all just seemed to know the drill and rarely had to be told what to do. This was something the likes of which we Americans had never seen. It's hard to explain how completely wild this whole thing was. These guys were a team. They ate together, lived together, worked together, and were literally a family. They all had worked together in Japan and knew what the job was. Every one of them contributed to all matter of work for the second unit and appeared to read their leader's mind when it came to stunts, rigging, fighting, the works. It might have been the best decision BZ ever made on the TV show. As they settled in, the Alpha Stunts guys became friendly with the American crew, and even though they spoke little English and we spoke zero Japanese, we had some funny conversations. And it was usually when they were shooting at the stage. It was not unusual to walk out and see the Pink Ranger double, helmet off, smoking a cigarette and laughing it up with his pals—a vision that startled me the first time I saw it, as I initially thought it was Amy Jo. But it was not. This diminutive in stature but gigantic in heart performer was the smallest of all of them, and his ability to mimic the female fighting footage from Japan was remarkable. One day we were all talking as the stunt guys were crouched down eating noodles for lunch, their staple, and the talk turned to the fact that the stunt team was going on an adventure for the weekend. They were all piling into the van and heading to Las Vegas. The excitement was palpable.

When we heard this, of course we immediately pictured this team of guys having the time of their lives on the streets of Vegas, eating, going to clubs, gambling...hmm. Gambling. That was a worry. I remember speaking to Larry Litton about it, and he was concerned that they were going to go there, blow all their money, and have no way to get back. This was the story that many tourists told when they went to Vegas. And the idea that our guys were going there with their hard-earned dollars and lose it all was a bummer to even think about. But these guys were grown-ups. They could do what they wanted and should experience everything their new country had to offer. If they lost money, so be it. It was something they would only do once, hopefully.

On Monday morning, the stunt guys rolled in after having an incredible time in Las Vegas. They were over the moon. Great food, great fun. I walked over from *Troopers* to see how they were doing before they went out to shoot for the day and immediately learned that they didn't lose all their money. In fact, a short time after arriving, the Pink Ranger stuntman won over $30,000 on a slot machine, if I'm not mistaken. And, in a very NON-American move, he did NOT lose it all back and they all had an amazing weekend. Guess we didn't have to worry about Alpha Stunts falling prey to the American underworld.

As for Koichi, he became increasingly important to the production. He and his stunt team were one thing. They were second to none when it came to recreating the style of the source material. However, his second unit directing was beyond fantastic. It was creative, dynamic, and always memorable. And his destruction of the command centers every year became legendary—a tip of the hat from him to the Japanese series from which the footage we used was derived.

There were a lot of traditions in the *Sentai* shows, events that year after year rarely changed. This was where Koichi and Ann and I weren't always in complete harmony. Koichi, as you would expect, had great reverence for the *Sentai* shows. They were what he (and all the guys from Alpha Stunts for that matter) grew up watching and eventually working on as performers. So, of course, they felt our show would be better served being done closer to the original. One of the big bones of contention was wardrobe. Koichi, along with BZ (for his own reasons), was hell-bent on getting the Rangers into the same outfits for every episode like they were in Japan. This was a discussion that we dealt with at the beginning of each season. At times if felt as though we were once again having to explain to him that the show had to satisfy our American audiences as well. American kids love clothes. They love fashion. To take that out of the equation was a huge mistake. The Rangers, in their brightly colored clothing that matched their Ranger color, was a staple of the show, and it was a cool inside thing that the Rangers and our audience alone knew. The civilians in the show weren't allowed in on the joke. And kids LOVE to see their heroes dressed up in something new and cool when they show up in the next episode. Every year we would drill this into Koichi and BZ. We knew what our viewers gravitated towards, and we intended to give them that. After all, if you pay all that money for a focus group, you might as well listen to what they have to say when it's something that is so obviously a common theme.

BZ had other reasons for wanting to lean the show more towards being like the Japanese version, and most were budgetary. Clearly the savings would be huge if we got rid of the varied wardrobe. What did he care if it would take away some of what made our American audience connect with the show in the first place? It was one of the reasons we always had such an issue with BZ. Who was he to unilaterally throw away years of development by some very brilliant people, Ann included?

When Ann and I left the show, that was the first thing they did. All the Rangers suddenly wore the same thing every day. Of course, the first season shot completely without us was "Rangers in Space," so it actually made sense to have them in *Star Trek*-looking uniforms. But after that? Not so much.

Koichi stayed with the show for many years after Ann and I left. I'm not sure if he was there at the very end of the initial Saban years, but it wouldn't shock me. He was one of the people most responsible for keeping that show going and making it work—even if he was wrong about the wardrobe.

Years later, when the show moved over to Disney and Ann and I were in charge, we of course brought Koichi with us. The first thing he asked when he got to New Zealand was whether we were going back to the wardrobe as before. I will never forget the look on his face when we told him we were indeed. At least then it was without BZ, so it made it much easier. One of the many wonderful things about Sakamoto-San was that he didn't harp on things. If one of his suggestions got shot down, that was the end of it. No argument or bad feelings. He would usually break out laughing, then just smile widely and say "Okay. No problem." Then off he'd go to blow something up.

Koichi was incredibly talented, kind, and easy to work with. I believe there is a part of him that appreciated some of the things we brought to the show regardless of what his pal BZ thought. I hope Koichi is still doing what he loves wherever he is.

CHAPTER 43
STRONGER THAN BEFORE: POWER RANGERS ZEO

As I'm sitting here writing this book, it has become obvious to me that the less chronicling of the show in terms of when things happened and in what order, the better off we'll all be. I don't remember everything that went on 30 years ago, and even if I did, most of that information can be found on the internet or in the massive book that Saban put out a few years ago for the bargain price of $200 a copy. What I'm trying to recall are stories that haven't been talked about as much. So that's where we're going as we move forward. Hope that's okay with all of you. I figure you'll be cool with it.

The first thing to note about the behind the scenes of *Zeo Rangers* is that we had an incredibly diverse team of writers. We brought in a few new ones, used some of the OGs who had been around forever, and everything in between. Everyone was pretty much on their "A" game that season. My friend Al Winchell had worked on *VR Troopers* the entire run of that show and was a truly gifted writer and director who knew the format. Ironically, they falsely criticized Al's directorial work on *Power Rangers Turbo* to begin the process of relieving me and Ann of our duties. More on that later.

I had kept thinking about those "Ranger Catastrophe" episodes and how they could have been so much better, at least in terms of my directorial skills. I had been studying my butt off since then, watching whatever I could get my hands on that I thought relevant, and I felt like I was ready to give it another go. This time, however, I wanted to do something different. Something special. It had to be unlike anything that *Power Rangers* had ever done and something that no one expected. First, I needed to take care of something that had been bugging me since I arrived at the Power Ranger stages.

I had been occupying the producer's chair for a few months, supervising the writing of the show with Ann, as well as looking after whatever creative things had fallen into my lap along the way. This could be anything from approving a prop that was unique and not a duplicate of something in the Japanese footage to looking at a casting tape, to watching a director's cut of a show with Ann and provide notes to postproduction. As I've mentioned before, it was completely arbitrary at Saban as to which producers looked after things like editing notes, mix notes, etc. These were tasks that on any other show in any other world would have obviously been part of the creative producer's duties. That's what showrunners did— they ran the show. On *Rangers*, it was not so cut and dry. But the bottom line was that we were doing enough other work to keep us plenty busy and to make my job far more involved and time-consuming than *VR Troopers* had ever been. With *Rangers*, there was always a PSA or an ad spot that needed to be written and shot. And it was always just assumed that Ann and I would handle it. Then there was Jason Frank. Just spending time attending to Jason's concerns was a job in and of itself. As I was now in immediate proximity to him whenever they were shooting on the stages, he would spend time in my office either talking about how great things were and what was on the horizon for him, or how crappy things were and how he wanted to quit. I should have clued in at that point as he was giving some pretty strong signs of what we later learned he was afflicted with. But I just didn't get it. It wasn't something you really looked for in 1995, I guess.

Ironically, as we moved through *Zeo*, the Jason conversations began to be more about how great things were than how bad. Haim and Shuki had started to find creative ways to reward Jason for his loyalty and the billions he was generating in revenue as the favorite Power Ranger. There was no getting around it. Tommy was God, Jason was Tommy, and ergo, it was time to open the checkbook and give our Ranger God a little something for the effort. And the same seemed to be happening for Amy Jo Johnson, who was cast as the lead in *Susie Q*, the movie I had helped write and was finally starting production. So it seemed that at least two of the Rangers were finally being remunerated for their patience and hard work.

One day Jason arrived in my office with a small notebook. Apparently, he'd done some math and had added up all the money he was going to make that year. He was pretty excited about it and wanted to show me. I told him he didn't have to. That was his thing, and I felt weird about being all up in his financials. He didn't feel the least bit weird and literally couldn't help himself. He remarked that it never would have happened without my help (probably not true) and so he wanted to share it with me (not the money but the information that there now WAS money). He laid the notebook down on my desk for me to peruse. Between the show, the Karate Club, the second movie, and other assorted extras and bonus payments he was in line for, Jason was slated to make close to $750,000 in the next 12 months. I was blown away. He probably deserved to make twice that, but it was an impressive sum. If he could repeat the year he was about to have a couple more times, along with the success of his schools, I told him, he would never have to worry about working again. He had done it. And that was awesome.

As we both took a deep breath, Jason said to me, "What about you, dude? They must be paying you a shitload by now." I was embarrassed to admit to him what was going on with my salary. But at that point, what did it matter?

"Dude, it's still the same as when I started as a staff writer on Troopers."

He stood up, with a look in his eye that was a little scary. "What the fuck? Are you serious? How much?"

"A grand a week."

Jason was near volcanic. As much as he was happy about his own good fortune, he was going to have trouble enjoying it when his mentor and friend was being taken advantage of in a pretty big way.

"I'm gonna go talk to Haim," he said. "This is messed up, dude."

"Jason, do not talk to Haim. Do not talk to Shuki. Just leave it." I told him about the time I went to ask Haim to give Bulk and Skull raises and how Haim pointed out that we were not sitting in the Social Security office.

JDF and I went back and forth for a few more minutes, Jason angry, me embarrassed, until he was called to set. His last words to me were, "This isn't over, buddy." I made him promise that he wouldn't say anything, which he did promise, and off he went, screaming down the hall, "This isn't over!"

As I sat there, my head was swimming. What right did I have to ask for a raise after all they had done for me? I had gotten to direct for the first time (without pay of course), I had acted in the shows (again, no extra fees), and they pretty much let me do what I wanted. This is how completely inadequate I felt. Partially because of my own inner demons, and partially because of the environment I was in where I was constantly being told by BZ that I sucked, my scripts sucked, my directing sucked. What I really needed was a second opinion. Fortunately, I knew just who to call.

CHAPTER 44
"AM I CRAZY?"

Ginger Perkins is a fiery red headed woman who was my first agent when I was an actor. She discovered me in the computer store where I worked, and she and the owner of the agency where she worked, Terry Lichtman, signed me for representation. Although my acting career had gone by the wayside once I became entrenched in *Rangers* and *VR Troopers*, Ginger and I remained great friends. To this day, she is one of the funniest, nicest, most genuine people I've ever met in my life. She cherishes her friends, and if you are fortunate enough to become one of them, you will truly be blessed in your life with the knowledge that out there is someone who unconditionally loves and cares about you.

Ginger's husband was a guy named William J. Immerman, or "Bill." He was a very successful lawyer who had started his career as a deputy District Attorney, but eventually became a film producer, a studio head, and a personal attorney to some lucky industry insiders. Bill was a fascinating guy in so many ways. He was one of the big dogs at 20th Century Fox back in the 70s and was one of the people who signed the green light paperwork that sent *Star Wars* into production. As a producer, Bill made close to 100 movies, all while keeping his law practice humming along.

And on top of it all, he was everything you would expect out of someone who was lucky enough to be married to Ginger. Bill was a terrific guy and a "Dad Humor" virtuoso. He was an obsessive sports fan and loved the Dodgers and Kings in particular. He was also an expert when it came to contracts and knew everything you ever needed to know about the law as it related to the entertainment industry. Bill had been my attorney since I left acting and always gave me great advice.

Ginger, who to this day is VERY protective of me, was disgusted when I told her what I was making, as she knew the insanity of what my job entailed. How could they move me over to a huge hit show with more responsibilities and still pay me what I had made three years ago on another show in which all I did was write and sometimes direct? As was her patented response in such cases, she immediately told me, "Honey, you better talk to Immerman." And so I did.

Bill agreed that the number I was getting was low, but he knew Saban and the attorneys there and did not relish the idea of going toe to toe with them on a kids TV contract. But he did. After warning to me that we should not expect too much, he started to haggle with Haim's attorneys. In the end, I was given a nice raise that took me from $1,000 a week to $2,600 a week. Plus, Bill had gotten me incorporated in California so the tax benefits would land me more take-home income every paycheck. All in all, I was over the moon. That was the most money I'd ever been paid for anything in my life, except for maybe the soap. It was insane.

> SIDE NOTE: Back in 1996, the lowest paid show runner working on a property that the Writers Guild of America sanctioned was making anywhere from $20,000 to $50,000 per episode, give or take. They were also paid for the scripts they wrote, and any directing or other side work was a separate issue. Additionally, they would receive residuals throughout the run of the show and beyond. So, although my bump seemed like a lot, it was well below the norm for the work I was doing.

But who cared? If you asked me, I was freaking rich! Bill and Ginger had come through, as they always did. Life was getting a little better all the time. It was time to get back to work and come up with something really cool to earn my new massive salary!

I won't call this next paragraph a side note, because that risks sounding dismissive. Bill was an important figure in my life and a true friend, and I couldn't bear that.

Several years ago, I was working on a series in Los Angeles and commuting, as Mindy was working in Arizona and the animals were all there and it was just easier. I would stay with Bill and Ginger in L.A. then drive back on Friday, having worked all week, and I would do it all over again the following Monday. Bill, unfortunately, was not in the best shape. He had gotten sick on a cruise to the South Pole and had to be life-flighted back to L.A. to be treated. Over the time I was there, I watched Bill's health deteriorate. His case was like a medical Jenga tower, where one treatment to help one ailment would be devastating for another of the issues with which he was dealing. Ginger was super-human over those months. She was by his side 24/7, sleeping when she could, pushing the doctors to try whatever they could to help her husband of 30-plus years. Ginger's goddaughter Zoey and I did what we could to help, but all we could really offer was support and love. Bill passed away on a Saturday morning in June, a few hours after I had left to drive back to Phoenix. He was brilliant, kind, and one of the most well-liked people I've met in all my years in the industry. It's been a loss to so many people; it's hard to explain how truly loved this man was. RIP William J. Immerman. And BTW, they did it, Bill—the freaking Dodgers won it all…twice!

CHAPTER 45
SNOWBLINDED

I came up with a cool idea towards the beginning of the season for a three-part episode I'd call "There's No Business Like Snow Business." It was a ridiculous and pointless exercise in that most of it took place at a ski resort and contained chases through the mountains on snowboards and skis, cog fights in the snow, romance on the slopes, etc. I was excited about the idea and so was Ann, but we were both pretty sure that BZ wasn't going to go for it. God knows how much it was going to cost us to go to a ski resort with an entire crew for a whole week just to shoot three episodes of *Zeo*. Regardless, Ann and I approached the great and powerful one with our plan and all the reasons why taking the Rangers to the snow for an action-packed skiing and snowboarding adventure was a great idea, fully expecting him to poo-poo the suggestion and have Jabba throw us out of the office.

Ann and I were completely caught off guard when BZ thought it was a decent idea and something that was perhaps "doable." WTF? Ann and I looked at each other in disbelief. Was he really going to get behind this whole thing? At the time, it seemed to go against everything BZ stood for. When looking back, however, that wasn't really the case. In fact, it made perfect sense that he would want to get behind it. In his heart of hearts, BZ desperately wanted to be a filmmaker. I wouldn't be surprised if he literally saw himself as a future Oscar-winning director, accepting his statue in front of the Hollywood elite, thanking Little BZ for his brilliant script, thanking Haim for giving him his start. Truth be told, BZ liked the idea of pushing the envelope and doing something that was previously thought to be impossible on our budget. I'm sure part of it felt like helping us realize this insane plan of ours would nudge him toward the creative fold and give him a way to help shape the story we were going to tell. Plus, it would look great to Haim and Shuki if BZ had managed to pull off this incredible feat for no more money than was allocated for the episodes. Before we even left the office that day, he was on the phone making calls and rounding up crew members to discuss our idea. I have to say, I was impressed and even felt a little guilty about everything I had thought of BZ in the past. I needn't have worried, however. BZ would prove, by the end of the ordeal, that he was still the same condescending, backbiting a-hole we had all grown to fear.

So, I got to work on the scripts for the episodes. The first thing I had to make sure of was that there was some sort of impactful character story involved in these episodes. I didn't want to just have the Rangers go away for the weekend, while back home the machine army attacks Angel Grove while they're having the time of their lives. There had to be more to it. My thought was that the most emotional component of the Ranger story to date had been the relationship between Kimberly and Tommy. Kimberly was said to be down in Florida working on her gymnastics, preparing for the Pan Global Games, but had been communicating with Tommy regularly and vowing to return to him so that they could be together.

Of course this was never going to happen, as Amy Jo Johnson had screeched out of the parking lot months ago like the Delorean in *Back to the Future* and hadn't looked back. If she ever did return to Rangers, it wasn't going to be this soon. She might have even been on another series by this time, but don't quote me on that. It *was* certain that we needed to end the relationship between Kim and Tommy. as the main idea for the three-part extravaganza was that Tommy meets a cute snowboarder named Heather and the two of them hit it off and seemed as though they were headed for romance, slowly of course. We could never have done this without first letting the audience know that Kimberly wouldn't be heartbroken, and that Tommy wasn't being a dickhead cheater. So, we decided the best thing would be a "Dear Tom" letter, delivered in the Juice Bar, explaining to Tommy that she had met someone at the gymnastics training and had developed feelings for him. This would be brutal and give Jason the chance to conjure up some real feelings.

We were all looking forward to the casting of Heather, as it presented the chance to find an actress that would have great chemistry with Jason and who could give the episodes the feel of something very special. After all, it was going to take someone with high volume "pixie dust" to melt Tommy's heart and to make him forget Kimberly for even a moment. We called our casting director, Katy, and asked her to put out a notice to the agents regarding what we were looking for. What I heard back from Katy was that she was under the impression that the role had already been cast. I told her it couldn't have because I had just written it, and the only people who had read it were internal to the show, such as Shuki, BZ, Ann, and Jackie. Katy told me I should probably talk to Shuki. As I was placing the receiver down and getting up to go fill Ann in, my phone rang. It was Shuki. *Perfect*, I thought. *Now we can straighten this out*. I mean, WTF was going on anyway?

I soon found out what was going on. The person who was cast to play Heather was none other than our very own Sarah Joy Brown from *VR Troopers*. This completely threw me off. *Troopers* was wrapped and not coming back, which made it odd that we would be throwing Sarah a role like Heather out of nowhere. Usually with Saban, there was some sort of strategic motive for hirings like this. For the life of me, I couldn't figure it out.

What I later learned was that as per usual, there was more at play than was on the surface. As we all now know, but did NOT know back then, Shuki and Sarah had been forming a connection that was more than a casual producer/star relationship. In fact, they would end up dating and living together for years and even have a daughter. Of course, at the time this would have seemed insane. I mean, Sarah and Shuki? There were so many reasons why that was preposterous, even beyond their nearly 30-year age difference. But, as with Divatox and Maligore, Zedd and Rita, Bulk and Skull (platonically speaking of course), the heart wants what the heart wants. Shuki and Sarah were happy together—and let's be clear, Sarah Brown is a tremendous actress. She is powerful, confident, emotional, everything you want in someone who is going to be the guest lead in a miniseries. As usual, Shuki was spot on with this one. And she wasn't going to take any crap from Jason or anyone else for that matter, which was something we needed for sure. In a way, it wasn't the worst decision.

> SIDE NOTE: Far be it from me to comment on any relationship that anyone has regarding anything that may make it unusual. Especially when it comes to age. Hell, Deborah was 12 years older than me, and my two longest relationships after that were both nearly 20 years my junior. So, I have no room to speak. It is so hard to find a relationship based on true unconditional love that isn't with a dog or a cat. If you are lucky enough to find one, you grab onto it and enjoy what time you have. That's what Shuki and Sarah did, and God bless them for that.

So, the scripts were written, and it was decided that Billy (who was not a Ranger at that point but had somehow worked his way back onto the show he had claimed to hate with such profound intensity), Catherine, Jason, Sarah, and some of the stunt guys would all go on location. The only part still to be cast was the role of a reporter, who we figured we could find up at the ski resort. I mean, there had to be *someone* who could read a few lines looking into camera, right?

With the scripts and the cast set, the next thing we needed to figure out was how we would manage to shoot the snow episodes up at the resort while shooting the other planned episodes without falling behind. Fortunately, the way the *Power Rangers* production was set up made this possible. The show, since its inception, had run two completely distinct and separate film units. The first unit shot all of the dialogue stuff and non-martial arts scenes featuring the principal cast. The second unit was for stunts and action sequences like precision driving, fighting, and explosions.

The second unit on *Power Rangers* was a slimmed-down guerilla version of first unit in that they carried no lighting equipment and no sound equipment. They basically survived by using reflectors to illuminate the scene with natural sunlight and a fast-moving director of photography who, although he was a Type One diabetic and had to check his insulin levels every couple of hours, moved the crew along at a record pace. They also were not in possession of many of the toys that the first unit was given. This didn't stop them, however. If they needed a dolly (the rail and wheels setup that rolls a camera along to track with the subject), they made one with two long pipes and a couple of chopped-up skateboards. If they needed a crane, they fashioned their own by nailing together old pieces of wood, pipes, and barbells. It could only go up a few feet and became known as the Jib, a useful tool that became even more useful in the hands of those skilled crew members.

The plan was that the second unit, for the most part, would go to the ski resort with us. They would be given what they needed to shoot the scenes, which included a sound man and his equipment, a proper dolly, Steadicam, the works. The first assistant director on the second unit was a guy named Chris Auer. Chris was great at his job. He was truly an excellent AD. But God love him, he was a freaking lunatic! He had a bizarre combination of seeming to not give a crap in the least while also taking incredible pride in his job. On the surface, you would have thought he just couldn't be bothered. But working with him, you realized his little group of film misfits was everything to him. He was a wild spirit, and the set often felt like being in the middle of a hurricane. Oh, and he never wore shoes. Ever. On set, at the office, in the parking lot, at lunch, the dude was always barefoot.

> AMUSING SIDE NOTE: Shuki loved to bring famous people to set with their children. It was fun for him to show them around and watch the kids go nuts meeting the Rangers. On one particular day, he landed quite the big fish and was escorting Marcia Clark, the prosecuting attorney in the O.J. Simpson case, to the set. This was at the height of the trial, so it was SUPER weird seeing her in person and away from the courtroom, standing next to a line of latex monster costumes on stands. Everyone in the cast and crew tried to keep things at least a little civilized during her visit, so as not to embarrass our boss in front of America's most famous prosecutor. Chris Auer, of course, didn't give a rip. Just as Shuki and Ms. Clark were arriving at the lunch tent, he appeared, dressed only in his short shorts, top button undone, all tan lines, jewelry, and bare feet. No shirt, just the shorts. He was screaming into his walkie something close to "Countess, I need your ass up there by 14:30 with every bug we got, hats on, ready to roll." (Translation: "John, I need you to have the monster costumes and the actors at the location at 2:30 p.m. with their heads on and attached, ready to fight.") For a moment, everyone stopped and stared at Chris. Shuki must have whispered something funny to Marcia, as we saw her laugh and the two continued on with their lunch. But that was Auer. I loved that guy. LOVED!!!

For the snow shows, BZ decided that Chris's methods and temperament would best be used at the studio. So, BZ switched out Larry Litton, the slightly calmer first unit AD who was familiar with shooting dialogue, keeping the set locked down and quiet, and understanding each Ranger's individual quirks as well as anyone. We were blessed with the director of photography from the second unit, glucose meter and all, and several other crew members from the second unit, including a dude named Cyrus who, while we were shooting the show, introduced me to, of all things, blaxploitation films, most notably, a movie called *Dolomite*, which he would watch upon our return to the condo. Every night, he would pop a beer, then lay back and laugh hysterically. And yes, Cyrus was/is of African America descent and had made it clear that it was cool that I enjoyed the film as much as he did. Cy saw *Dolomite* as a piece of historical significance, a work of art, something to be analyzed, celebrated, and shared with friends of any race.

> SIDE NOTE: I'm not sure if Chris Auer worked with First Unit at the stages while we were on location or not. But I'm sure they found something for him to keep him occupied, something that didn't require shoes.

The final piece to the "Snow Business" puzzle, actually BZ's idea and on the face of it, a good one, was his plan to contact the Warren Miller company (the famed ski film company back in the day) and hire one of their operators/directors to come with us and shoot all the stunt skiing footage. Having seen all the Warren Miller films and growing up skiing as often as I possibly could, I was elated. This was exactly what we needed to make these episodes really stand out. We needed someone who understood setting up spectacular ski shots and could move quickly, across the mountain, knocking out entire scenes in a matter of hours. So BZ pulled the trigger, and we were told that the guy would meet us at the ski area for our first day of shooting. This was going to be epic. I was really excited about it. There were no GoPro cameras back in the day (the little ones you strap to your body to create amazing shots) and there were certainly no camera drones, so we needed someone who understood the technology of the day and could use it. This was supposed to be our Warren Miller guy.

Initially we thought that the best place to shoot the mini-series would be at one of the nearby resorts like Bear Mountain up in Big Bear Lakes, CA. This was the closest ski area to our studio, about a three-hour drive, and it would keep us close enough to the city in case we needed to send for equipment, or someone had to return to the studios for some reason. In the back of my mind, I was a little nervous that the resort would provide enough terrain for us to successfully shoot all the scenes that we needed. We would have to piece together what we could get on a mountain that was, as resorts go, relatively small. Thankfully, the decision was made to drive the extra couple of hours and shoot at Mammoth Mountain, also in California but north of L.A. on the eastern side of the state on the way to Lake Tahoe. Mammoth lived up to its name in terms of sheer size. It provided us with 3,500 acres of skiable terrain, great accommodations, and a friendly local staff who were not only willing, but excited, to work with a TV series.

So off we went to Mammoth Mountain with three pretty good scripts and visions of cinematic grandeur. I should have known I was going to be screwed from the start when, as I pulled into the little town of Bishop to make the turn up the mountain towards the ski area, enjoying the newest Collective Soul album, I was pulled over and given a ticket for going 35 mph in a 25-mph zone. Later, I would come to find out that this was a well-known speed trap, although nobody had mentioned it to me. To this day I cannot listen to Collective Soul without getting a little annoyed. With my ticket in hand, I headed up the mountain to prepare for our weeklong shoot. I was meeting Larry Litton at the condo we were sharing with Cy to discuss the schedule and decide whether we were fooling ourselves and needed to make some cuts to give us more time. What I wasn't prepared for was the insane amount of rewriting and rescheduling that was to follow.

The cast had all made it up to Mammoth and were settling in, along with a surprise guest in the form of Erik Frank, Jason's older brother, who was now a part of the Ranger family and set to appear in future episodes as who else—Jason's long-lost brother. I was a bit worried that Erik was going to be a distraction for Jason. It turns out I was just being my usual paranoid self. Jason was there to work, and nothing ever really got out of hand in terms of Erik's presence.

The scripts had been written so that every scene would be shot outside. We weren't given access to the lodge or any of the buildings, so we were locked into getting our work done on the slopes and the lifts. This was fine with me, since Mammoth is one of the most beautiful places on the planet when the sun is shining and there is fresh snow. We were going to have some amazing looking stuff to cut together once we were finished. I was psyched.

Having grown up in Southern California and being an avid skier, I had made many a trip to Mammoth over the years. The weather on the mountain had been near perfect every time I'd gone there on a class ski trip or with friends in college. It always seemed bright and sunny, and when it snowed, it did so for a couple of hours, until the sun broke through and you were back on the slopes, tearing into a layer of beautiful fresh powder. Turns out the cinema gods had something else in mind for our little crew the week we were there.

Larry first started to become concerned when the weather reports were calling for three straight days of white-out snowfall. My thought was that regardless of how bad it got, we could still get out there and shoot what we needed to. It would just be a different look. The snowfall might be cool. Turns out I was so freaking wrong that it was almost comical. On day one, we shot a scene with Tommy, Billy, and Katherine walking at the base of the mountain discussing plans for the trip. As the reports had promised, the snow started to fall. It was heavy, steady, and accompanied by thick fog and a sky that was gray and foreboding. There was nothing cool nor beautiful about it. The scenes we shot just looked flat and dull with no contrast at all. The colors were getting washed into the background, and there was nothing we could do to mitigate the issue. We had to figure out another way to pull this off until the storm had passed.

At that point, we had limited options. We could sit in our condos until the storm made its way through the area. But it was supposed to be almost a week until that happened, and there was no way we could pay an entire crew to do nothing while we waited. We really had no choice. We had to shoot. The issue with that was not only that we weren't cleared to go inside the buildings on the property, but since we had planned to shoot outside only, we hadn't brought any lighting equipment. Nothing. And with how dark it was outdoors; we would have to blast the interiors with light if we were to get anything that looked halfway decent. Larry spent a long time on the phone with BZ, and the decision was made that someone would load up a vehicle from the fleet of BZ's trucking company with a lighting package and head up to Mammoth right away. I would have to get busy writing, turning every scene I could think of that was outside and not an action scene into an interior. We had no choice. And it sucked. What a pain in the ass for everyone involved. But what could we do?

I rewrote every possible scene that could be moved indoors and handed them over to Larry to remake the schedule. As it turns out, the folks at the resort were fine with us working inside as long as we didn't disturb the customers at the resort. In other words, we couldn't stop people from walking through scenes or talking in the vicinity. Fortunately, the guys on our crew were used to guerilla film making and were able to sweet talk the skiers who were crazy enough to be out there in the first place to leave us to our business and not yell or look into the camera. And so, we shot. Scene after scene became an interior by necessity, and it looked like we were maybe going to have a couple of days, if we were lucky, to get the action shots.

One thing that had slipped my mind during all this crap was the fact that we still hadn't cast the reporter part we needed to. We couldn't really cut the scene, so it was decided there was only one answer. I would step in and do the part. It was the simplest answer and, in the end, it didn't turn out horribly. It was the least of the disasters that week and gives me something people can laugh at when they look through the old shows.

On the day that we ran out of scenes we could shoot inside, Larry informed me that he wasn't sure the storm was going to clear by morning, but we didn't really have much choice but to go to sleep and plan to shoot outside. We got so freaking lucky. The storm not only passed but it had dumped five feet of beautiful brand-new snow on the mountain. There wasn't a cloud to be seen, and the conditions were perfect for filming both the stunt scenes and the sequence where Heather had to be rescued after she flew off a cliff while snowboarding with Tommy and Billy. The only issue was time. We were going to have to bust ass to get everything done. And our Warren Miller cameraman, who had been sitting by the fire, was going to have to help us out by shooting the chase scene with Katherine and the Cogs. This is NOT what we hired him for originally. He was there to create amazing shots that we could use to dazzle our viewers and make it a magical experience for them. Now, he was going to have to just help us tell the story of the chase and get what cool shots he could along the way.

As it turns out, the guy they sent was one of the more senior filmmakers at Warren's place, and as a result was a bit salty, moved very slowly, and wasn't concerned with being creative when it came to anything that wasn't 100% skiing related, or so it seemed. One thing was for sure—he was not excited to be rushing around getting the specific shots we were asking him to get. He was used to just doing his thing and bringing home a handful of beautiful action sequences, then calling it a week. Looking back, there was absolutely nothing we could have done. We had to get the Cogs and Katherine, and we had to get the shots of Heather and the boys snowboarding and having a blast before she crashes out. And because we had been snowed out for three days, there wasn't time to get fancy. We just had to tell the story.

CHAPTER 46
BIT BY BIT, PUTTING IT TOGETHER

Thankfully, when all was said and done, we were able to finish up the work and had all the material that we needed. The chase scenes came out okay. They did the job, but they certainly weren't the Warren Miller spectacle I had hoped for. But, at the end of the day, you HAVE to tell the story first and add the flash later if there is time. In the end, we got all the story and ZERO flash.

When I got back to L.A., after literally kissing the ground at the stages upon arriving for work, I asked BZ how the edit was progressing, as I was certain he was checking every day to see what was coming in and how it was looking. He was only too happy to tell me what he and his pals thought of the material we had shot. He told me it sucked. Not that he thought it could have used work, or that the weather really killed us, or that it was a shame how things had turned out. No, he stated as fact that our work was total shit. There was nothing cool or interesting about what we had spent six days up there doing, never mind the fact that we had two actual shoot days on the mountain. In BZ's eyes, it all looked like crap and he was very disappointed to have employed so many resources to get what we did. Of course, he told me this in front of all his cronies, which made it that much more unbearable. I said nothing at the time and headed down to my office to commiserate with Ann and Jackie and tell them that the great and powerful BZ had given me a full thumbs down as my welcome home present.

Part of me wanted to ask what he would have suggested to make it better given the amount of time we had. But I really didn't give a crap what his answer was, so I kept my mouth shut. I CAN, however, imagine that he would have extended the shoot by a couple of days, and maybe brought in a couple more camera guys on skis to make all the snow shots look amazing. Of course, we were never given those options. But that's what he would have done to save his own ass, I'm pretty sure.

I thought there were good and bad things about that miniseries, as with all episodes of *Rangers*. But I certainly didn't think it was the disaster that BZ portrayed. Then again, who knew with him? He could have just been saying it to get it on the record that he thought I was a shitty director, among all of my other shortcomings. He did crap like that all the time. It's what satanic denizens of the dark underworld do, so I'm not sure why I was ever surprised. At least he did it with a smile. Anyway, onward.

> SIDE NOTE: There was a small group of crew members who had been on the snow shoot who hypothesized an interesting theory about what had gone down. If BZ was going to hire Warren Miller's guys, knowing this whole thing was going to hinge on the ski action, then why didn't he get a couple of them and one who could actually get the great shots? Why did he hire the most tired, bitter guy they had, who never really had any ideas that would make things dynamic and cool looking. It's a far-fetched thought that BZ would sit back and let us go down like a pile of rocks in terms of the snow material. But there would be a time in the very near future that something similar would take place. This was when I finally had to admit that it made me think. Was this guy beyond passively aggressive? Were we finally seeing under the hood, having a look at

the engine that was supercharged by evil and the bloodlust to take creative control of the show at any cost? I guess if you want to look for a positive, at least he got an extra couple of days of production renting his trucks out of the whole deal. So that's good.

CHAPTER 47
GUY RIDES UP ON A HORSE

As I mentioned earlier, Jason Frank's brother Erik had become part of the *Ranger* family. There are some very sad and tragic parts to this story, but it's an important story to tell, for better or worse. So I hope you will all forgive me.

Jason arrived in my office one day for his usual weekly chat and somewhere in between "Dude, BZ is such a dick" and "Who's going to be the Gold Ranger? Hey, can I be the Gold Ranger?" he mentioned that his older brother Erik was coming to set to visit and that he was starting to take acting classes. The implication behind this, of course, was that Jason would love it if there were a way that we could put Erik on the show. Nothing was said out loud, but both of us knew that was what was implied. I told Jason to stop by with his brother later that day and introduce us and that I would have Ann there as well.

That afternoon, Ann and I were going over some story ideas when there was a knock on the door and in walked the brothers Frank. Jason was very excited, like a little kid, that his big brother was on set. You could see that he looked up to Erik just as any little brother would. The irony was that Jason was the big star on the cover of TV Guide, and Erik was teaching karate at the dojo Jason recently opened. Erik had long hair much like Jason, was very tan, and he also had the eyelashes. It was uncanny.

Erik was incredibly polite and seemed so grateful to be meeting us, which was a nice change around there. Jason had most likely already promised him that he could be the next Ranger or something and that this meeting was a formality. Of course, we'd never seen the guy act, and this was the first time we were laying eyes on him. But, as things tended to work for Jason, we couldn't help but agree. This dude needed to be on the show. He could play Jason's brother. There would have been so many great opportunities had we given the Rangers siblings on the series. We could have created episodes around the real-world problems that brothers and sisters face. Imagine if Billy had a jock brother who was going to be kicked off the team if he didn't get his grades up. Or if Kimberly had a jealous sister who got caught up in making her life miserable, only to discover that Kimberly is a Power Ranger. Just a few ideas, but stuff like that would have worked great. But you can't go back and change things, so let's talk Erik and Jason.

Although Erik was super polite in our meeting, there was an edge to him, an element of danger, that both Ann and I picked up on. He just had this vibe that was different from the loving, deeply emotional one that our beloved JDF had. I made note of it and kind of stuck it in the back of my mind for later.

Ann and I decided to immediately pitch the story of the brothers to Shuki, who right away thought it was a great idea and signed off. When I think back on it, what the "F" were we thinking? We had no clue if this guy could even say his name on camera. He was relatively quiet in person. If that magnified itself when "action" was called, we'd be screwed. The other issue was that Jason could be a handful with his practical jokes, manic behavior, and sometimes zero attention span. Now we were going to have two of them on the same set. We never really thought of that, and I'm kind of glad we didn't. We probably would have backed out.

But we didn't back out, and all we had to do now was come up with an idea for the episodes with the two brothers. We sat in my office for three days straight, and all we could come up with was a scene where a guy rides up on a horse and looks out over a valley. Every day we could come into the office and either Ann or I would say, "Okay, a guy rides up on a horse." From there, we were stumped. Next day: "Guy rides up on a horse." Every day…nothing. It got to be ridiculous, until finally one day it was suggested that Jason looked a bit Native American in his features and coloring.

SOUND OF BRAKES SQUEALING!!!!!!! SOUND OF CAR CRASHING!!!!

CRITICALLY IMPORTANT SIDE NOTE: I want to get very serious here in discussing the issue of the Native American storyline featuring Jason and his brother Erik. Please keep in mind that this was back in the day when we were so much less sensitive to the plight and the struggles of Native American people. Their treatment has been abhorrent and deserves every ounce of scrutiny that treatment is facing so many years too late. And now that I am in Arizona and live among the populations of the many tribes from this area, it's right there in front of my face and hard to ignore. Had the *Rangers* idea come up today, there would have been no question that this storyline would have been shot down instantly. But it was 1995. The Black Ranger had been an African American guy, the Yellow Ranger, may she rest in peace, was from Vietnam. There was a lot of learning that needed to happen to even get us to a place where we could identify words and ideas that were hurtful so as not to use and perpetuate them.

I ask that you forgive us and understand there was no ill will intended, just ignorance and a lack of education. As I said, we decided that Jason was part Native American and the guy who rode up on the horse was his long-lost brother, adopted by the local Native American tribe many years earlier, separating the two, neither knowing they had a brother. Now, David Trueheart has come into Tommy's life to help our hero transition to the idea that he has a whole other side of himself that he never even knew existed. At the time, we thought it was a beautiful story. Looking back, it could have been, had it not originated from a misguided place.

And if that wasn't bad enough, I've had a production company since 1997 that I formed with Ann that haunts me to this day because of the name...Somehow, we decided that it would be funny to create an anagram of Guy Rides Up on a Horse. And so, GRUH Entertainment, Inc. was born. Epic fail to be sure. To this day, I still have the company in my name, and I still have to deal with the questions about the origin of its name. Anything would have been better. Anything but GRUH.

Mark Hoffmeier and Mark Litton wrote the script that introduced David Trueheart to our audiences. I thought they did an amazing job. It was a great script. Then Litton wrote the second on his own, another great job, and we were ready to see if we had shot ourselves in the foot or whether by some miracle Jason's brother had that same innate ability to work hard and pull off the role. Turns out he did. Whether it was with Jason's help or on his own, Erik showed up prepared and did a fantastic job. I'm not sure that so many fans remember that little bit of *Rangers* history, but I am super proud of those episodes. We had several Native American performers who also acted as advisors to make sure we didn't get anything too glaringly wrong. To me, I've always looked back on those as compelling and well-thought-out episodes. And as we've talked about, if you start with character, you always have a better chance of creating something that resonates with your audience.

This was where BZ's creative tended to go a little off, especially as a director. He insisted on putting the cheap gag or the splashy visual ahead of what was in the hearts of the characters. And this trickled down to Little BZ in his writing. (Or maybe it trickled up the other way. But I don't think so.) Having been under BZ's thumb all those years, Little BZ never even explored the idea that if you start with an issue that is important to the character, it will mean more to the story and ultimately to the audience. This is a concept that is easily forgotten to the detriment of many writers in the screen world. Characters in books have the opportunity to be very well developed, so the reading experience is often so much more enjoyable. This is why book to movie translations often fall short. There's no effort taken to set up the characters, and the story cannot be supported as a result and collapses. But that's for another book and another day.

The true tragedy of Erik Frank, of course, was his untimely death at the age of 29. According to the media, including many of the Ranger-specific fan and Wiki sites, it was from an "unknown illness." Now, I would never presume to tell a family how to handle such a tragic event, and this was many years ago that this all happened. However, there was an opportunity here to take away a positive through Jason's fame and access to the public. Most of you outside the Ranger Universe are probably wondering what the hell I'm talking about. Allow me to explain as best I can.

First let me be clear that I wrestled with this for months. Is this really the place to write about the circumstances behind Erik Frank's death? And is it even necessary for our purposes to reveal my perception of the situation? The decision to get into it came when I was notified of Jason's passing in 2022. I was so angry and so completely devasted that I felt there needed to be some context given to what lead to Jason taking his own life. Just days after Erik passed, I received a call from Jason. He was a complete mess, as you would expect, and I think just wanted someone to talk to as we had done so many times in the past behind the closed doors of my office at *Power Rangers*. I like to think he saw me as a voice of reason who would always be there if he needed me. Just as I would have done with my own children, or a brother, I dropped everything.

Jason informed me on that call, without hesitation, that Erik had taken his own life. He had, in fact, hung himself using the black belt he so proudly wore as a brilliant martial artist. According to Jason, what led Erik to take this drastic step was the relationship he was in that had become a source of pain and frustration Erik could no longer bear. He just couldn't take the pain anymore and decided the easiest way out was to end it. Sound familiar? It should, because years later, Jason also hung himself, also during an ongoing struggle with his wife/ex-wife. It was a repeat of Erik's suicide.

Clearly, there had to have been some sort of mental illness at play in the Frank family, at least with the two boys I knew. I was aware that Jason had displayed signs of being bipolar and manic depressive. It didn't take a genius to figure this out if you spent any amount of time with him. One day Jason was on top of the world, loving life, enjoying his unique fame, caring for his family, growing the martial arts community just by being part of it. And there were days that he was in the pits of despair. He would get in dark moods that could not be talked away. He just had to let it subside. (As I mentioned earlier, back in the *Ranger* days, I pleaded with him to go to a counselor just for a single appointment. He wasn't crazy about that, but he did it, I think to appease me. He never went back.)

If the truth about Erik's death had been acknowledged back when it occurred, I can't help feeling that Jason would have taken up the cause of suicide prevention. He would have met doctors and clinicians that could have helped him stabilize his own condition—and who knows? Perhaps he would still be with us, living a much less dramatic and far less stressful life. Maybe we would be having a completely different discussion. But we're not. We're having THIS shitty and painful discussion. Whatever happened is over, and there's no going back. It breaks my heart every day to think of both of those beautiful, talented, charismatic brothers and what they must have been feeling when they decided there was nothing worth living for. It makes me want to scream.

CHAPTER 48
BZ LOSES HIS VOICE—CREATIVELY

Earlier, I described a meeting that I had with Haim in which he asked if I wanted BZ fired so that Ann and I could operate in a more harmonious way with the production team. My response to Haim had actually been a request that he speak with BZ and suggest that he stick with his production duties and I would handle the creative. The time had come for our first production meeting with the new rules supposedly in place. I had heard through the grapevine that Haim did in fact have a talk with BZ, and like a gentleman, he agreed to keep his notes to himself and let us worry about the scripts.

"Heard It Through the Grapevine." Great song.

Unfortunately, the grapes on this particular vine appeared to be dead and shriveled, as the production meeting we were having showed no signs that there had been any sort of talk between Haim and BZ. Let's all travel back there now and, like flies on the wall, observe that meeting.

First, a little bit of set up. When new scripts were distributed and nearly ready to shoot, the department heads from the production would get together and discuss any questions or issues they had after digesting the new material. The art department would ask about any new sets. The prop department would discuss weapons, simple props like pencils and notebooks for school scenes, sporting goods for episodes in the park, etc. Hair and Makeup would talk about any special looks we needed for those episodes as would the wardrobe department. And of course, BZ and one of his crew were there to talk about what we could afford to spend and if anything appeared to be beyond the limitations of our financial resources. At least that's what was supposed to be happening. After all, this wasn't a script meeting. The scripts were locked. They were approved by Shuki. And a production meeting was not the place for anyone to start tearing apart something that could not be changed by any of us, or anything that wasn't related to production. It was a "production meeting." Seemed simple enough to me.

Imagine if every department spent just ten minutes talking about the changes that they thought would be good for the scripts. That would work out to be about an hour of us listening to experts in their field which was NOT storytelling, instruct us on how to tell our stories and respond to suggested changes that could not and would not be made. That's why none of the other departments ever did that. No more than we would tell them how to apply makeup or build a super mega blaster or how to spend the money that was in the budget. In fact, the entire time I was there, I never even saw the budget for the show. I never bothered to ask because I knew what the answer would be. So why did these imbeciles think it was okay for them to start tearing the scripts apart after Haim had supposedly told them not to waste time giving us their thoughts on the script? (I'm talking BZ and his team.)

On this occasion I felt like I had the backing of Shuki and Haim, so the moment BZ brought up a script note, I calmly told him that Ann and I would worry about the scripts, and he should worry about the budget. If he would just stick to that, it would be much appreciated and it would speed up the process. Saying that in front of all the department heads was probably not the best move on my part. I could have walked him outside and done it in the hallway in private. But at that point, I was fed up, and it needed to be said for everyone's sake. BZ, as predicted, did NOT take it well. I can't remember if he got up and left the meeting with Jabba trundling behind him, snorting to herself in a combination of what must have been anger and confusion, or if he just sat there in stunned silence, pissed off and already plotting his revenge. Either way, I felt better in the moment, but had quite possibly effed up in a big way. I knew he wouldn't let it slide, and it would come back to bite me down the line...which it most definitely did.

After the meeting, I asked Jackie if she thought it was too much. Ann was at another meeting, so it was just me and Jackie that day. Jackie agreed that we had given him every opportunity to get back in his lane, but he just couldn't. He had to tell us everything that was wrong in front of all the departments. Not only was it irritating and disrespectful, but it proved over and over how completely self-involved he was to truly believe the show could only survive if his script notes were taken. Well, they weren't. That day, Jackie and I agreed that he seemed really pissed off and that this would come around to a very bad place at some point down the road. But on that day, it felt kind of good just to shut the guy down.

CHAPTER 49
ZEO KEPT A ROLLIN' ALL NIGHT LONG

During the *Zeo* season, there were a lot of enormous shifts upcoming in the stories we were going to tell. There were the new villains, the changing of the costumes, the way the Rangers got their powers, and a whole host of other moments that were new and different, some created by us, some based on the footage. The idea of having Billy in the command center and not being a Ranger just kind of happened without any of us chiming in as to whether it was a good or bad idea. But there he was, all buffed out and happy, helping the Rangers do their best to protect Angel Grove from the Machine Empire.

I think it's safe to say that *Zeo* was a mixed bag of some great acting, directing, and story moments, combined with others that just kind of fell short and didn't do much to lift the franchise. I could not find a better example of this when looking back than the appearance of the Gold Ranger.

In the footage from Japan, there was a 6th Ranger who came along, and he was most definitely a badass. He had this cool black and gold suit and kicked some serious butt, to the point that the Rangers were mightily impressed by his ability, although they had no idea who he was or where he came from. The mystery of the

Gold Ranger would end up in a great place. But the way it got there, to me, was a freaking disaster. Let's look at the mechanics of the whole thing just for some context. As with any Ranger anecdote that involved the creative, it all started with Shuki.

Shuki always had an eye open for the next star he could cast on one of the current shows or even sign up for the creation of a new show. In *Zeo*, it was a set of male triplets from Rhode Island, who Shuki insisted should be stars in the Saban galaxy immediately, if not sooner. I'm not sure whether it was Katy and Thom who found them or what, but the truth of the matter was, the brothers were stunning to look at. They were of Sicilian descent, if I'm not mistaken, and just had that look, that thing, say it with me…"the pixie dust!" In their late teens/early twenties, they had most likely been discovered by Katy and brought to Shuki's attention, although I cannot confirm that. What I CAN confirm is that the triplets had never acted before, and it showed. This was always the first red flag. I'm certain that Shuki didn't give a crap about that and just wanted to see how they would handle being in front of the camera and whether they had the charisma to carry a show or even be part of one.

So, how was Shuki going to gain this knowledge? The same way Shuki always did, with zero fear and blind belief in his instincts which had served him extraordinarily well up to this point. Much to all our grand disappointment, we soon learned that no one can be right 100% of the time, not even Shuki.

The first issue that we encountered with the triplets was their strange desire to look directly into the camera. This is a common mistake that new actors will make once or twice as they are getting up to speed and used to being on set. But it seemed like with these guys it was just impossible for them to avoid the lens. Wherever the camera was, they seemed to find it. On one of the end credit gag reels, you can hear the director telling them NOT to look into the camera and getting frustrated doing take after take of them staring right down the barrel (into the lens). In response, the guys would quickly look away, then right back into the lens. It was wild. It's almost like there was some sort of tractor beam being sent out to their brains, demanding that they look into the camera. It was almost comical. No, check that: it WAS comical.

The second and much more serious issue we had with the triplets was what they had brought with them all the way from Rhode Island. It was their heavy, and I mean HEAVY, New England/Rhode Island accent, much like the Boston accent but with a twist. The way they formed their R's was almost like Barbara Walters. When you look back at Ms. Walters, she had a very specific way she spoke that, although brilliantly spoofed, was not really like the Gilda Radner "Baba Wawa." Ms. Walters was close mouthed and landed somewhere between an "R" and a "W." The triplets to me sounded very similar. I'm not sure how this escaped everyone during the casting process, I mean there were three of them. They must all have been talking nonstop. And we missed it? Yep. We missed it, so we had to deal with it.

Unfortunately, the name Shuki and Shell had chosen for the character the triplets played was immediately going to be an issue. The moment they said their own name, "Trey of Triforia," it became Twey of Twifowia. Holy shit! I don't bring this up to make fun or to shame anyone. It was just something that became more and more impossible as the days progressed. A Rhode Island inflection is not one that can be hidden or is easily changed. Especially when you are talking about three dudes who shared a womb and have been speaking this way their whole lives. There was no way it was going to change. And it was frankly a bit unfair to ask them to do so. I mean how does that happen in a couple of weeks, for three brothers? I was asked to try to help them but was forced to remind the powers that be that I was an acting coach, not a speech pathologist or the potions teacher at Hogwarts. (Writer's embellishment, of course—Harry Potter came out after I was gone from *Rangers* the first time.)

When we started to look at the film that was being shot of the triplets, it immediately stood out as sounding completely bizarre. Why would Trey of Triforia speak with such a distinct Rhode Island intonation? It was really hitting my and Ann's ears and Scott Page's ears and Shuki's ears as basically being something we had to fix.

That is why, to this day, I say, "Thank the good Lord for Brad Hawkins."

Brad has always been one of the most agreeable, nicest, low stress actors I've worked with. He'll come in and do any part you ask him to do, not complain, and always do a great job. When we asked Brad to revoice Trey of Triforia, he didn't even hesitate. In fact, because of his training on *VR Troopers*, he was able, within a couple of sessions, to replace all of Trey's dialogue and do all the Japanese footage overdubbing to boot.

> SIDE NOTE: If you really think about the whole thing, what we should have done was put an effect on Brad's voice to disguise it. That way it would have been believable when we revealed that Austin was the Gold Ranger. Brad sounds NOTHING like Austin, and both of their voices are SO recognizable to our audience. The whole thing was kind of a comedy of errors. In the end, it was great that Austin came back. I love the guy. He IS a Power Ranger. But wouldn't it have been nice if the Gold Ranger had been Ryan Steele? No? Eh, well, what do I know?

But I digress. Once Brad came in and finished the overdubs, it seemed like things with Trey were going to be all right. Phew. Once again, saved in ADR. Since the beginning, any story point or issue could always be fixed in that nice little studio across the parking lot at the hands of the brilliant Scott Page-Pagter.

As I was saying, a lot of what was great about the Gold Ranger storyline was the return of the one and only Austin St. John. I had been sad to see him go when he and Walter and Thuy left. When he returned, I think it breathed new life into all of us in the writing room. We had another character that we could fold into the mix, one who was familiar and yet had clearly matured over the time he was gone. Austin was always a great superhero, and you can never have too many of them on a show about superheroes, unless you happen to be Marvel in the last couple of years. In that case? Yes. It is possible for there to be too many superheroes in a superhero movie.

When Austin returned, you could see that he had been humbled by the earlier departure and never mentioned money or any of that. He'd been there and knew what the deal was. Austin just showed up, did his job, and went home. It was awesome, and I commend him for returning after the way he and the others were muscled out of the show back in the beginning. I have more thoughts on that which I will expand upon at some point.

As I said, there were some really cool things about *Zeo* that were unique to that season and that I remember fondly as contributing greatly to the success of that show. I wanted to mention a few and contrast those with some of the negatives, at least for me.

The Bulk and Skull storyline for *Zeo*, to me, was freaking awesome. They started off as cadets still under the watchful eye of Lieutenant Stone and unbeknownst to anyone had adopted Goldar and Rito as indentured servants who had lost their memories and would clean the house at the ring of a tiny bell. For their next storyline, Shuki and Shell hit it out of the park. Making Bulk and Skull private detectives in business with Lieutenant Stone was just a perfect way to transition them out of the junior police academy. What took this storyline over the top was the way it was shot. And to this day, I'm not sure how we were allowed to go for it.

The number one rule in the production of a kids TV series is that the screen must be always flooded with bright primary colors. Anyone who has worked in the kid biz will tell you that this is a hard and fast rule. For some reason, we were able to smash that rule to bits and create a space for Lieutenant Stone, Bulk, and Skull that was a cool homage to the film noir detective movies of the 1940s and 1950s like *The Maltese Falcon*, *The Big Sleep*, and *Strangers on a Train*. These films were dark, moody, and cynical, using lots of shadows and always in black and white. Of course we couldn't do the latter, but our cinematographer Ilan Rosenberg did an amazing job along with our production design team to come up with a look that closely resembled these old movies without taking it too far. For the first time, our show had a completely different look, one with some mood depth and some character. We actually had shadows! I was completely blown away by it at the time. I'm not sure how we slipped it by, but it sure was cool. I'm not sure the stories lived up to the look, but you could only devote so much time to Stone and his goofy partners, as it was only a 22-minute show and we had rubber monsters to blow up. But every time I saw scenes shot in that office space, it made smile with pride that these talented folks were working on our dopey little show, doing whatever they could within our tight budget constraints to create special moments along the way.

I believe in fact that the detective office on *Zeo* was a perfect microcosm for what the entire series was about. For better or for worse, we took some risks that season. It seems like every show pushed the boundaries in terms of what we could achieve, and most of the time I felt like we pulled it off. We went to a bunch of unique locations, had the Rangers trying new activities, introduced Ernie's Beach Club and brought in the uber-cute Lesley Tesh, who was just getting her acting career started. She was maybe the coolest girl ever. So funny, and she could hang with just about anyone. She was a great addition to the cast.

Zeo, to me, marked a great season for guest actors. I felt like we finally got ourselves some truly good performers to fill the roles of new characters coming into the series. The guy who played Raymond was Darren Press, and he was amazing. Darren was quirky, had great timing, and just fit in with the gang. He was fantastic. As was Erik Frank as David Trueheart. For someone who had never been in front of a camera, he did an amazing job. And, as always, our Mrs. Appleby and Principal Caplan were in fine form that season. I don't think people realize how difficult it is for guest actors. They come on a set, not knowing anyone, having to jump in with folks who are like a family and give a great performance. It's not easy. But somehow that season, all our guests and day players managed to do a great job.

We also had a plethora of different writers and directors. All of them brought their own style and point of view to the show without straying too far from what *Power Rangers* was all about. When I look back, we were really lucky that year. I felt like it was a great group all around, with everyone adding their creative flair. It was a season when *Power Rangers* really spread its wings for the first time and took some chances.

We added the gag reels to the end credits, which were always funny and showed the true personalities of the actors, who all had great senses of humor. They changed the theme song, which was a HUGE risk, but to this day I LOVE that *Zeo* theme. It manages to include the original Go-Go Power Rangers riff while introducing new elements at the same time. I thought it was awesome.

There were also some things about *Zeo* that I wasn't crazy about. The one worth mentioning is the Machine Army. That footage, to me, was not the best. I see what they were trying to do over in the Land of the Rising Sun. It was an attempt to capture that old school Metropolis feel but turn it goofy at the same time. I never really felt as though the Cogs were the best foot soldiers, and I didn't think the king and his court were all that threatening. And having voiced Prince Gasket, I feel like I'm allowed to say that. But Scott did the best he could with what we were given, and I suppose it could have been much worse. There was just not a lot of charm in the faces of those fat, weird-looking robots. That being said, we did what we could and later on, when Divatox and her minions darkened our doorstep after leaving their giant skid mark on the second movie, I would come to appreciate the Machine Army for their simplicity and comparatively sublime acting skills.

You might want to grab a latte or some chips or some other type of distraction, as I will now officially begin my rant on movie and TV villains. You'll definitely get sick of hearing me say this, but it is my firm belief that any superhero or sci-fi show or movie is only ever as good as its main villain. There has to be that serious threat, or there won't be any empathy for the main characters. The viewer won't worry about them, and that's the last thing you want. If you have any doubts about this, watch some of the successful TV shows and movies from recent years. *Breaking Bad, Prison Break, Iron Man, Guardians of the Galaxy*—all of these had amazing villains that truly left a doubt as to whether our heroes could defeat them. I never felt that with the Machine Army. They looked like all you had to do was shove them and they'd tip over and not be able to right themselves, much like the children's toys Weebles. Although it should be mentioned to avoid any future litigation that according to them, Weebles "wobbled" but did NOT fall down. Overall, though, I do think the good outweighed the bad. And, to me, *Zeo* was a fun, action-packed, entertaining season that is beginning to be recognized for some of the cool stuff we did.

CHAPTER 50
LATE NIGHT ATTA BOY

As we produced more and more episodes of *Power Rangers*, there weren't a lot of times when any of us working on the show would get any sort of "good job" or "great show" or even "great script" for the work we were doing. And this was completely understandable. The company was growing at a rate that was insane. From new shows to new movies to taking over networks and taking over companies, the daily activity going on in the corporate office was staggering. And in most cases, Haim was right in the middle of the hurricane of activity. He loved growing his business, and he was certainly having success at it. However, this meant that the idea that he or any of the other higher-ups would even remember a specific *Rangers* episode to call out as being anything but another *Rangers* episode was a fantasy.

One night I happened to be at Shell Danielson's for a housewarming party she was throwing. It was a new house for her, since she had technically separated from Shuki and seemed to be taking a moment to digest the upheaval that had surely left her anywhere from devastated to happily moving on, although she was showing signs of neither and kept that ever present smile firmly in place.

The modern cottage was perfect for her. Little did I know I

would soon be seeing much more of it, driving there every day, slaving over a tiny 9-inch Macintosh computer screen while having my face licked by a strange little animal with awful breath. Right now, a large portion of you are wondering, "WTF" is he talking about?" I'll save the reveal and crazy story for later. It's worth the wait. Promise.

Halfway through the party, I felt the phone in my pocket buzzing. I pulled it out and looked at the number. There was just a name—Haim. How did he find me all the way down here? And it was Saturday. Well first off, he didn't have to find you, dumb ass. That's why cell phones have become the standard form of communication in modern society. The real question was, "Why was he calling? Shouldn't he out with Benjamin Netanyahu or Bill Clinton, or Hillary Clinton for that matter?"

Haim's voice was chipper, even cheerful. This was a huge relief. We had all received the other kind of call from Haim, and you could instantly tell that this was NOT one of those.

"Doug, this is Haim," were the first words I heard.

No shit, I thought. What I actually said was something like, "Mr. Saban! This must be important."

He explained that he was giving his pursuit of world domination a break for the evening and had decided to stay home and catch up on his *Power Rangers* episodes. I told him to be careful how many he watched in one sitting. I had read an article that claimed we were inserting secret messages into the show that were turning kids violent, and I didn't want him getting into any trouble just when things were going so well. He laughed and proceeded to explain the reason for the call.

There was a group of four episodes that he had watched that he thought were "incredible." He said the scripts were great, the acting was spot on, the directing was fantastic. He couldn't come up with a single negative note. He wanted to be the one to tell me personally.

"Well, that's good news. I love hearing that we're on the right track," I answered.

"Oh, you're on the right track. Keep this up and we may never let you leave," was his reply.

This was SO very Haim. While the statement was a huge compliment, it also had deeply hidden shades of "don't screw up" in the subtext of the statement, as I was not supposed to be going anywhere, at least that I knew of. Whether he did it consciously or not, it was a brilliant way to remind me that no one was ever truly safe. That's not how I read it back in the day. Trying to decode Haim's business lexicon was not easy, and it would probably just make sense to me when I crawled into bed later than night. Anyway, at the heart of his phone call was that he was happy with the show and took time out of his evening to call and personally thank me for the hard work. Awesome.

After the call, I switched off my phone and dashed into the guest bathroom at Shell's to blot the sweat that was pouring down my face. *Holy shit.* I would never get used to that. Yes, he could be a brutally tough at times. But he was a force of nature, one of a kind, and when he gave you a bit of praise, it was like you had just won an Oscar. I looked at myself in the mirror and started to get a bit emotional. This probably had to do with a lot of unresolved childhood issues and not getting enough pats on the back as a kid. Or, it might have been the realization that I was safe at the company, at least for a while. Whatever the reason, I gave it a couple of minutes and headed back out to the party, thankful that I had my ancient cell phone set to vibrate, or I never would have heard that someone was calling.

The idea that no job is safe has always been a reality at Saban. Haim surrounded himself with a very small group of people that he trusted implicitly. But beyond that, it's never wise to get too comfortable. I recall a time when I called down to post-production and my old friend the post producer was frantically trying to locate his assistant to get the day's work going. He had never known this woman to be late and was baffled that she was over an hour behind. He decided to call her and ask if she was all right.

Haim's daughter Tiffany answered the phone at the 25,000-

square-foot home they all lived in up on Mulholland Drive. Yes, Tiffany had been hired as the post-production assistant and, according to my buddy Paul Rosenthal (a super talented guy and one of the guys in charge of post-production), she was doing a really good job. When Tiffany picked up the phone that day, she regretted to inform Paul that the whole family had been involved in an argument at dinner the previous night and Haim, in a fit of anger, had fired her from her job.

Paul smiled, shook his head, and asked if he could put her on hold. He then called Haim and asked if this was true. Haim said it was and that it was her own fault for starting an argument when they were trying to enjoy dinner. Paul informed Haim that he needed her at work. She was a valuable member of the team, and she had to be there. Haim asked, "You mean she actually does something besides sit around all day?" Paul assured Haim that she did and again asked if they could reinstate her. Haim's response was along the lines of, "Well, I suppose if she's doing something useful," followed, after a brief pause, with "Fine. She can go to work." Paul hung up and told Tiffany the good news. I think she must have been greatly relieved. Nothing worse than getting axed by your father a couple of weeks after you start. And to those of us who were around then, it was proof as to the vulnerability of anyone who wears a Saban employee badge regardless of their last name.

CHAPTER 51
"IT'S A LITTLE LONG, NO?"

I had always gauged my status at Saban through my relationship with Shuki and relied on that for the feeling of job security I carried with me into my daily battles with BZ. This is not to say that I used that connection in any way to treat BZ differently than I would have under normal circumstances. But a small part of me did feel safer knowing there was a layer of familiarity there that would perhaps come to my aid if things every got really ugly. And even though the call from Haim I had received while at Shell's was a welcome one, I was not an idiot. I knew that the big boss would clip me in a heartbeat if I did the slightest thing to get in the way of him taking control of the kids TV business or whatever white whale he was chasing at the time.

It seemed like Haim was cool with me for the moment. But this was nothing concrete that I could see that guaranteed this. Nope. My suit of armor at Saban had always been and would hopefully continue to be Shuki. And there were two definitive reasons behind that. First, he appreciated my work. He truly did trust me with a lot of stuff he wouldn't have handed over to anyone else in terms of the actors, the writing, etc. I felt like he knew he could rely on me and as long as that feeling of confidence was there, I would be okay.

Then there was the Deborah of it all. Because of Deborah and Tamara, Shuki had a soft spot that also contributed to his desire to see me succeed. And for my part, I treated him with the respect of a valued mentor and friend. I had never, in the entire time I had been there, publicly questioned his creative choices or anything he did for that matter. He was sensitive about this kind of thing. The meetings with Ann and me about casting, writing, directing or anything else were mostly just to run ideas past us that we would usually tell him we really liked, because we usually really did like them. Lately, however, there had been a recent development that had me a bit concerned, as I was truly unaware as to how it would affect my standing at Saban. Something that should not have been an issue, but of course, was because the world of *Power Rangers* was not like other worlds. It had its own rules, its own hierarchy of things that were important, which made it unpredictable at best and a minefield at worst.

The recent development that had me concerned, ridiculous as it seems now, was that Deborah and I had broken it off and had stopped seeing one another completely. This time it was for good. It wasn't a big, weird blow-up thing. It was just time. When I look back, I really should thank her for never allowing me to believe there was any permanence to our relationship. She held firm on the idea that I was too young for her and would lose interest years down the road, as do most men when their wives enter their golden years. The irony is that if you were to run into Deborah today, she is still as stunning as ever and I'm pretty sure I would have still been right by her side. But were it not for her doing what she felt was the prudent thing, I would never have met my true soulmate, my wife Mindy. So, thank you for that, Deb.

As far as Rangers was concerned, the question at hand was, "Would our split leave Shuki feeling less loyal to me?" Were my abilities enough to keep me in my job? Or did I need that extra "he's part of the family" thing? I decided that I could never go on and concentrate without having the answers to these questions. It would be too weird if we never discussed it, and it was something that down the line could become an issue.

> SIDE NOTE: Okay, all of you reading this, let's take a beat while I ask you to go a little easy on me here. We're all friends, right? You've torched me on the internet for years, so I feel like we have a special connection. And we've had some laughs along the way. I've revealed deep, dark secrets I thought were buried forever. So, you know enough about me to know that these thoughts I was having were somewhat out of character and could be chalked up to stress, being overworked, my fancy new car that kept breaking down... From the outside, it must have looked so disjointed from any kind of reality that it's almost embarrassing to admit that I had these fears. Because let's face it, who the "F" would fire someone because they stopped dating his ex-wife? Just saying it out loud is completely laughable. Look at Shell and Shuki, for the love of God. Who knows what those two were up to or where their relationship was? I knew where SHE physically was, two hours away down the 405, tucked away with her Mac and her Italian Greyhound, still working on the series and I assumed seeing very little of Shuki. Most importantly, she didn't seem to be going anywhere anytime soon.

So, yes. You are correct. I was a borderline mental patient for even allowing my mind to travel that road. That's not even the way the business works. Personal friendships/relationships may be the propellant that sends you through the door and gets you your shot. But it's not what keeps you there. What secures your place is the work. If you are doing your job well and the results show this, then the other stuff is unimportant. Now, here, today, I understand that and would never let myself get all wound up over it. But back then I needed to know for sure, or it would consume me.

Unfortunately, I couldn't just call up and ask Shuki such a

bizarre question. That would have been ridiculous, unprofessional, immature, you name it. Whatever the label affixed to it, the conversation would have started him thinking of me in a way that I did not want. So, I did the only thing a self-respecting, hyper-paranoid dude with a messed-up childhood who just broke up with his non-girlfriend could do. I hatched a simple, mostly harmless plan to settle this so I could move on with the work at hand.

Later that day, as it turns out, I was scheduled to give Shell notes on a *Rangers* script. When we were finished with our call, Shell mentioned that I didn't seem myself that day. (I had been a little less than my "Up with People" self on our call.) I told her that I was still bummed out about the whole Deborah thing (not THAT bummed in reality) and I was worried that Shuki was going to react and my place at *Rangers* might be a bit tenuous as a result. Shell was SO sweet. She reassured me of course and made sure that I knew there was no way this was going to happen. Shuki loved me and he would never even think of getting rid of me over something like that. I told Shell that I was quite relieved and thanked her for sharing that with me. I also asked her to please NOT fill Shuki in on our conversation, as it was a bit embarrassing. She didn't promise but said "of course."

I knew that the first thing she was going to do, because she was worried about me, was tell Shuki and ask him to call and reassure me. Yes, it was a sissy move on my part that I'm not proud of to this day. But that was what I needed in the moment. In asking her to keep it quiet, I was relying on the fact that she would have to tell Shuki, as her allegiance was to him and it was my own fault for sharing with her and knowing where her loyalty lied. They were too close to keep things from each other, so I figured it might take a couple of days, but he would call.

It took an hour for Shuki to ring me up on that same day. And, in a very kind and loving tone, he let me know that I was being a lunatic, to come in off the ledge and stop worrying about things that weren't real. From that moment on, I felt great. I will always deeply appreciate Shell for her loyalty to Shuki and her inability to keep anything quiet where he was concerned. I also should apologize to Shell for the minor deception. She is such a pure and good person that I'm sure she wouldn't imagine me doing something like that. But, as it turns out, I am not as much of a good and pure person and sometimes I do stupid things. So, please forgive me, Shell.

For the moment, all was well…right up until the time a rusty, leaky submarine broke the surface, the hatch flung open, and it was time to climb aboard for the journey to the bottom of the sea, in the wreckage now known as *Turbo*.

CHAPTER 52
THE TRUTH ABOUT TURBO (AKA THE CATASTROPHE THAT WAS CARRANGER)

B efore we even go down this road that is littered with ruined careers and hurt feelings, I want to offer my two cents and proclaim right here and now that *Turbo* never stood a chance on our side of the Pacific and should NOT have been used in our series. That's right, I said it. Sitting in a vault in Japan, this series consisting of 48 fully realized episodes was never going to succeed on our U.S. television airwaves or in our theatres, at least not as a *Power Rangers* entity. This, again, is an opinion, but one I share with legions of fans and critics of the series and the movie.

One might ask, "What told you the show would fail? How could I know that? Hey, Mr. Big stuff. Who do you think you are?"

Let me try to explain myself, as I have researched this tirelessly and concluded that this statement will be unpopular with at least 25% to 49% of our fan base allowing for a plus or minus 0.5% standard deviation. Actually, I don't have numbers, I didn't do research, and I haven't thought about it in years, but I felt like there would probably be a lot of people disagreeing with me about Carranger, so here's my perception of the whole thing.

The first four seasons of U.S. made *Power Rangers* featured dinosaurs, ninjas, a dragon, a white tiger, and giant mechanical robots for *Zeo*. These were all cool in that it allowed kids to use their imaginations and take these incredible journeys with the Rangers aboard these enormous, majestic metallic creatures.

Then, all of a sudden, came the Turbo cars along with their Zords and weapons. Anyone who has spent even ten minutes with me knows that I am freaking obsessed with cars. I believe with all my heart that cars can be and definitely are works of art and must be revered and honored as such. So, of course, when I first thought about it, the idea of us doing a season of the show based on cars, it was just too good to be true. I was over the moon. Before I ever saw it, however, I knew that we would truly live or die by the footage on this one. This season had to be great.

"And why is that?" you ask. For starters, every kid out there has a real-life car parked within a few hundred yards of them at any given time. So, these needed to be some pretty dope whips (as the kids used to say). Oh, and there were a few other things at play I should mention.

1. Hot Wheels has been a successful kids' property for decades. Hot Wheels are awesome. I love Hot Wheels. I still buy Hot Wheels if I'm at Walmart and there's a cool one to be had.
2. The cars from Turbo are NOT awesome. They don't look much different than the cars that moms were taking their kids to school in back then. They were NOT Hot Wheels. They were not awesome.

The show that Turbo was derived from in Japan was called *Carranger*, and it was very different from any other show we had used in the past. This series was the first in their history to SPOOF the *Sentai* shows. It was a sendup of the whole concept, making fun of itself in the narrative.

1. There ended up being a lot we couldn't use from the footage, as it was way too goofy and didn't fit the brand we were trying to keep at the top of the kids TV food chain.
2. We had to create our own villain. We all know how that turned out.

Perhaps the most important issue we faced was the fact that before the new series began, we were producing a movie for the theatres, called, what else, *Turbo: A Power Rangers Movie*. This was concerning to me, but Shuki and Shell were writing away on the script. The second movie was going to act as an introduction to the new season, which would be called, what else, *Turbo*. Shell was living in her house down the coast a couple of hours and had seemed to be setting down roots there without Shuki. It was hard to say how exactly she and Shuki were working on the script together, as there was no Zoom or FaceTime yet. But they somehow managed, and in a matter of a month or two from when it was announced, they had a script. And what a script it turned out to be.

CHAPTER 53
FREAKING TURBO

We were in the final stages of finishing up *Zeo*, so things were slowing down around the office and the stages, at least for the writing portion of the series. One day, Shuki came by my office and dropped off the script for *Turbo: A Power Rangers Movie*. It made a loud thud as it hit the faux wood top of my desk, causing me to immediately notice that the screenplay seemed a little hefty. When I picked it up and flipped to the last page (as most everyone does with a new script), I was hoping that it was just printed on heavier paper stock Shell had picked out to give it that special touch, and I would still see a number between 95 and 105 in the corner of the last page of the script. That would let me know that we had a shot in hell of rewriting it and getting it to a more manageable length so that we had the money in the budget to make the thing. I knew that anything over 90 pages was going to be tough. If we were closer to 100, it was going to get harder and eventually impossible. And speaking of impossible, the script that I had just been handed, Shuki and Shell's first draft, FADED OUT on Page 136.

QUICK SIDE NOTE: Shuki and Shell, back then, wrote things a bit on the "cute" side. The comedy was sometimes a little young and too on the nose. This was never an issue, because we could fix these problems before we went into production. Shuki and Shell would have moved on to the next script by that time and had less of an attachment to one they had written months ago. With this movie, it was different. Ann and I didn't even know what they wanted us to do, or if they wanted us to do anything. So, whatever was in that script might have to live there and could wind up on the screen. It wasn't that their writing was better or worse. It just strayed from the voice of the show at times, and that's why we were there, to bring it back in line. We might not have that opportunity on the second movie, and that was scary.

I asked Shuki whether he planned on cutting the script down. He told me that he knew it was a too long, but he and Shell had packed it full of the coolest stuff the kids would love, and they would thin it out at a later date. Well, that date never arrived. Apparently, they didn't want to cut anything they had written because they loved every bit of it. This is NOT an uncommon thing to have happen. It's just that unless your last name is Cameron or Tarantino or Scorsese, you better get to cutting, because nobody else cares what you think is the coolest stuff and they sure aren't going to hand you an extra $10 million to find out what.

Shuki asked me and Ann to read the script and to prepare written notes if we had any, providing we weren't too busy. We both gladly agreed and were relieved as hell. We felt like maybe there was a way to pull together whatever lay in those many… many…many pages and turn it into something that was realistic to shoot while still telling the great story Shuki wanted to tell. At the end of the day, Shuki and Shell always came up with good ideas that sounded awesome when you heard them. The ideas usually ended up being strong TV episodes after some work in the writing room. And the movies they had written together in the past, although low budget, always had similarly great ideas behind them and were just a notch above most of the other mindless crap that was out there like, I don't know, *Silk Degrees*.

So, Ann and I both sat down to read. And we read. And we read. And we read. Holy shit, when I turned over page 136 and closed the script, it was as dark outside as it was in my brain, which had shut off several pages earlier due to exhaustion. Finally, when we had both finished, we met in her office and let out a huge sigh in unison that probably sounded more like a whimper in the moment. What did we just read? As usual, there was a decent story, but it suffered from on-the-nose dialogue, a lack of structure, and a frenetic narrative. Most importantly, at least to me, the villain was weak and her sidekicks were weaker. Oh, and it was 50 pages longer than it should have been.

It was immediately clear to both of us what had happened. Shuki had, at some point, realized that he and Shell were completely free to write whatever script they wanted for this next movie. They were the single creative voice, at least in the beginning, on what was to become the sequel to the Fox movie. But this time, the movie studio had completely handed over the reins to Saban. The reason I believe this is simple: If Shell and Shuki had pitched this story to Fox, and had been given notes on it, and the notes had been addressed, there wouldn't be a 136-page script on all of our desks.

> SIDE NOTE: Very quickly: I am in no way criticizing Shuki for telling the story he wanted to tell. He had a vision for the movie and wanted to do it his way, no interference from executives and producers who didn't know the show, didn't care about the show, and didn't want to have anything to do with the show. So, in a way, I say, "Good for Shuki." He was probably still bummed out that they had completely shanked what was the equivalent of a five-foot putt and managed to screw up the license to print money that the first movie should have been. All

they had to do, this behemoth of a movie studio, making films since 1935, was figure out how to create a piece of entertainment that kids and their parents could enjoy together, so that the studio could take advantage of the repeat business on which kids' films build their box office numbers. And, in truth, all they had to do was figure out how to keep the parents interested in the films for a couple of hours. The kids were already captivated. So, part of me completely understands where Shuki was coming from.

I got the feeling that Shuki wasn't crazy with the creative on the first movie. Haim felt the same about the box office receipts and looked to his partner to make certain that they didn't fall down that corporate rabbit hole again. Haim left the team of Shuki and Shell to come up with a movie script that would do better than the one the "think tank" at Fox had. Besides, Haim was mapping out his takeover of the world. He was dealing with huge companies, political candidates, important people at every level who could help him when he needed it. This left Shuki on his own, and he and Shell had created the opus they had always wanted to write. This was the uncensored, unrestrained, unimaginable answer to the studio's first movie. It was Shuki saying, "Okay guys, THIS is a how you do a *Power Rangers* movie." That was the only explanation we could come up with for what we were looking at, the only thing that made sense to those of us who had read it. What else could it have been?

The irony was that it was incumbent upon us to make sure this script was readable before anyone else had the chance to react the way we did. Locked in a room for a couple of weeks, Ann and I could have done just that. In fact, I always thought we could have crushed it. It would have been amazing (not to toot our own horn, we just knew the franchise really well at that point). However, as was always the case at Saban, things didn't get done in the normal way Hollywood things get done.

At a normal movie studio: The idea is borne through some

meeting or focus test or a kid telling his dad who happens to be the studio head he should make a movie about "insert idea here." Writer is hired based on fleshed-out story idea. Writers come, story gets pitched, story gets approved with changes, script is ordered, script is written with changes, script comes out. Script is bad or Script is good. Script needs massive rewrite or some changes that aren't structural and can be completed in a few weeks. Original writer gets fired. Script gets the massive rewrite it always needed but nobody wanted to admit it did. Movie is saved.

As it happened, ironically, our process was SO MUCH simpler than that when it came to important shows or movies. It kind of went like this: Shuki has an idea. Shuki gives Haim the elevator pitch. Haim loves it. Shell and Shuki get to work. Shell and Shuki distribute script for notes. Shell and Shuki ignore notes. Shuki realizes he should probably take some of the notes that make sense. A rewrite is done. The script is green lit. The script is shot.

What the hell were we going to do? What were we going to tell our beloved leader about his creation, of which he seemed so proud? Ann and I literally considered having a conversation with Shuki where we would just tell him we thought it was great, it just needed some cuts, and he would be off to the races. That would have been so easy to do. Although we would NOT be doing the jobs they hired us for, and Haim would end up pissed off at us before he would be pissed off at Shuki. We were the creatives behind the series, and we were supposed to watch after shit like this. If something wasn't right, we had to fix it, regardless of who wrote it.

It took a couple of days for Shuki to come around and face the fact that there needed to be a plan of action. Part of me was thinking he would find someone else to read it and hope that they were a little less focused on the negative than we were. But that's not what happened. What DID happen defied belief. I was called into his office for a brief meeting. I was informed that he understood the issues that we had pointed out. He was aware that the length and the story structure was an issue, and that it needed to be brushed up a bit. Unfortunately, and this is according to him, he just didn't have the time to do it. I felt a tiny glimmer of hope inside me. Did this mean he was going to turn it over to me and Ann? Would we be allowed to help put the project back on the road to success and maybe pick up a little extra cash for our trouble? Would this be our first theatrical feature film credit? I remember sitting on that leather couch in his office imagining how great this was going to turn out. We DID do the right thing by being honest—and now it was paying off. Ann and I were going to reap the benefits of our honesty and our loyalty to Shuki and to the entire—

STOP! Come on. You guys didn't fall for that! Of course you didn't. Because you all are smart and pay attention, unlike me back then who was the Chief Executive Officer of Fantasyland and employed "hope" as my chief strategy in all matters personal and professional. And, as you also know, hope is NOT a strategy. It's the name of the title character in one of Sandra Bullock's less remarkable efforts back in the 90s—*Hope Floats*. Well for me, hope sank like a lead weight tied to a cement cinderblock tangled up in a boat anchor.

You had to know this was going to a place no one saw coming, and it definitely didn't have me and Ann unwinding the 136-page behemoth and turning it into a tight, engaging producible script all to the grateful applause of Haim, Shuki, BZ, and the rest. It was our "hope"—it was not reality. Shuki had something different in mind. And it was different in a way that was more bizarre than I could have ever imagined.

Shuki, of course, was not going to hand over the script to me and Ann. What he WAS going to do was send me and my sorry, once-hopeful, now-sunken ass alone, down to Orange County to Shell's to sit with her and rewrite the script. And I would stay there for as long as it took to "fix it." For this, I would receive the standard Saban rate for work done outside the scope of one's normal contracted duties. In other words, I'd be getting normal pay for the

TV show, which I would still be working on at night after driving home from my work with Shell. This wasn't a request, either. These were my marching orders. Anytime I was ready, I was free to hop in my ride and hit the L.A. freeways for the miserable drive down the coast and begin my punishment for being honest and truly concerned that this script was on life support before it even left the womb.

I was bummed out. But I was not surprised. Shuki must have assumed our reaction to the first draft would be very different. We had a meeting to go over the specific notes and you could feel his disappointment and frustration. At least this is what I believe. I'm sure he would see things differently if asked today. He would probably just say that I was the head writer and it needed my voice or something like that. But, at his core, Shuki is a sensitive, driven, proud artist. Artists pour their soul into their work and can easily be hurt by criticism of it regardless of how successful and talented they are. I think, looking back, this was the case here. And I was going to have to deal with the fallout, although my issues with the script were echoed by those who had also read it. I was just the one who decided I owed the man who had written it the truth. As good and as kind as he had been to me, I wasn't going to let this get any farther down the road. Thinking back, I often wonder if that was the first time he ever had been told the truth about something he'd created. He wrote tons of scripts for TV and movies at Saban. Some were good. Some were just okay. I started to feel like perhaps no one had ever told him what they really thought. How else would we have gotten to the place we were now?

Along with his artist's mentality, Shuki, much like me, was not a fan of face-to-face conflict. Unlike me, he's always seemed to be a lover of people, someone who wanted anyone he met to like him, men or women, it didn't matter. He was incredibly kind to those in his life and did his best to keep personal exchanges positive and happy, IN PERSON, that is. On the surface, Shuki was the ying to Haim's yang. Where Haim didn't mind getting his hands dirty from time to time, Shuki rarely dealt with face-to-face reprimands, from what I was privy to. That was left to BZ or Ronnie Hadar, or if the situation called for hell fire raining from the sky, Haim.

Those three, all in their own way, could "straight out ball" when it came to a verbal beatdown. But Shuki was never the one. And, in many cases, he would simply excuse himself, announcing he had another meeting to get to, and leave the room. I literally spent my first couple of years at Saban under the impression that he was in such a good place spiritually, that nothing so meaningless as issues with a TV show would even register on his Zen meter. He didn't need a "steam valve" to purge himself of the built-up pressure caused by the stupid mistakes that those around him were making. He accepted us all for who we were and was there to help us succeed—together. He was the perfect boss, the idea coach, the calm, kind shepherd to his flock. He was the ideal guy to have in your corner. Boy, I was one lucky dude. And only looking back all these years later, writing this book, do I see how ridiculously idealistic and immature it was for me to even imagine that this was what was really going on inside my boss's brain. And on top of that, it was completely unfair to assign these god-like qualities to a man who was just that…a man. I wish I could have figured that out back then, but there was a lot I didn't figure out back then.

From what I've been able to gather throughout my life, studying this in college, experiencing it every day, is that human beings, based on how they were raised OR their genetics OR their environment, traumatic events, etc., or a combination of any of those, end up developing into the person they are as grown-ups. I must believe that there are many factors that contribute to our psyche, and it really is true that we are all very different in how we deal with life, face adversity, handle success, and anything else life brings us. It is very unusual for one person, except in cases of mental illness, to be completely 100% devoid of any one specific human character trait, whether it be considered a "positive" or a "negative" by the society in which they live. Human emotions reside in all of us. There are times when the rigors of the modern-day world just become too much, and our brain triggers an emotional response that, although seen as negative in the moment, is a safety valve to keep us sane and moving forward. This is not a new argument or anything earth shattering that I'm bringing to the table here. There are those who argue that "blowing off steam" has the exact opposite effect on a person, only serving to elevate all the disruptive chemical reactions in the brain and make it harder to get past what has caused the release valve to open in the first place. Those same people would say that the ability to examine your feelings and situation in a very analytical way—count to ten, take a walk, do whatever it took to train yourself NOT to release the toxic feelings boiling up inside of you—is the goal every human being should shoot for.

As I've said before, I write this book with only my own experiences as the research from which to draw; things I've read, seen, heard, learned in school. My experience with controlling one's anger was interesting, to say the least, and is directly responsible for my firm belief that you really do have to let it out.

I was 9 years old. I was a very angry kid. For whatever reason, I was surrounded by a cloud of nervousness, sadness, and anger that followed me around like the dirt Pigpen had to deal with in the Peanuts comics. My parents, God bless them, were very concerned and decided it would be wise to get me to a therapist to straighten all this nonsense out before it got to be uncontrollable and became permanent part of my brain mapping. When I was growing up, child psychology was still finding its way as far as treating the general population of kids out there. What was seen as acceptable treatment amounted to Pavlovian-derived methods of behavior modification, more concerned with making life livable for those around the child and not really being too concerned with what was troubling the kid and causing the offensive behavior. So, the goal was for me to get to a place where I was able to suppress my anger instead of putting it on full display for the world to see. To achieve this, they deployed a seemingly endless array of exercises we could use in the home that would allow me to forever quell my nasty thoughts and be the good kid they were convinced I would grow up to be.

This was the one I most remember. My allowance was, at the time, 50 cents per week. Adjusted for inflation, that's around $4.58 in today's money. This is what I would use to go into the tiny town of Hartsdale and check out any new affordable toy cars, toy planes, etc., at the local drug store. That money gave me my freedom, at least for a couple of hours on a Saturday, to just be a kid, ride my bike, see what life had to offer out there in the big wide world of Westchester, New York.

My parents were instructed by the psychologist (a woman in her 70s named Mrs. Stone, who chain-smoked through our sessions and coughed like she had a pile of shucked oysters in her throat) to place that 50 cents on the windowsill in the kitchen in the form of 50 pennies, ten rows across, 5 pennies tall. Then, every time I lost my temper, expressed my anger or raised my voice, they would remove a penny. One after the next, throughout the week, they would take those pennies away until most weeks they were all gone and I was left trying to remember what I could possibly have done that was so wrong as to cause the complete loss of my allowance again!

You may be asking yourself, "Did this new-fangled way to fix messed up kids find success?" Well, not with me, it didn't. I could NOT control it, for whatever reason. And so, for the next half century I was sentenced to simmer in my own venomous psycho stew of self-loathing and regret. Ashamed of myself for all the people I hurt over the years. So many mistakes made out of emotional desperation. Who knew there was a little pill called Zoloft that could have afforded me a few more years of peaceful existence?

So, clearly, I've never ascribed to the world famous "count to ten" exercise. If you're pissed off and someone has done you wrong, you let it out in whatever way is socially acceptable for the time and location you are occupying. That's how I feel. And I don't mean let it out in a way that is hurtful to others. There are so many ways you can go too far, which I think we can see just by turning on CNN or firing up YouTube and searching "Karen punches cyclist and gets instant Kharma." I warn you, however. Karen is a nasty piece of work. He or she will draw you in to those videos the point of waking up on the couch at 4 in the morning, computer in your lap with videos still playing and your partner pissed off that you never came to bed. So, proceed with caution.

All kidding aside, road rage makes a good example. There are drivers out there who believe that if another car cuts them off, slams on their brakes in front of their car or otherwise puts them in danger because of their bad driving, they are well within their rights to follow the offending car, remove little Teddy's pint-sized bat from the back seat, and smash the front windshield of the other car at the next traffic light. This usually results in the other driver deploying a taser, or worse, the Glock that she keeps in the glove compartment in case her Tuesday afternoon Hearts game with the girls goes sideways and she has to put one in Mrs. Johnson's foot to snap her out of the rage she's experiencing as she's waving a cleaver over her head (true story, by the way, but the names have been changed).

"Blowing off steam and blowing off heads are two very different things." Not a bad credo to live by. Let's keep that in our "obvious shit to live by" box along with "hope is not a strategy."

What I'm trying to get at, not very well I'm afraid, is the concept that people DO exist, real people, living breathing beings with no brain trauma or anything like that, who live among the hustle and bustle of today's world, who do not experience the need to vent, either by cussing, punching the air, screaming into a pillow, or anything else that helps dissipate the rancor that can flow through us in times of extreme anger. Are there really people who have simply risen above this or never had an issue to begin with? Maybe. I don't have a clue. My mother is from a wealthy and idyllic New England town where nobody has expressed anger since the Boston Tea Party. Instead, they drink, drug, and die from diseases that eat away their insides. It's still pain and hurt and angst.

When it came to my mentor and friend Shuki, I was convinced there for a while that he was a shining example that these people did exist, that he was the personification of someone who had it all on lockdown, who didn't need to vent, never got pissed off due to his heightened state of enlightenment. That was right up until I literally "got the memo"—that wonderful, revelatory, out-of-the-blue memo that cleared up a lot of stuff for me.

One day in going through my interoffice mail, I opened an envelope that had been delivered to me mistakenly. It had no name on the outside and one sheet of paper inside. It was a memo to Paul Rosenthal, our co-producer in charge of Post, but it had somehow arrived on my desk. The memorandum was from Shuki regarding the editing of an episode he had just watched. Now, Paul is one of the most on the level, straight-shooting guys I've ever worked with. He has the patience of Job and is as smart as they come; a 100%, no-BS dude who always did a great job under incredibly difficult circumstances and was never really given the credit he was due.

Even though it was intended for Paul and therefore had zero effect on me or my life at that moment, after reading it I had to pick up the phone, call over to his office and ask, "See if you can tell me what I'm holding in my hand?"

"Bro. You know I don't like that hand game," came the reply.

I gave him the obligatory chuckle for the dad humor and continued, "It's from Shuki. VERY intense. One might even go so far as to say *pissy*."

Paul laughed. "What, you've never gotten one?"

I had not and I had to ask, "Has Scott ever gotten one of these?" This was often the question when our little group was discussing something that related to the production that could be considered…controversial.

"Hell yes. He gets them."

"What?"

Apparently, Scott had gotten more than a few similarly

constructed interoffice "Fuck you's" from Shuki. In fact, these memos, dictated to Shuki's assistant Nancy Kennedy, were apparently legendary, landing with the force of a hand grenade on the desks of those Shuki felt had disappointed him or screwed up to the level that it could not go unmentioned. What was strange was that no one ever spoke openly about these memos. It was as though they didn't exist. I had never even seen one until now. What a completely mind-blowing moment. What an insanely pivotal day this was for me and my relationship with my boss and mentor.

I know it seems like I'm making a huge deal out of something that in the bizarre upside-down world of *Rangers* shouldn't even register as a blip on the radar. Normally you would, of course, have an excellent point. But please stick with me on this. Let's maybe look at the memo for some clarification. It always helps give context to what you're discussing if all those participating in the discussion have been privy to the object of said discussion. In other words, let's see just what the big freaking deal was.

Thankfully, Shuki doesn't mince words and gets right to the issue:

I am sick and tired of giving the same elementary notes on a daily basis to our so-called "editors." The next "editor" who leaves one shot on the screen for 19 seconds during dialogue will be fired. This is disturbing considering the episode is 3:41 too long and obviously needs to be sped up, not slowed down. You will re-edit the entire thing. And do not ever give me cuts that are 3:41 over, especially ones full of stupid mistakes.

Okay, first off, OUCH. Second, Paul told me he responded and explained to Shuki that, as with the 95 previous episodes that Shuki had been sent, the first cut was often times long because it included ALL of the available material that could be used in the episode. This included the Japanese preexisting footage and what we shot up in Valencia. This way Shuki would know what footage we had and could use it, or not, depending on how he wanted the episode cut. Also, in this case, there was a shot by our director that was a single long take with no close-ups to cut into and had to be included to tell the story. It wasn't that Paul was delivering a 26-minute episode and expecting that to be okay.

Apparently, there was a lot of back and forth after that first memo. Unfortunately, none of those subsequent howlers were sent to me by mistake. But if I know Paul, he gave as good as he got with Shuki, and I'm pretty sure Shuki respected him for that. Maybe if I'd been a little more like my friend, things would have turned out differently for me at Saban.

Eh, probably not.

So, here's where this lands us and why it is pertinent to our story. We are talking about the same mellow supportive dude, half teddy bear, half tortured artist who was always a perfect gentleman, never openly critical in any sort of mean or threatening way. Now, suddenly, we have him firing off a very "Haimesque" memo that surprised the shit out of me but seemed to be a regular part of his workflow when letting out his frustration at something that wasn't up to snuff. I guess thinking about it, at least if you were on the receiving end, you could digest it in private and weren't subject to the humiliation of a Haim tirade or a visit from Ronnie Hadar with his German Shepherd and his Glock. In truth, this memo was the quintessential Shuki version of a Haim tongue lashing. And the people who had gotten them seemed much less torn up than, say, me when I got the speech about taking the food out of the mouths of the Saban children because BZ had hired shitty untrained chimpanzees to replace two gifted actors. More on that later.

I'm not sure why I even cared back then. I have no idea why learning about the memos fascinated me so much. Probably, it had to do with the image I had of Shuki as this almost Yoda-like figure and the idea that I had finally spotted that rarest of creatures in the wild, the man with no temper. I was now fascinated that there was this whole other side to him, a side to which I had never been exposed. If I'm honest, I really wanted to dissect this whole process, just in case it was something I had to deal with down the road, of course. After reading a few more of these memos and speaking with a few more employees who had received them, Shuki Levy, my friend, mentor, and boss made a lot more sense to me, and my opinion of him shifted. And it wasn't a negative shift. It was one of relief in a weird sort of way. Relief that he had an outlet with which to expel the frustration that he must have felt having to oversee so much crap at the same time. And for that matter, why WAS he overseeing so much crap at the same time? How did he end up being put in that position? That's an excellent question. I won't get all long and boring with it, but read on for the abridged version.

CHAPTER 54
HOW IT ALL CAME TO BE— THE READER'S DIGEST VERSION

In 1980, Saban Productions, Inc. was formed primarily as a music production company. Shuki was the composer, the guy in the recording studio creating the music cues for animated as well as live-action shows, while Haim was out there selling their tunes and at the same time laying the groundwork for what would one day become the Saban Empire.

In a genius move, Haim offered DIC Entertainment (run by his longtime friend and successful animation producer, Andy Heyward) the full library of Saban original music for use in all the DIC animated shows…for free. Yes. You heard that correctly—zero charge for all DIC shows being produced. The "only" thing that Haim and Shuki kept was the publishing rights. In other words, they retained ownership of the contents of that music and were entitled to receive royalties for every time the music was played in the future. Today we know that the publishing is where the real money lies, and companies do everything in their power to hang onto it as they too have discovered that it is a VERY lucrative industry. The agreement Haim reached was the musical version of the *Star Wars* deal at Fox, where George Lucas was given the merchandising rights and would receive the lion's share of all future income produced by the sales of T-shirts, toys, books, etc. Think for a moment about all the *Star Wars* lunchboxes, action figures, and light sabers you saw back in the day, and you can maybe get an idea as to what Mr. Lucas pulled off. And it was all to settle a budget dispute in which Fox refused to pay for additional production on the movies. That turned out pretty well for Mr. Lucas, and it did for Mr. Saban.

Having written the lyrics for the *Dino Thunder* theme song, I can tell you that it takes nine months for royalties to begin arriving from ASCAP or BMI, the two companies that keep track of music use all over the world and distribute the monies they generate. I can only imagine that when the checks started to arrive, things changed for their little company very quickly. They suddenly had a source of income that would continue as long as they generated music for all of those series.

Cut to 10 years later, and Saban had become a full-scale content creator with movies and TV series under their belt. They were starting down the road that would eventually lead to *Mighty Morphin Power Rangers, VR Troopers, BeetleBorgs, Masked Rider,* and other Japanese sourced shows. In another genius move, Haim licensed each full season of the dozens of Japanese series available that he felt would translate to America, 52 episodes per show from TOEI, the large Japanese production company who created and made the series in Japan. Then, he created a business model to produce a kid show, combining 11 minutes of Japanese footage which held an amortized cost of just $20,000 per episode, with footage shot in the U.S. for around $200K to create a full-length half hour show at the cost of half of anything else that was on the air back then. AND there was a huge toy component to *Power Rangers* that was serviced by a long-standing deal with the Bandai company, which was already making toys for the Japanese show.

So, when I first met Shuki for the *Susie Q* movie, he was the most mellow individual I had ever come across, at least in the

MORPHERS, MONSTERS & MAYHEM 319

industry. He was just making his music, writing his movies, helping Haim out with his dopey little kids show. Life was good. Somehow, along the way, Shuki must have added something spectacular in the development of *Power Rangers*, because after the two movies I wrote with him and Shell, *Susie Q* and *Someone to Die For*, everything else faded into the background and it was all *Power Rangers*, all the time. Any Shuki call I got from the Jason Frank coaching call on, was *Rangers*-related. There were no other projects (except the other TOEI offerings) that were even mentioned to me. I never worked on another outside project that wasn't *Rangers*-related in all the years I worked at Saban, in fact. "How did this happen?" you ask.

As I wasn't there for the decision that officially made Shuki the *Power Rangers* whisperer, I can only speculate. But if I had to guess. I would say that it went something like this: At some point towards the beginning of the project, Haim decided that the show was a disaster and no one he had currently working on it could fix it. What he needed was a fresh set of eyes. He needed a creative genius. Naturally, Haim looked to Shuki for help in coming up with some fixes. Shuki comes in (probably after brainstorming with Shell) with his usual plethora of ideas that range from pretty decent to awesome. The other producers who have been trying to crack the thing are pissed off that Haim didn't give them a real shot, but they aren't going to say anything and risk losing their jobs. Haim feels a huge sense of relief that the show is back on track. His old friend and partner has bailed them out of a jam. The next day, Haim declares that Shuki is the new king of *Power Rangers*, all while Shuki was still creating hours and hours of original music every week. Not only that, but he was also now directing movies and TV shows for Saban. And he seemed happy as can be.

I think what Shuki loved was the variety of the work he was doing. There was no one job that he was stuck performing. His workday encompassed so many projects that he never was able to get bored. What would become a problem, however, was that *Power*

Rangers and the other Japanese footage shows had become the most important thing to the company by a long shot. And, for some reason, Shuki had demonstrated, by helping to get *Power Rangers* on track, that he had a knack for these shows. Like it or not, Shuki was the one person Haim really trusted and turned to when it came to the creative decisions on the series. Haim at some point had literally appointed Shuki to the position of "head creative genius in charge of everything *Power Rangers*." I'm thinking it must have happened when I first arrived at Saban and was working on *Susie Q* and the other movies. Because the shift was pretty noticeable. One day Shuki was all about those endeavors, and the next day he was standing at Whiteman Field in Van Nuys directing the *Power Rangers* episode "Foul Play in the Sky," from the script that I had helped him with one Saturday afternoon.

> SIDE NOTE: I recall very clearly a time before I went to work at Saban, Deborah espousing Skuki's directing genius when it came to the movies he was doing at the company (many of which were starring Deborah). When I asked her about *Power Rangers*, she commented that it was a dumb kids show they were doing that was doomed to fail. Shuki was just helping Haim try to save it, then Shuki could go back to doing his movies. I wasn't sure this is how Shuki would have described it, but that's how it was presented to me by Deb.
>
> At our first meeting for the *Susie Q* movie script I was helping with, Shuki actually seemed to confirm Deborah's take on the whole situation. The feeling I got was that he had no clue what *Power Rangers* was going to become (who did?) and he would never have believed that his destiny was to be the creative heartbeat of this weird little show for the next seven years of his life. I wonder what he would have done had he known? By the time I started working there regularly, Shuki had so many things on his plate that he would have needed a full setting of Royal Copenhagen Porcelain "plates" to hold all the projects

MORPHERS, MONSTERS & MAYHEM 321

(what a crappy metaphor! sorry, I tried, but it just wouldn't come together).

It was impressive. Especially since he never seemed to get bent out of shape or flustered. He saved that for the Howler Memos he churned out every couple of weeks to his underlings who had screwed something up that bared pointing out.

So, all of this was to point out that Shuki, at the time that all this was going on, was dealing with more crap than any one person should have to deal with, especially when that person doesn't seem to enjoy dealing with that much crap. Some people can't get enough of the day-to-day hurricane of activity that comes with being an executive at a huge company that has its hands in a zillion different projects.

Haim is that guy. He thrives on this giant game of full contact chess he plays 24/7, tearing apart his competitors, friend and foe alike, and anyone else who would dare get in his way. That's his thing, and I kind of loved having a front row seat for it back then. I was just glad I was behind the front lines and could see the back of Haim's head and wasn't on the other side of the battle, not yet at least.

Shuki was NOT that guy. And I only say this based on my observations of him over the years and having worked with him closely on several projects and having been near his family through Deb and Tamara. I can only assume that this time must have been at least a little bit soul sucking for him. He loved things quiet and mellow. His house was always dimly lit, at least when I was there. Things were peaceful, unless he was composing or watching a movie or there was a party. But all in all, I don't think he really wanted to be that closely involved in the daily hurly burly of a growing company that was dealing with a hit TV series and the slate of other similar shows that were all in development. Shuki was creative, meaning he wanted to create. His head must have been full of ideas for all kinds of movies, shows, the works. So, while I don't think the memos were that cool, I understood that this was his only way to vent. And I think he basically had to do it or live a much less peaceful life. That's my take at least. If anyone out there feels differently, make sure you include that in your book, which I look forward to reading as I've stated in the past.

CHAPTER 55
MY WONDERFUL WACKY WEEK WITH SHELL

Okay, let's get back on track. To recap: I told Shuki his movie was kind of a disaster. He told me to go fix it with Shell. I had no choice but to make the two-hour drive and pray my boss would forgive me once the rewrite came in and he could see how much better it was (I hoped). And, so, off I went, leaving Hollywood at 6 a.m., hoping traffic would be merciful and allow me to arrive at Shell's Orange County home on time.

After a couple of hours on the 405 Freeway, I arrived at Shell's house, the same nice, upscale home where Haim called to congratulate me on the terrific job I was doing. At this time I had never actually worked one-on-one with Shell and had no clue what to expect. She had always been so sweet and so kind. But I wondered how strongly she was going to fight to keep this 136-page epic intact. I needed to be careful, of course. I had no clue which ideas were hers and which were Shuki's. So, I had to treat everything equally and pray she didn't get too insulted and call Shuki complaining that this opinionated jerk (me) was ruining their masterpiece. I don't think that ever happened. But who knows?

If I gave you a thousand guesses, you could never imagine what greeted me when Shell Danielson opened the door to her house on that first morning we met to work on the movie script. I actually took a step back when she appeared, as it took me a moment to focus on what I was looking at. Shell was wearing a long flowing peasant dress, which was standard issue for her. I think she had a comfortable pair of sandals on and was ready for the day. Again, all pretty normal. What was completely unexpected was the fact that she had accessorized her ensemble with a living and breathing (and trembling) miniature greyhound dog in what can only be described as a baby sling that she had strapped to her chest and secured with Velcro. The dog looked like it wanted to be anywhere but where it was but made no attempt to extricate itself. Shell greeted me with a hug, pressing the greyhounds face to my chest, a position with which both the dog and I were less than comfortable.

Shell was not only a writer but a successful actress and had been on *General Hospital* for a while as one of the lead characters. So, in my mind, I figured this whole thing was just an actress adding a little dramatic flair to her "entrance" and was certain the dog would be napping comfortably on its favorite pillow soon enough. So, in I went.

As we sipped the tea, she offered me upon entering, it became clear that the dog was not going anywhere. The trembling had dissipated slowly as it adjusted to having a visitor. In fact, this seemed to be the reason it was so agitated in the first place. From there, the dog appeared to be just fine swaddled in the device. At least I assume that was the case, as Shell was a true lover of all things breathing and would never allow another creature to experience a moment of discomfort while in her care.

Shell and I chatted away, talking a little about life, love, investment strategies, anything we could think of to avoid starting in on the script. After we had exhausted the subjects on the table, we both had to admit that we could delay no longer. It was best that we get down to work. I figured at least the dog would be un-swaddled, and we could go about our business.

Shell sat down at her desk, which was not so much a desk but a wall unit with a place for a computer. She immediately opened the script and was ready to go. Shell was going to be the one typing apparently, which is NOT the way I prefer to write. I have always been a massive control freak when it comes to work, so this would be rough. But I just had to accept that this was her deal, and it was best if I said nothing. I DID wonder how effective she was going to be, seeing as she still hadn't released the dog from her clutches. Her typing slowly became a chore. As the dog grew more and more restless, I grew more and more uncomfortable, and Shell grew more and more distracted.

Finally, thank the good lord above, she stood up, took the dog out of the carrier, and let it scurry away. She made no comment about any of this and merely proceeded to get back into the script. If this was all a "bit," and she was doing it for effect, it was freaking genius. No acknowledgement whatsoever of the dog. None. It was a living accessory she had picked out for the day and was now setting back in its proper place until her next visitors arrived. Thankfully all this meant that we could begin for real this time. And so, as they say…FADE UP, bitches!

Page one. Shell asked if there was anything that needed to change on page one. If not, she suggested that we move on to page two. "What about page two? Nothing? Page 3? That seems good to me."

"Hang on," I said, then asked if it was her intention to continue like this until we had gone through the entire script. I was confused. Shell had the notes from me and Ann in front of her, large sweeping changes. But she seemed to think we were just going to go through page by page and tweak the thing until we had gotten through all 136. I asked if we could try something different. The first thing that had to happen was that we needed to make cuts. We needed to "Sophie's Choice" the crap out of that script. We needed to get rid of anything that was not 100% necessary, regardless of how much she and Shuki were in love with it. In screenwriting, the rule of thumb is that if something, whether it be a scene or a line, doesn't advance the story or the characters, then it doesn't belong. Cut it out. Sadly, they should have cut a lot before showing anyone this script. Turning in a 136-page screenplay for a *Power Rangers* movie sequel after the first one was 90 pages and didn't exactly rewrite box office history could be considered borderline insane. But there it was, right in front of us. The script was the family film equivalent of the guy on *My 600-lb Life*, a large, nearly impossible challenge that would most likely never reach the page length we all knew it had to reach to stay alive. All I could do was start slashing pages and hope we made a difference.

Although we started off slowly, neither of us wanting to push too hard for our own ideas, but both of us feeling like we knew how to fix the thing, we did fall into a rhythm after a while. Shell and I started to click. We riffed on some of my ideas and some of her ideas and eventually got to the place where we were plowing through the thing, cutting 10 pages here, five pages there. It was a gigantic relief. We actually had a really good time, and when we were done, we had a script that was at least producible, if not the most coherent story ever. This, I felt, was the very best that I could have hoped for. The idea was the idea, the story the story. This was about as good as it was going to get with the mandates that had to remain in place. The last night of our work together, I remember guiding my car onto the 405 Freeway in Orange County, headed for home. I took a long deep breath, probably lit up a Marlboro Light with the lighter Jason Frank had given me, and said out loud to myself, "Thank God."

As far as what we were able to cut from the script, there were certain nonstarters that were never going anywhere right from the beginning. These were characters and scenes that Shuki and Shell really loved. They loved the pirate ship set piece with the fight on the deck. It seemed kind of like it was in the wrong movie, but it was their movie, and they wanted that in there. They also LOVED, LOVED, LOVED Divatox for some reason. On those days we were working on it, whenever a Divatox line would come up in the script, Shell would break into hysterics. She just thought the character was so damn funny with her "witty" dialogue and crazy/whacky antics. And look, maybe she was…on the page…in the script. But it was clear it was going to require an actress with superhuman ability to pull it off on screen. One thing I knew with 100% certainty was that if I suggested changing Divatox for something more interesting, and if by some miracle Shell had gone along with it, Shuki was going to put her right back in the movie. That being said, we did try to polish up the dialogue as best we could, although it was hard to rework lines that were making Shell laugh heartily every time she heard them. We also tried to make Divatox believable as a being who could destroy the Rangers with a mere flick of her wrist.

Unfortunately, once she was cast, the only way to make the character less annoying would have been to make her a mute. The character's voice, as played by the actress, was a thousand nails on a million chalkboards. And this was NOT her actual voice. It was an acting direction she had either adopted or been given. Again, what the hell did I know? Maybe she was a brilliant undiscovered talent and I just couldn't see past the voice. It's happened to me in the past. Wait. Hang on. No, it hasn't. I can't even pretend that's true. I'm pretty good at predicting the outcome of a casting choice. I seriously couldn't remember a time when I was as clearly wrong as I would have had to be for Divatox to be anything but what she presented as.

To be clear, I have no animosity for the actress who played Divatox in the movie and later in the series. I don't even remember ever meeting her or speaking with her. I WAS able to observe her on set several times and got the feeling that she could be a bit of a "diva" at times, but that was her character, and she wouldn't have been the first thespian to stay in character all day. But she didn't do much to make life easier on the crew or the cast with whom she was working. I had been an actor for years and had worked with high-maintenance thespians. You can spot them a mile away. It always comes from insecurity. Whatever their "deal" is, it usually stems from nothing movie related, but a long-standing personal issue. So, all I have to go on with this actress was what I observed on set. You should definitely take it with a grain of sea salt.

As I arrived home from Shell's that night, I thought maybe we had dodged a bullet and there would be some forgiveness based on the hard work both at Shell's house and on the 405 Freeway getting to and from her crib. However, that was not to be. In fact, I never received any sort of "thanks" or "well done" on that script. I can't remember if it was ever brought up again. Even beyond that, I could sense a shift. Shuki was never the same around me. At the time, I chalked it up to hurt feelings and figured he would get past it, and we would laugh about the whole thing one day. Little did I know the seeds of discourse had been sown for a forest of doom from which Ann and I would not escape, at least not while we were still at Saban.

What we didn't know, and what would have explained a lot, was that there was some dark shit going on after hours, in the dimly lit corridors of the main Saban office that DID NOT say Social Security on the outside. Things were starting to get weird, and maybe because things were always weird on the show, I didn't pay much attention to it. But I was now aware that Shuki was not all rainbows and flavored tobacco in a darkly lit hookah room. As we now know, I had recently discovered that within his kind exterior lurked, not a God, or the perfect boss, but just a kind, yet flawed human being, who was capable of the same harshness that his partner of fifteen years (at the time) was capable of and who wouldn't think twice about dictating a memo to Nancy that could, in one reading, leave me speechless as well as jobless. If only that's how it had gone down. At least I could have framed the memo.

CHAPTER 56
LITTLE BZ BIDS FAREWELL... SORT OF

One day, a bit after the movie script fiasco had settled down, Little BZ knocked on my door asking to speak with me. Suspiciously, I ushered him into my office and asked what I could do for him. He told me that he merely wanted to let me know that he was going to be leaving the show. This, of course, led to a moment where I was kind of euphoric. One "cheek" of the giant ASS that was the BZ machine was going to be gone. BZ's support system would be weakened considerably. Elation! Then sadness, as Little BZ informed me that he was leaving to take care of an ongoing health issue that, unfortunately, had a grim prognosis, at least at the time.

In that moment, standing there in my office, I became very emotional. You can be pissed off at someone for all of the stupid day-to-day drama, but when that person is given what equates to a death sentence in their prime, it hits hard, as it did for me that day. All I could think to do was give the guy a genuine hug and tell him if he ever needed anything just to call. He could write a script whenever he wanted. The door was open.

As Little BZ left, I felt sick to my stomach, both because of what he had just revealed and also for what I had just promised him. A script any time he wanted? What a dopey, sappy move that was. Seriously though, no one should have to go through what he explained he was perhaps going to be dealing with. It took me a couple of days to even be able to focus again. I would later find out that perhaps there was more to this tidbit of carefully placed information than met the eye. But, for the moment, it was as it appeared to be, and it was truly playing tricks on my brain.

CHAPTER 57
TURBO—IT IS ALIVE!

The actual making of the *Turbo* movie was not something that I was heavily involved with once the writing was done. Ann and I were busy trying to come up with ideas for the new TV season, which would be based on the movie of course. I remember thinking at the time that this was going to be a serious challenge. "Challenge, you say? What possible reason could there be for that?" Well, let's see. Off the top of my head, I can think of a couple of big reasons:

Number 1: See if you can guess what the number one reason was… Never mind. Let's not make a game out of it. Any writer or director worth a crap will tell you that the success of a movie, whether it be a thriller, cop drama, fantasy, or spy movie is wholly dependent on the villain. The bad guy must be formidable, otherwise there is no serious obstacle for the hero, and his journey will be one the audience cares little about. I repeat. You MUST HAVE A GREAT BAD GUY. The villain can be funny and steal the show, but they must be clever in the way they do it, and you must believe they can bring about the demise of the hero in an instant. Let's look at some great film villains who are perfect examples:

The Joker played by Jack Nicholson in the original *Batman*,

Miranda Priestly played by Meryl Streep in *The Devil Wears Prada*, The Joker played by Heath Ledger in a later iteration of the Batman franchise, Hans Landa played by Christoph Walz in Tarantino's *Inglorious Basterds*, Bellatrix Lestrange played by Helena Bonham Carter in the Harry Potter series, Loki played by Tom Hiddleston in the Marvel Avengers Thor series, Regina George played by Rachel McAdams in *Mean Girls*, Hans Gruber played by Alan Rickman in *Die Hard*.

All these bad guys and gals were smartly written, well-conceived and in most cases, funny as hell. The fact that there was humor in these characters pushed the movies to heights they would not have reached otherwise. Meryl Streep was cool, calm, and never raised her voice in *The Devil Wears Prada*. Her mere reputation and presence in the room was enough to elicit fear in everyone she met over the course of that movie. Just the prospect of what she could do to another character was frightening enough.

Christoph Walz was in the first scene of *Inglorious Basterds* and basically took over that movie. For 18 minutes, he sat across from another brilliant actor playing a dairy farmer and the two just talked. Walz actually smiled through most of the conversation until the very end. He didn't need to do anything more than just have a dialogue. The stakes were clearly so high that he was able to play with the words, enjoy what he was doing, and every moment was brilliant, from the milk he drank to opening his pen set and filling the pen. It was subtle genius and, in my opinion, one of the greatest villains in modern film history.

It's ridiculous to sit here and compare Hans Landa to Divatox, of course. But even in a kids' movie, the villain doesn't have to be a one-note screaming buffoon. The Divatox character was intended to be a layered, comical villain who would add legit humor to a movie that desperately needed it, but at the same time be scary and feel threatening until Maligore came along. We had tried with every ounce of writing ability we possessed at the time to make her that way. She had a real love story with heartbreak that was causing her to spin out of control and try to take it out on anyone within her line of sight.

In the end, Divatox ended up being a two-note buffoon in a low-cut leather outfit and a push-up undergarment who was either screaming at her underlings in that painfully screechy pitch or cooing weirdly at her beloved rubber eel. There was nothing in between. Even her intro was a bumbling mess. In it, Divatox enters the bridge of the submarine and immediately bangs her head on the ceiling with a loud Three Stooges clank sound effect added. She then punches her main henchmen like a five-year-old lashing out in a tantrum and proceeds to reach into a repurposed painted coffee can to remove a ridiculous rubber eel that she gushes over and calls "Eelie." Any of those things on their own would weaken a character's perceived strength and ability to destroy the Power Rangers. But together, they set her up for a long hard road that never really went anywhere.

When those of us working on the TV show saw the footage from the first day of the submarine work, we were just, well, bummed. Not because of what it would do to the movie so much as the fact that she was going to be the villain who would continue in the *Turbo* series. We would now have to write for her, and we had no clue what we were going to do. I know what I had to do right away, and that was to enforce a moratorium on submarine dailies being shown in my office. This came after one particularly awful scene where Divatox gives a raspberry to one of her henchmen to put a "comic button" on the scene. What well-constructed villain even thinks to stick their tongue out and blow a raspberry at a big latex diving bell cohort? Again, nothing against the actress. I assume this was what she was directed to do, as for some strange reason, Shell and Shuki found it to be hysterically funny.

Number 2: Justin as the Blue Ranger. If any of you ever had the pleasure of watching *The Brady Bunch*, you will remember that at the end of the series run, they brought in a character called Cousin Oliver, played by an actor named Robbie Rist. He was hired to inject some young blood into the cast who were now starting to show their age and were not quite as cute as they once were. A similar thing happened on *Power Rangers Turbo*. I'm not sure what the reasoning was for Justin to be a kid, except maybe that Shuki met the actor Blake Foster and was so blown away by his martial arts ability at such a young age, he came up with the idea on the spot. And to be fair, Blake was a talented little guy with amazing martial arts skills. I never had an issue with the casting choice. It was the whole idea I thought was kind of a bust.

It has been proven time and time again that kids are "aspirational viewers." For the most part, they don't want to see boys and girls their own age as the superheroes. They want to see the next age group up, at the very least, like their older brothers and sisters. This has been borne out in focus group after focus group for years. And it was well known back in the day. But of course, it was never brought up because this was one of those decisions that was made above our heads and we were just told, "Here's how it's going to go." And "Isn't this kid amazing?"

One of the battles I lost in the writing process on the movie script remains to me one of the most egregious errors in the story. And it took a year before anyone really mentioned it. And what was this truly offensive and mind-blowing (at least to me) mistake that remained in the script and ended up in the film? It was the scene where Justin discovers the identity of the Power Rangers by hiding under a hospital bed for five minutes and overhearing a communicator conversation with Zordon. Tantamount to Batman/Bruce Wayne, Superman/Clark Kent, Bruce Banner/The Hulk, there had been a lot of effort put into keeping these guys' identities a secret. It was a secret that had been well kept for years in Angel Grove. Hell, Bulk and Skull, as misguided as they were, spent 50-plus episodes trying to figure it out, and they never even came close. Then, a little kid shows up, mistakenly gets trapped in Rocky's hospital room, and overhears the Rangers talking Ranger stuff while hiding under the bed? Once the Rangers (minus Rocky) teleport out, Justin pops out, then Rocky just folds without even trying to come up with a good story to explain what Justin thinks he heard and saw. During the writing process, I remember suggesting that we could have turned it into a great opportunity for comedy, like Rocky coming up with wild excuses and Justin not buying any of them. To this day, it bums me out that we just let the cat out of the bag so casually.

All in all, I remain torn on this whole Justin as a Ranger thing because Blake was a GREAT kid and from what I've heard has become a great adult, an ambassador for the show, and a fan favorite. He was awesome to have around the set, and everyone really liked him. But was the character right for the franchise? Did we really want a child wearing spandex which, on him looked a little ridiculous and baggy in the back?

Number 3: Lerigot. Okay, help me out here. Knowing what the character was required to do in the movie, how did everyone look at the concept art for Lerigot and think it was going to work? For anyone out there who might have missed it, Lerigot was a four-foot-tall, hairy wizard creature with enormous eyes and the body of a Pacman with none of the speed or agility of the character in the game. The physics alone would make for an unexciting one-sided chase to start the movie. When working on it with Shell, I could have never imagined that this was what we were unleashing on the unsuspecting *Power Rangers* fans who would end up seeing the movie. Every time those costumed padded feet came on screen, it immediately flashed an image in my mind of the Cowardly Lion costume in the *Wizard of Oz*. And the way the whole thing maneuvered, you just knew it was a little guy in a suit who was having considerable trouble mastering the operation of the costume. The idea of opening the movie with him being hunted down by dudes on horses with bows and arrows was absurd. There were so many other things we could have done to make that scene stronger.

The beginning of any film is supposed to WOW you, suck you into the movie, leave you wanting more. This opening chase scene was the antithesis of that. And it was never going to be any different with the way they had set it up. There was never going to be a good way for a chase to be staged when the character being pursued could only waddle around until he eventually lost his balance and fell over. And the first part of the scene is barely a minute. Let's face it, Lerigot was clumsy and odd looking and no match for the dudes after him. It looked ridiculous and anything that followed on screen was going to be severely tainted by it.

But let's assume for a moment that we were stuck with the costume and we had to do the chase. Was there ANY way to make it look at least a little cooler, a little scarier? Of course there was. And many of you are probably thinking the same thing I was back then. There WAS a way to fix the whole cheesy mess, and it was as simple as five letters on the page: N-I-G-H-T. Shooting puppets or any kind of weird looking fake furry creature or latex monster that's not supposed elicit memories of H.R. Pufnstuf but needs to have an element of danger and foreboding should be shot at night, or in a dark interior at the very least. I was always kind of surprised that BZ didn't catch this while they were scheduling the shoot days. Or, if he did catch it (which I suspect he did), why he didn't suggest switching it to night? Shuki probably wouldn't have even cared. Especially after seeing what Lerigot was going to look like in daytime footage, and that it was going to bring zero jeopardy and deliver the emotional impact of an AFLAC commercial without a duck.

To be fair, there are any number of reasons for why that scene was shot during the day. The location could have been booked, the neighborhood could have had a rule against night filming, perhaps the permits were too hard to get, etc. Or maybe Shuki, or the director, David Winning, really wanted it shot during the day in order to show off the beautiful location, which would NOT have been an issue if you ask me. Either way, Spielberg (BZ) whiffed on that one. Epic fail. And what really sucks is that the sequence could have looked super cool at night, with long shadows and a big full moon courtesy of the lighting department. Even beyond that, they could have had guys with flaming torches, running through sweeping shadows made by search lights. Anything that hid the fact that

Lerigot was a knee-high, hairy Pacman character with a glowing Ring Pop on a necklace.

> IMPORTANT SIDE NOTE: As I'm spewing out all this opinionated bull crap that really is just that, my opinion, I think about the legions of you who believe that *Turbo: A Power Rangers Movie* is a fantastic film. When I read through comments on YouTube about the movie, I am continually surprised to find that many people have very fond memories of it and even feel like it is a much better representation of *Power Rangers* than the first movie. Many of you out there feel that the story was imaginative and exciting. Lots of you think Divatox was a fab villain and just as many believe that Justin was a great way to freshen the cast and the franchise. As I've said before, we all have an opinion and we all see things very differently. So, please, please, don't take offense to my commentary. I don't mean to insult anyone or sound like some guy in a basement somewhere who read one screenwriting book and feels qualified to discuss anything and everything related to film. The truth is, I'm just calling it like I saw it and still see it today. I did go back and watch *Turbo: A Power Rangers Movie* several times to see if perhaps I was just being too hard on it back in the day. As it turns out, for me, for what I know about making movies, I feel secure in my assessment (at least that's what I'm going with right now).

I think it's important for all of you to understand that a part of me feels as though I have no right to say anything negative about the movie. I was there for the rewrite, and that made me a direct participant in these issues. I suppose I could have been more vocal about some of the super cringy stuff that ended up staying in the final film. Many of those things read okay on the page but materialized on set in a way that no one could have imagined. The truth is, for better or for worse, no ONE person has the power to completely change the course of a movie when the shooting has begun, unless, as I said, it's a James Cameron or someone of that ilk, who has the latitude to spend millions of dollars to fix things they believe MUST be fixed at any stage in the process regardless of cost.

One final thing about the movie I feel like I really need to say: there IS a part of me that despises it, but for very personal reasons as it signaled the start of the break in my relationship with Shuki and my eventual exit from Saban. Thinking back, I don't know what I would have done differently. The truth about the script was going to come out at some point. We needed to get on top of it, and with Ann feeling the same way I did, I figured it wouldn't be a big deal. But things were never the same again with me and Shuki.

At the end of the day, nothing Ann or I said or did back then was going to change the movie once the script was locked. Shuki was especially uninterested in what I had to say, I guess since I had been so hard on his first draft. As we re-examine the film ad nauseam, the same things keep coming up as the big issues that should have been taken care of right off the bat, and funny enough, those were issues in the script that could have easily been changed with a couple of days of writing. But they were never going to be re-worked unless Shell had vehemently agreed with me that they were a problem, which I don't think she did. At times Shell and I worked together like champs, and she was very receptive to my ideas. Other times, it was as if her Italian Greyhound was whispering more worthy contributions in her ear when I wasn't looking. Whatever Ann and I could have done at the time, we will never know. But, as a member of the *Power Rangers* team, I knew we could have done better and it kind of sucks that we didn't.

CHAPTER 58
WHERE OH WHERE HAS OUR BZ GONE?

I was trying to remember if there were any funny or ridiculous BZ stories that I could tell just to illustrate that regardless of the size of the project, he was always true to his arrogant, know-it-all self, regardless of the risk. This one came to mind:

It seems that during the production of *Turbo: A Power Rangers Movie*, BZ had been spending a lot of time hanging out with a very sketchy oddball named Yakov who BZ had brought in. They seemed attached at the hip for a great portion of the film. Yakov's actual job was to direct the underwater sequences in the movie, and then I guess help BZ with anything he needed, which made a certain amount of sense since Yakov seemed to list every film credit imaginable on his resume short of helicopter stunt pilot. It was explained to me that Yakov was some kind of savant who had the inexplicable ability to slot into just about every job on a show and was known for saving the day on many occasions. I didn't see it, if I'm being honest. To all of us, Yakov was one of the Steve Martin and Dan Aykroyd "crazy guys" brothers from SNL come to life, with the accent, sense of humor, the whole thing. Those of you too young to remember, check Peacock. They stream everything that's ever been on SNL, and a lot of it is hilarious.

Yakov quickly became known to the crew, and just about anyone else involved with the movie, as Jackoff. I think the only person besides BZ who was happy that Jackoff had arrived was Jason David Frank. By this time Jason, had become an expert at creating comedic, over-the-top impersonations of the cast and crew. And his "Yakov" was truly his crowning achievement. It was genius. He had the voice, the walk, and the material that made it must see viewing in and around the set. Man, was that entertainment.

And speaking of entertainment, we learned one day that BZ and his sidekick Yakov had been working on a secret side project for months that was literally going to save the movie and turn them into heroes overnight. I was intrigued. Not because I actually thought anything these two came up with would have any effect at all on the film, but because if BZ did try something and it failed, it could possibly redirect some of Shuki's dark energy back to BZ and away from me and Ann, which would have been nice at that point in our Saban journey.

When the whole thing started to unfold, the first thing we learned was that BZ was indeed trying to conjure up a cinematic miracle that would save the movie. The plan involved coming up with a group of visual effects shots that were so technologically advanced and so brilliant to behold that dropping them into the film would distract the audience to such a degree that they would ignore the movie's shortcomings. (A little over dramatic, I know, but not too far off what he was probably thinking.) As it turns out, those weren't the shortcomings that these two should have been worried about. What they should have concerned themselves with was their complete lack of understanding of the final postproduction process and what adding or subtracting material to a finished film can do to the film as a whole. In addition to their lack of basic knowledge when it came to this kind of thing, they decided that they would execute these changes on their own so that everyone would be surprised and hail the conquering heroes.

There was an early "test screening" of the movie scheduled

where a cross section of kids, parents, grandparents, etc., were invited to watch the movie and fill out comment cards with their thoughts. This was happening in a theater south of L.A. and would be the first time the movie would be shown to the public. A print of the movie would be played on the giant projectors at the theater so everyone could enjoy it in the environment for which it was intended. Shuki and Haim must have been super excited to hear what people thought. This was certainly not an ideal time for things to go wrong. Somehow BZ and Yakov decided it would be the perfect time to reveal their brilliant contribution to the film.

> SIDE NOTE: Before we continue, I think it's important to explain how the handling of audio in moviemaking was changing at that time. Thanks to the use of computers and a software program called Pro Tools, there is no limit to the number of audio tracks that can be used in a modern-day movie to create an audio experience that complements the visuals. All of those files live in a computer on a massive hard disk or disks, and every sound in the film is assigned its own track. There are dialogue tracks that contain the spoken words of the actors. There are music tracks that make up the score, usually broken down into every instrument (these are called stems), so that if a tuba is too loud, for example, it can be brought down in the mix. There were sound effects tracks, Foley tracks (the guy who does the shoe clomping in time with the actor on the screen to enhance his steps in the film), and even a track that holds the tone of the room where the scene was shot to layer with all of the other sounds as background silence. All of these tracks, in the end, line up to the picture and when the film is played do exactly what they are supposed do when they are supposed to do it. If a picture or visual shot is added that is too long or too short once the film's sound has been mixed, it can put the entire film out of sync, and it will be that way until the last frame of the movie unless someone corrects it.

So BZ and Yakov had made the bilateral decision that their last-minute visual effects shots sprinkled throughout the movie would dazzle (distract) the audience with enough cinematic sleight of hand so they would hopefully not pay attention to "Eelie" the rubber sea snake who lived in a coffee can or Lerigot, the overweight wizard/Muppet who kept tipping over. Their thinking, I imagine, was that it was too late to save the story or the performances or anything else for that matter, so "Let's give them a sparkly light show and hopefully they won't notice the rest of the movie." That must have been the logic, as I can see no other reason to start chopping into the movie the night before the screening. In Shuki's mind, the film was locked, done, no turning back. All that was left was for the computer to spit out the massive file that the postproduction team would run to the lab so they could create a print in time for the screening.

Since there are always issues (at least there were back then) with the technology still being somewhat new, my buddy in postproduction had allotted extra time for the simple process of taking the finished film from the computer, making the print, and returning it to Saban headquarters. The whole thing should have been easy. Unfortunately, BZ and Jackoff somehow managed to get hold of the finished print and insert their new shots—the shots that would make them the heroes of the day. I can see the two of them patting one another on the back, laughing at how pleased Shuki would be with them for the magical moments that would now be a part of his movie. Unfortunately, those magical moments died at the hands of two up and coming filmmakers who forgot a few of the most basic rules of their chosen profession.

My friend the postproduction god had spent until 3 a.m. the previous morning making sure that the final copy of *Turbo: A Power Rangers Movie* was exactly as Shuki wanted it. And why wouldn't it be? Shuki had been there all through the post process. The movie was locked and ready to view. All they needed to do was make a print. So, that night, while they all thought that print was being made, my buddy and his editors went home to get a well-deserved rest and forget about *Turbo* for at least a few moments, maybe enjoy a nice meal, return a few emails, get a good night sleep. Then saunter back to the office first thing in the morning to check the print one final time and

"What the—"

My friend was livid, as you can imagine. All the hours he had spent getting things just right, or at least right in Shuki's mind, had been destroyed by the desire of these two boneheads to be seen as creative geniuses and, ultimately, heroes. Unfortunately, they had not only NOT done anything remotely heroic, but they had, well, I'll just come out and say it, "screwed the pooch." (In honor of Scott Page-Pagter, who loved that phrase for some reason. Perhaps it was because he didn't have a dog.) But Jackoff and BZ had messed up. Things were bad. Really bad. And time was not on their side. The screening was in three hours, and the movie was out of sync, a complete mess. Whatever the degree of damage, I cannot attest to, as I wasn't there in person. But my friend assures me it was significant and...

Hey, wait a minute. Why wonder? Why not go right to the source and find out how this insanity was eventually ironed out?

This is word for word his explanation of what happened. I thought it was far more interesting than anything I could have written, so I figured I'd pass it along. A couple of details to remember: The Avid is the computer and software they use to edit the movie. The "cuts" refer to the edits. Aaaaaand, go!

> *Essentially, we had to pull out of the print what BZ and Yakov cut into the print.*
>
> *The print has to match what we cut in the Avid. At a certain point leading up to the screening, we had to stop cutting in the Avid to allow ourselves time to conform the print to match the cuts in the Avid.*
>
> *I had to explain to them that they needed to tell me what they put in because everything they put into the print was knocking the movie out of sync. Then the assistant editor and I had to cut back into the print the shots they had removed.*

I can't remember now exactly how we checked what was in the Avid vs what we had cut back into the print was accurate. We had to trust that what they told us they put in and what we put back in was correct.

If I remember correctly there were a couple of quick shots we missed but the timing must have been close to the original shots because nothing was thrown out of sync (that badly), but the new shots that they had cut in had no sound FX under them.

Another thing they hadn't thought of while up to their shenanigans - they cut in these new VFX shots but didn't tell audio—they claim they didn't have time to tell audio, so there would have been no sound effects under their new shots. So, like I said, I think we missed a couple quick shots because I remember sitting in the theatre watching the screening and seeing a couple that had no sound effects under them. That was fun.

So, that pretty much tells that story. Not only did they almost cause the screening to be cancelled, but they left shots in the movie with no sound effects at all, greatly reducing any impact they could have brought to the film. How in the world does someone attempt something like that and not know the risks and the consequences if you do it incorrectly? How do you forget to tell the audio department about your plan? How do you not ask for help to keep it in sync? All this just so you can be the surprise hero in the end? Or was it that BZ knew he would not be allowed to touch the file to begin with and that someone would call Shuki if he tried? Either way, incredible. But so perfectly BZ.

And, in the end, because my friend is such a good guy and put the success of the movie before his desire to let BZ crash and burn, everything worked out, and it's questionable whether Shuki or Haim ever even found out. Irony at its cruelest and most, well, ironic.

CHAPTER 59
A DEVELOPMENT IN THE DIVATOX DEPARTMENT

When we began writing the new season of *Turbo*, we quickly learned that the actress who played Divatox in the film would not be appearing in the TV show, as she was apparently going on maternity leave. What wonderful news! Another child being brought into the world and thus into the *Power Rangers* family. Our sheer bliss was unmistakable as it would be upon learning that any of our beloved actors or crew members were going to become parents. Our bliss was cut short, however, and quickly turned to COMPLETE ELATION as we realized that we would have to re-cast the role of Divatox! NO!

But wait, what about continuity?!! Screw continuity! This was *Power Rangers,* and we had been given a gift, the opportunity to bring in someone who could perhaps right the ship (or submarine, as it were) on that entire storyline. In the movie, she was so over the top goofy that it completely neutralized any threat to the Rangers. We needed to find an actress who could play her relatively straight with some ability to instill fear in the hearts of our audience as well. Then we would let the sidekicks be her foil and get the comedy from them somehow. We were incredibly lucky and found the perfect actress in a woman named Carol Hoyt. I had never worked with her before, but her audition tape was amazing, and she was a fair representation of the woman who originally played Divatox when in the suit, at least height-wise. Carol had a more elegant air about her, which also worked, But the look was definitely there.

TURBO BEGINS: We shifted into *Turbo*, the TV season, by picking up the Rangers' story after the movie, with Justin as the new Blue Ranger and Divatox still pissed off that the teens messed up her wedding to giant lava dude. (Not sure what that wedding night would have looked like, but the heart wants what the heart wants I suppose.) I figured the first thing we needed to do was tie at least a couple of the Rangers into something that was related to cars in a cool way. Tommy was the logical choice, so we researched what it would take to rent a stock car, a stunt driver, and a track for the day. Turns out it was doable, so the idea of Tommy becoming an aspiring race car driver was born. Of course, it was tossed out once Ann and I left. But they didn't really know what our plans were at that point. They were unaware that I had contacted and toured California Speedway and spoke about a partnership with a nearby race school to help us put together an amazing final arc that would include Tommy racing in front of thousands of people and a Zord fight just outside the track. It would have been cool. But alas, it was never to be.

It was finally time for the kids to graduate high school, so along with Tommy, the other Rangers were given new pursuits that would perhaps lead to future careers. Kat would be a teaching assistant, Tanya worked at a radio station, and Adam was in the Angel Grove Amusement park stunt show, which for some reason was being directed by Tanya in her off time from the radio station. This whole set up led to one of the most bizarre Ranger episodes ever. We'll get to that in a bit.

Then we had Lt. Stone taking over the Juice Bar as Ernie had been, brace yourselves, called up by his Foreign Legion division to go to the Amazon and build a bridge to connect two communities or something.

MORPHERS, MONSTERS & MAYHEM

SIDE NOTE: Okay, I know this was supposed to be a funny sendoff for the character, but the idea of poor Ernie humping it through the jungle carrying rebar over his shoulder wearing a hard hat and singing "It's off to work I go" was just insane and frankly a little degrading to think about. Rich Ganelle, the actor who played Ernie, could barely find the energy to light up a cigarette at the end of the day, waddle out to his enormous Caddy and crank up the air for the ride home. He was not in any way athletic, or even able-bodied if I'm being honest. (I imagine poor Rich is still rolling over in his grave over the way we sent him off.)

Lieutenant Stone was, as I said, no longer a cop or a detective or anything useful story-wise but the owner of the Juice Bar and the keeper of Bulk and Skull, who were now being played by two chimpanzees. Bulk and Skull lived out on the back patio of the Juice Bar surrounded by a plethora of toys and crap that they could play with so they wouldn't be bored. Now would probably be a good time to explain that crazy last statement. We'll call this an extra-long side note.

As it happened, the beginning of *Turbo* brought with it another problem that was a bit more difficult to solve than the normal issues we tackled daily. Jason and Paul, the actors who played Bulk and Skull were going to shoot a pilot for what was to become their own spinoff TV series. Although Ann and I had, at one point, written a script of a pilot for them, I can say with relative certainty that this was not the script they were planning on shooting. The problem that was the most serious was the fact that we would have no Bulk and Skull for the next several months. We had to deliver new shows, and we needed the comedy desperately, as it was pretty obvious that Divatox was not going to be helpful in this area regardless of who was wearing the leather suit.

As I've mentioned before, Shuki was the guy who could usually fix any issue when it came to last minute "Hail Mary rescues," be it script, production, whatever. It was uncanny. He always seemed to have a good grasp on what was needed to plug the holes in our often-leaky ship and keep the engines running at the same time. In this case, I can't be sure that it was his idea or whether Haim had said it in jest and Shuki followed it up by doing it, but I was told one afternoon as we were planning our next set of scripts that Bulk and Skull would no longer be in the episodes. Wait. Was this the writing on the wall? Were they exiting the show for good? Not exactly. Their presence would still be there as characters, but no longer as human characters. Nope. They would appear in the form of two chimpanzees, each dressed in its own monkey size Jr. Police Patrol uniform. I'm sure all the Ranger fans remember this moment. Suddenly these two talented actors were gone, and in their place were two apes with significantly less talent and considerably more fur. There were a lot of reasons this was not a stellar idea. But, to me, number one on that list is that we'd suddenly be working with chimpanzees. Let me explain why this is never a good idea on a low-budget production, because on its surface it sounds fun and interesting and a great way to break up the monotony on set.

Using animals for TV or movies is a very tricky business that rarely works out as you had planned. Trained animals are expensive, unpredictable, and can even be dangerous. There is a famous story of an orangutan who was working on a low-budget film set, quite a few years ago. The orangutan was described as being sweet as can be, but with a naughty streak that could be unpredictable under the best of circumstances. Let me be clear, unpredictability is NOT a quality you want in a wild animal, trained or not. Add to this the fact that orangutans are strong. VERY strong. This particular animal was so strong, in fact, that its lone toy, one that he would throw around his fenced enclosure on set to keep him amused, was a full-sized refrigerator. Not one of those little portable ones. Full sized!

Adding to what was already a dicey situation was that his movie had a couple of dozen little people in the cast. And in this cast of little people, there was one particular chap who suffered from the same affliction as the orangutan—having a naughty streak. And one day those two streaks intersected and it got crazy. Grumpy orangutan grabbed grumpy little person who was flipping it off through its pen on the way to lunch. The orangutan jumped the fence, grabbed the little person under its ape arm, and raced up a tree, where it planted itself and refused to come down. The little person screamed obscenities at the orangutan and its trainer, who calmly informed the man of diminutive stature that the ape would come down when it was ready, and that the man was "probably not in danger." In the meantime, screaming would help nothing. The trainer continued that the orangutan was just lonely and wanted a friend. "I don't want to be friends with no fucking orange monkey," came the response. It took about three hours, but the orangutan finally came down and all was returned to normal, or as normal as it could be on a movie set with an orangutan that spends its day throwing a refrigerator around like a nerf football.

This story is one of the reasons you don't hire animals, especially if you are shooting on a budget. You may be able to get a second-rate Picture Animal service to supply one that fits the description in the script. But there's no way it will be the perfectly trained gem you had hoped for. This is exactly what went down with the two primates that were rented for us, by guess who…

Our old pal BZ was charged with finding us the two chimps that would replace Bulk and Skull. And so, the calls went out. By some miracle it seemed like almost immediately BZ had procured two chimps. As much as I was suspicious of this miraculous achievement, days later two chimps and their trainer appeared at the stages for introductions. This is when I began understanding why he was able to locate and hire them on our meager budget. Somehow, BZ had managed to find the two most lethargic, untrained, unattractive chimps in Hollywood. (For all you young folks, these chimps were Cringe AF.)

For some reason, BZ decided that it would be a good idea to rent two chimps that were new to the game, NOT trained to do much of anything. Not only that, but one of the poor things has such bad psoriasis that it barely had hair in some places. Instead there was this unsightly flaking "ape-idermis."

I couldn't figure out why BZ had decided to go in this direction. Haim and Shuki were very high on the concept and thought the chimps were the answer to all of our prayers. It seemed stupid to me not to spend the money for two well-trained primates. Why risk the plethora of things that could go wrong, like perhaps one of them running up the side of the studio with Billy under its arm because it was lonely?

I asked BZ what the deal was, and he told me that this was what we could afford, and if I had a problem with it, I should talk to Haim. BZ quickly pointed out the fact that Haim agreed with what they were going to devote financially to the chimps.

"WHAT?" My BS alarm immediately stared blaring in my head so loud that, had it been an actual alarm and not a crappy metaphor, it would have been heard across the entire Santa Clarita valley. "So, what you're telling me, BZ, is that with the importance of this entirely new storyline, and the reality that it was the only comedy for miles in this new series, Haim decided that we should skimp on the one thing that could allow it to succeed or fail?"

"That's what I'm telling you," was BZ's answer. And off went my BS alarm again.

What was more likely was that BZ had assured Haim and Shuki that they could get quality apes for what we could afford, and spending any more of Haim's precious budget was just throwing money away. Or it could have been that Haim was never even consulted and that this time, for whatever reason, BZ was NOT going to turn the coffers upside down and shake them as he always did when we needed something extra because it had been requested by Shuki or was actually a solid idea. You could say what you wanted about BZ's weird personality, his need to control every little situation, his insincere gentleman act, etc., but he always found the money in the budget for something important. He was a master at hiding little pockets all over the place that he could reach into if the need arose. And, for the stupidest things that didn't seem nearly as important as these chimps did. The reality was, this was a mess. And there was no way BZ was going to subject himself to the wrath of Haim over it. BZ had to feel like he had some sort of safety net to avoid any repercussions if things went sideways. And his safety net, whatever it was, felt very unsafe for me and for Ann.

CHAPTER 60
"YOU ARE STEALING FOOD OUT OF MY CHILDREN'S MOUTHS!"

The apes began work and it immediately became obvious that they literally could do nothing. When I say nothing, I don't mean "nothing we asked of them." I mean they could do literally zero that they were told. As a result, the two sad-looking critters just kind of laid there, propped up against the nearest piece of furniture like two brown floor mats, one shag and one Berber. They were two hairy lumps, lying around the Juice Bar in police uniforms, looking like grotesque taxidermy we had placed there as a Tim Burtonesque sight gag. It was insane. But we soldiered on, doing the best we could with what we had, which was nothing. I was just waiting for BZ to get the call from Haim to receive the ass scorching of the year, if Haim happened to watch the dailies, which, unfortunately, he rarely did those days. This would possibly be a fun moment, had it come to fruition. It did not, at least not in the way we had imagined it would.

While the apes were sleeping their careers away on the *Power Rangers* sound stages, Ann and I decided we should try to find ourselves an agent so that when this job was over, we could take advantage of the momentum that *Power Rangers* had created. There was a guy I had gone to grad school with named Ian Greenstein.

He was in our little group that always shot our films together and was a decent enough guy. What always struck me about Ian was that he was smooth. VERY smooth. He dressed well and had the attitude like he'd been there before, wherever "there" happened to be. One summer, during film school, I interned at the William Morris Agency, so I was around agents for three solid months. Ian felt much more like one of those agents to me than he did a filmmaker.

This was not meant as an insult in any way. There are those who belong behind the camera, those who belong in front of the camera, and those who belong behind a desk collecting 10% of what the money that the people on both sides of the camera make. They are called agents (or managers), and it takes a very special combination of brains, balls, and a complete lack of empathy towards the person against whom you are negotiating to be successful. Ian clearly had that skill set. He was a lovely guy, but he could also be a guy who didn't seem to mind crushing anyone who got in the way of him getting what he wanted in a business deal, or any deal for that matter.

I told him one day when we were on a break from shooting a scene on the streets of New York that I felt he was uniquely suited for the role. Surprisingly, he didn't completely dismiss the idea, and a part of me thought it had probably been mentioned before by one of his friends or family. He had most likely stored it away in his subconscious as a kind of escape hatch if, God forbid, his dreams of rising to the top of the directorial ladder hit a snag. But we were at film school to make films, and that's what he was concentrating on at the time. Years later I would learn that Ian HAD become an agent, and a VERY successful one at that. So, I called him up and asked him if he would have lunch with Ann and I to discuss our future. He was more than happy to oblige. I figured at the very least he would offer some help or guidance to get the ball rolling in our search. Why not help an old friend out?

Ann and I met at a restaurant in Beverly Hills for what should have been a pleasant lunch with Ian, who was a bit older and a bit grayer than the last time I had seen him in New York. Who wasn't? But he was the same old Ian. As we were getting our salads, my cell rang. It was Haim calling me from his personal cell, being connected through his assistant. I didn't think too much of it as I reached for my phone. Haim had called me that one time to offer congratulations on a few episodes he had watched and loved. Getting some props from the big guy wouldn't be the worst thing to happen at lunch with Ian sitting there. At the very least it would show that we were valued by a powerful person in the industry, that we knew what we were doing. Unfortunately, this was not the call it was to be. The call that it was, had me exiting the restaurant and running to find a place where I could hear and Ian couldn't.

"Mr. Sloan. It's Haim."

Uh oh. He usually called me Doug or Douglas when it was something good. Never "Mr. Sloan." He continued with, "I'm sitting here, and I suddenly realized that you are the bastard who is taking food out of the mouths of my children."

Obviously, he was speaking metaphorically, as the reality of this was impossible. I had never met his children, and I was pretty sure that anything I said or did would have zero effect on their caloric intake, especially since his new home had THREE kitchens, one of them being a sushi bar with a world class sushi chef on call. Haim continued.

"Can you answer this for me?" he said. "What is with these fucking monkeys?" Shit. It took me a moment to clue in on what was going on, but once I got my bearings, I started putting the pieces together. First shot over the bow by BZ, and it was a well-aimed strike that had Haim good and riled. This was going to be rough.

"They just sit there," he continued. "Why don't they do anything? You must make them do something."

The next moment was an example of a miscommunication that can sometimes happen when you are dealing with a boss who, although they speak perfect English, doesn't always take things in the way they may have been intended.

What I said next was, "Haim, they can't do anything. They just…they can't." What I should have said was, "Haim, they aren't trained. They can't do what we tell them to do." I'm sure what Haim heard was some version of me not wanting to go the extra mile for the show and think of something for the chimps to perform. This was when the tirade began. The full intensity of the legendary Haim temper was thrust upon me courtesy of Verizon wireless's excellent coverage back in the day.

"Listen to me, you motherfucker. I'll tell you what they can do. They can suck each other's monkey dicks. They can throw their crap at each other. They can throw their crap at the Rangers. I don't care, but they can't sit around doing nothing."

I waited until he was finished and corrected myself by telling him that they weren't trained to do anything. They're bargain-basement apes. It's all we could afford.

"Bullshit. I spoke to [insert BZ's real name here], and he told me they were perfectly acceptable and that it was the scripts that were the problem. They're too complicated. The trainer said this to you!"

Wait. What? Had BZ gone full annihilation on us? Had he set his official *Power Rangers* obliterator to 11 and just fired away? Was that possible?

"Listen to me. You're the creative genius. So, I want you to stop whatever else it is you're doing, stop it, and fix these monkeys. I don't want to get calls that the children in our audience are scared of these things."

I immediately thought that if there were any calls coming in about the show, it would probably be about a laundry list of other things, but I was in no position to make that argument right then.

"I'll handle it," I told him. The next sound I heard was the phone cutting off. I was stunned. Did I just receive BZ's first shot across the bow? If so, it was a doozy.

BZ had hated the way I spoke to him in that production meeting when he ignored Haim's directive to stay away from the creative. The look on his face as he walked out of that meeting flashed in my mind. Maybe this was some super psycho military way of communicating to me exactly how much he hated it—and hated me. If asked, he would deny, deny, deny, because that's what he does. But the fact that Haim called to ram it down my throat—and only *my* throat—because BZ told him the issue was the writing, not the chimps, had the smell of an attack. It was beyond nasty. All I could do was go back to lunch and try to choke down my Chinese chicken salad.

Of course, lunch was miserable from that point forward. Ian had little interest in repping a couple of kids TV writers, regardless of our friendship. We parted with the promise that we'd get together down the road. Of course, that never happened, and I haven't seen the guy since. As I said, born to be an agent.

Back at the *Power Rangers,* Ann and I seethed in her office at what had just happened. Of course, we had no proof that BZ had anything to do with it. Sure, he told Haim our scripts were at fault, but that could just be an opinion. He had plausible deniability that he intentionally set us up. But it seemed like a fifty-fifty shot that the dude had, at the very least, used his ability to call the shots with the budget to create this ruthless plan, and it had succeeded quite nicely. It was undeniable that we were headed towards a boiling point. It was going to come down to him or us, and we needed to be ready for that. In the meantime, we had some ape scripts to write.

At the end of their limited engagement, the chimps were able to execute some basic commands that you would expect any pet chimp to be able to execute. We started to write bits for them that only required them to react to what was going on around them. It wasn't perfect, but we survived being without Jason and Paul, which was a victory as far as I was concerned. Thankfully, Bulk and Skull returned not too long after that, and all was right with the world. The chimps were gone, and we were free to look for our comedy in the guise of two very talented actors. Thank the lord. To this day, I feel badly that the Bulk and Skull spinoff didn't happen. I thought they would have been great in it, and they deserved it. Who knows why it never materialized. I'm not sure even they know. It's not unusual in our business unfortunately.

So, let's review what lay in front of us at the beginning of *Turbo*:

1. No Bulk and Skull. In their place, two chimps who were incapable of doing much of anything. In essence, we had swapped two trained actors for two untrained primates.
2. We were stuck with a villain who wasn't that threatening or interesting, but we were going to try to up the danger with a new actress.
3. Lt. Stone was the new Ernie. As good as Greg Bullock was, there are just some things that would be missed.
4. The Rangers were now the de facto parents of an 11-year-old Power Ranger who was a good actor and martial artist. But he was still 11.
5. Zordon was gone, leaving in his place Divatox in a veil, the floating head who only asked questions as her way to help the Rangers.
6. Alpha 6 was the robot version of *My Cousin Vinnie* and quickly became super annoying and had us desperate to subtract one digit from his name and bring back Alpha 5.

I don't know about you guys, but how great did that all sound? Let's definitely GUT our hit show after four seasons and turn it into something completely unrecognizable? What could possibly go wrong? *Zeo* worked, I believe, because we changed just enough so that the kids would still identify it as a *Power Rangers* show, but it also had enough freshening up that it had room to grow and expand the world. And why was *Turbo* allowed to happen? How? Who? When?

What the "F"?

Well, because it was too freaking late to go back. *Turbo* was the footage. *Turbo* was the movie. *Turbo* was big changes. That's what the series was going to be, and there wasn't really a choice. And can you believe I didn't do anything to stop this from happening? What was I thinking? Why was I so silent about all this? I had known Shuki long enough to step up and try to do some damage control. I was a 35-year-old, first-time producer who still thought my boss was a genius and never dared argue for fear that I would rock the boat and lose my job. Turns out it wouldn't have mattered. All I could do at that point was control the stuff I could control. We were bringing in good directors, had some exciting stuff written for the characters, and we were just going to make the best of what was set up to be a massive shit show. Or should I say a "massively shitty show?" Either seemed appropriate.

For the fourth and fifth episodes of *Turbo*, we brought in a director by the name of Al Winchell. Al was not only our first AD on *VR Troopers* but had gone on to direct some amazing episodes of that show and had written for us on *Power Rangers*. He was a talented, easy to work with, funny guy who had an amazing eye and a way with actors. I was excited to see what he could do on our show. When I started watching the dailies, I was really psyched. His stuff looked great, and I knew it was going to cut together well. And it did. Al's shows were among the best directed of the first couple of blocks of episodes. I couldn't wait to have him back. Of course, BZ shrugged it off as being pedestrian and was not impressed at all. He said that if I wanted to see great direction, I should look at *Built for Speed*, the episode Little BZ had just directed. So, I did.

The episode in question was one of the most bizarre, non-Ranger-like scripts we have ever commissioned, and the only reason it got through was that there was a car racing B-story to it. That was about it. It featured a bunch of guest actors who no one knew or cared about. The episode started off with a big Vegas dance extravaganza that was supposed to be for the stunt show that Adam was in at the amusement park but looked more like a scene out of the local high school production of *West Side Story*. And, as you may remember, Tanya was the director of the stunt show, for some odd reason, in addition to working at a radio station. The story would come to a climax with the five guest actors

MORPHERS, MONSTERS & MAYHEM   359

out on an abandoned highway, racing one another in vintage cars as some sort of grudge match that had been explained in the script as them being so into their 50s characters in the stunt show that it was spilling over into their real life. Ultimately, in lieu of creating something new and interesting, BZ and Little BZ just couldn't stop themselves from recreating the final scene from *Rebel Without a Cause* almost shot for shot, both cars heading towards a cliff, the Bulk and Skull monkeys locked in the trunk. Fortunately, they were rescued by the Rangers in the Megazord and safely returned to the grassy knoll they had just flown off. What a freaking mess. Does this sound like an episode of *Power Rangers* to you? Is there anything cool about a musical number if you were in our audience and a 6-year-old boy in the year 1997? Please tell me if I'm wrong.

When the script came through for this pile of crap, I realized that BZ, who was obsessed with using every scrap of Japanese footage he could get his hands on and intercutting it with stuff we shot, had outdone himself on this one. He and Little BZ (who I guess had decided that the stresses of directing were much less of a threat to his health than sitting at a desk all day and was very much back in the fold) had basically spent the entire budget on two or three scenes. The problem was that while doing it, they had broken the cardinal rule of the Japanese footage. You take out anything that references Japan, as it destroys the illusion of it all being one show. In this episode there are scenes with Japanese writing on street signs, road barriers, and even a wall that one of the Rangers rescues two Japanese people in front of during an action scene is plastered with Japanese characters. It was ridiculous. I remember protesting and being told that it had been cleared with Shuki and everyone was fine with it.

So, yeah, the episode looked expensive. But it was only made possible by BZ cheating the system to put the money there. He manipulated the budget that only he and Jabba had access to and helped Little BZ make his "cinematic work of art."

And I asked once again, what the "F" was Little BZ doing back? I had been seriously concerned for his health. Really concerned.

And here he was a couple of months later, fresh as a daisy. I was told there had been some astounding new developments in the treatment of his affliction and the prognosis was good. In the last two months? They figured the whole thing out in 60 days? How lucky is that? I suppose I would have been happier for Little BZ had the whole story not been so completely insane. But it gets better.

Directors, as a rule, would usually get two days to re-edit their four episodes and that was pretty much it. Any more, and the whole system would fall behind, as there were so many shows that needed to be cut. There just wasn't time to linger on any one episode. Also, if the director had done their job, they wouldn't need to spend any more time than that, as the episodes were never more that 22 minutes, with at least 8 minutes, ideally 11, of precut footage from Japan that had already been expertly assembled by the editors before production even saw the episode. So, this was the process. It had been working very well for the years that we had been employed on Rangers. So, it was a mystery to us why I received a call later that day that BZ and Little BZ had decided that this rule was to be lifted temporarily—and just for them.

The call was more of a plea for help than anything else. According to my good old friend in post, the BZ twins had spent DAYS working on their show…long days, pushing the editors well into overtime, which of course BZ would cover somehow since he oversaw the budget. To be fair, when Ann and I were doing the show and it came to postproduction, there were always small overages as a result of post being the last possible place to fix things when it came down to it, and that's where the money had to come from.

Budgets are like living, breathing organisms that change with time and adjust to the outside world and have pressures placed on them. They must, because the numbers in there are only estimates that can't take into account everything that is going to come along during shooting that wasn't planned for. Postproduction is often a place where there are overages, just based on the fact that it is the end of the line and a place to spend extra money to try to fix mistakes made throughout the process that came before it.

> SIDE NOTE: When Ann and I were on the show, there was an overage in post for every episode. That dollar amount was usually a little under $1,000. As I said, this is not unusual, as you always come across things that need to be fixed and it always costs a bit to make it happen.
> Years later, I learned that the per episode overage for postproduction after Ann and I were gone and BZ was overseeing the show was a bit more…robust than it had been in our day. Robust to the tune of $10,832 average per episode OVER the amount that was budgeted. For an entire season, that works out to around $411,000 that they were pouring into post that had never been spent there before.
> This is the only event of its kind happening that I personally could prove to be 100% factual; I won't speculate as to other departments and where the numbers were. But one must wonder if this was happening in postproduction, where else was it happening? And if there was all this extra money floating around stuffed into BZ's preverbal budgetary mattress, you had to wonder several things:

1. It was 1997 when this was first discovered. Could BZ have been "mad stacking Bengies" since the show started prepping in 1992? It would have been perfectly normal for a line producer to create a few little windows hidden deep in the budget, money moved from one place to another, one department getting cut to feed another department, but all of it bull crap since it was just a big shell game anyway. Was this all part of BZ's grand plan, his long game for when he finally ascended to the crown at *Power Rangers*? Having money squirreled away to keep his ass covered wasn't a bad strategy.

a. We know that Saban himself, in the early days, was redistributing a few thousand per episode off the top from the license fee of an already meager budget. So why would it be so hard to believe stuff like this was going on everywhere?
2. In terms of BZ stashing cash, my question was, how was it okay for him to be putting away this money through all the actor troubles that had gone on over the first couple of years? Could they at least have shown them a gesture of goodwill through some kind of bonus at the end of the season? That could have changed everything.
    a. But rewarding the actors would have done nothing to improve the series. BZ wanted to prove that he was the wizard of Rangerland, and he alone could conjure up the Power Ranger magic that he felt had been missing for so long. Well, good job, Voldemort. You did it by lying, cheating, and contributing to at least one mental breakdown and another bankruptcy (names withheld to protect the embarrassed).
3. Selfishly, it kind of pissed me off that going forward, these two clowns, BZ and Little BZ, were going to have the ability to do things Ann and I could never have dreamed of, all as a result of the financial restrictions imposed on us by their bullcrap budget being lifted when they took over. It kind of steams me up when I hear people say that the show was "fixed" and "so much better" once Ann and I left. Of course it was! They were working with a budget that was significantly larger than what we had, and no one was trying to jam them up in the process.

Anyway, we're not gone yet in this timeline. Back to *Turbo*. Things were going great for Little BZ. He had a full ride scholarship to the Beelzebub school of film making and budgetary bamboozling, shooting episodes of *Rangers* whenever he wanted, spending hours in the editing room, getting every shot picture perfect with all the extra time afforded to him by the keeper of the cash, BZ himself.

Little BZ was also remarkably chipper and full of energy, seemingly cured of the incurable illness that caused him to leave us in the first place. Honestly, I was truly happy for him, as clearly he was in a better place. But why did it have to be at *Power Rangers*? Why did his better place have to be our place?

Jesus. Not important.

As BZ had promoted Jabba to Little BZ's position, Jabba brought in an assistant to work directly in service of his "assholiness." Funny enough, the new assistant was a carbon copy of Jabba in every possible way. And, although she was nice enough and respectful enough when she started, she quickly became infected with the darkness and the need to make our lives miserable as the days wore on. She became more and more disrespectful and, in the end, basically ignored all of us and would even scream at us to be quiet when she was on an "important" call. Weird for an assistant, I thought, to be allowed to scream at producers with absolutely zero consequences. I'd never seen that before. Jabba seemed to love it, snorting loudly (her laugh) every time Jabba Jr. treated us with the disrespect and disdain Jabba felt we so richly deserved.

As for Jabba, she seemed happier than she'd been since we'd had the misfortune of knowing her, like she was sitting on some sort of bombshell information, walking around with a huge disgusting Jabba-sized grin on her face from morning to night. God, it was irritating. But who knew what was going on behind closed doors at the time, so what could I say. It had been more than a year since the meeting in which I told BZ that we would handle the creative and he should deal with the production. He hadn't said much to me since then. It appeared as though he was closing ranks around him and at the same time doing things to irritate me, like bringing back Little BZ as a director. He was also circumventing me to Shuki for approval on ideas that effected the creative on the show, and Shuki was not pushing back. So that was freaking weird as well. Although it WAS like Shuki to agree to whatever just to get off the phone and not have to deal with something. I always thought it was kind of hilarious when I watched him do it in his office, squirming like some sort of bizarre fish with a mane of multicolored hair and dark sunglasses you couldn't see past.

The episodes clicked by, one after the next, and somehow it seemed as though we were going in a weird direction. The whole block of shows that Little BZ directed were just...well...a little off. Little BZ's next episode was all about Justin getting the mind meld and turning into a lying little a-hole. All of this was against a backdrop of a car wash for the baseball team's new uniforms. Again, Blake Foster did a GREAT job delivering on the material he was given. It was just that the part was turning out to mostly be Justin disappearing, the Rangers trying to find him, and him getting into non-costumed fights with either one of Divatox's henchmen or the foot (or fin) soldiers. The Rangers were starting to feel so old! It really was becoming *The Brady Bunch* with superhero costumes.

As head writers, Ann and I had to get a handle on it, as it felt like a negative regression was in the works. Somehow the scripts were ending up nothing like what we imagined, and the series was going in a direction that was going to make it difficult to end up where we wanted it to at the end of the season. Later we would find out why that was.

CHAPTER 61
COUNTDOWN TO CRASH LANDING

Things had started to get more and more weird for Ann and me at *Power Rangers*. Looking back, knowing what I know now about the entertainment business and how some people operate, I should have seen it coming, as there wasn't much of an attempt to cover up. There was a cast change coming in which all the current Rangers were being replaced. The current cast was starting to show their age. And with them all having jobs now, there was no getting around the fact that they were becoming less relatable to our audience. So, the search was on for a new "extraordinary group of teenagers" to step into the spandex.

What was weird, at least to me, was that Shuki seemed to have no interest in what I thought about the actors who were reading for the new Rangers. Katy Wallin and Thom Klohn had been replaced by an amazing casting director named Julie Ashton. And, in looking for an assistant, she had hired my younger sister Alix to fill that void (another example of nepotism getting someone in the door, but only so far). I should mention that Alix is the smartest one in our family by far. She can pick up anything and excel at it in no time. She's just a super-cool, super-talented, super-smart woman. She picked up casting but didn't stick with it. She felt so badly for the actors who didn't get hired that she gave it up and now writes novels. Anyway, it was weird that Ann and my opinions were kind of being sloughed off when it came to the new actors. This was the first thing I noticed that was genuinely unsettling.

Additionally, we had been instructed not to tell the current Rangers about the changeover. Shuki, Haim, and BZ wanted to work as close to the end date as they could without things blowing up and actors walking off the set. So, we were all, for about a minute, walking around wondering how the cast would react when they were told. I say "about a minute" because that's how long it took Johnny Yong Bosch to read an ad in the L.A. actors periodical, *Backstage*, announcing that the current *Power Rangers* actors were being replaced and open auditions were being held. Anyone interested in auditioning should send in a head shot. I cannot think of a worse way to find out your job is coming to an end than to read it in the local casting rag. Then, for Johnny to have to tell the others? It must have been torture. I can remember that at the time I was happy that at least they now knew. It was just a classless way to handle this very delicate situation. These actors had made the company billions of dollars, and the thanks they got was an ad in *Backstage* and a "See ya later"?

Speaking of Johnny Yong Bosch, at some point around the time that *Zeo* was finishing and *Turbo* was being conceived, Johnny started to bring his new girlfriend around the set with him. It seemed like she was there just about every day, and the two of them appeared to really be into one another, Johnny rushing over to her every time they had a break, making sure she was okay, that she was having a good time, etc. Then, one day, I noticed that she had become an extra in one of the Juice Bar scenes. That was something that made sense to me. She was a stunning young woman, and to my utter shock and delight (maybe not "utter shock"), she was an aspiring actress! I guess Johnny had asked if she could be an extra on days when we needed them and that way she could make some money, get some experience, and not sit around being bored all day. I was fine with it. She seemed like a nice enough girl, and you must take any advantage you can get in our business. She needed a leg up, and Johnny was there to give her one.

My only concern in all of this was for Johnny, actually. He may be one of the nicest human beings on the planet (or at least in that cast) and always saw the best in people. His new girlfriend, although on the surface perfectly nice, was trying to become a successful actress. AND she was beautiful. AND she was very friendly. I was a bit concerned that there would come a point where the sharks who had begun circling already would get to her and just like that, she would be swept up by another guy who hadn't just lost his Ranger status, and she would be gone. That's pretty much what happened. And if that wasn't enough of a punch to the gut, the flying shit that had hit the fan got on me as well. Somehow, I had successfully blocked the story I'm about to tell you out of my mind for years. However, once I was reminded of it, the memory came flooding back like a tsunami. I suddenly remembered it like it was yesterday. And it made me sad, angry, and disgusted with myself.

It began like many of these stories did back then. Shuki was at the offices for a meeting, and the moment he entered the stage, his eyes locked onto Johnny's cute little gal pal. Shuki asked me about her, and I revealed to him the whole story of how she had become part of our Power Ranger family. Shuki was completely taken with her and asked if I had seen her act (this was before he stopped asking for my opinion on actors). Long story short, when the new Rangers were being cast, I had found who I thought would be a home run Yellow Ranger in a great young actress from New York named Selma Blair. Yes, that same Selma Blair who went on to appear in *Legally Blonde, Cruel Intentions*, and *Hellboy*. Of all the actors on the tape I watched that had come in from New York, she clearly had been blessed with the pixie dust. It wasn't even a close call. When I excitedly brought the tape to Shuki, I was more than a little surprised by his reaction. Shuki dismissed her without letting the audition tape finish. He felt that Selma was "just okay, nothing special." This was, of course, ludicrous. Selma Blair, to this day, is one of the most believable, talented actors around. Her comedy skills are fantastic, and she's able to play parts that seem ludicrous but somehow, in her hands, are grounded and fun to watch. Were it not for her tragic health struggles, I believe she would have copious awards and credits too numerous to list. None of that is pertinent to this moment of the *Rangers* story, but I felt it warranted mentioning. And if you think I'm nuts, just watch her in anything. She is truly gifted.

Shuki informed me that he knew who the Yellow Ranger was going to be, and the auditions taking place now were a mere formality. And they certainly weren't going to pay for anyone to fly from New York when the job was essentially taken. And who was this remarkable talent, light years ahead of Selma Blair (according to Shuki)? To my surprise, the new Yellow Ranger was going to be none other than Tracie Lynn Cruz, Johnny Bosch's girlfriend, the one-time extra, the girl with no experience who I had never even seen read for the part. What the "F" was going on in this twisted universe? I was clearly not paying close enough attention to the goings-on around the show. This was a bad sign. A very bad sign. As inexperienced as I was as a producer, even I knew that we were in trouble. This was another harbinger of things to come, big things, life changing things.

But wait, there's more!

Even though Shuki had decided, for whatever reason, that Tracy was going to be the new Yellow Ranger, he still thought it was necessary to have her do a screen test. I thought to myself at the time, "Finally! Some common sense!" Of course she needed to be screen-tested. I only hoped that it wasn't going to be my job to direct it, as I wanted no part of this whole weirdness. I needn't have worried. Apparently, Shuki had saved that honor for himself. Because apparently there was nothing more important than directing a walk-and-talk scene with an actress he had already cast in his mind. WTF? Well, at least I was out of it. Wait. No, I wasn't. I wasn't out of it. I was more in it than I could have ever imagined. And what a crappy way to get sucked in to this dysfunctional fun house. The very best job had been saved for me!

Shuki had the scene he wanted to shoot. In it, Tracy would be acting with…wait…WTF?

Tracy would be doing her screen test with Catherine Sutherland.

"Why is this a big deal," you ask? Think about it. The Rangers were being replaced…all of them. To ask an outgoing cast member who was not going voluntarily, and about to lose their job, to screen test with an incoming actor is, at the very least, offensive. Couple that with the fact that Tracy would be replacing Cat's very best friend on the series, Nakia Burrise, and you had a recipe for resentment, anger, emotion, and a good old *Power Rangers* dumpster fire.

I was wondering how the hell Shuki thought he was going to get Cat to even do it. The answer is, HE wasn't going to get her to do anything. Apparently, it had been decided that because of my close relationship to Cat, I was the one who was going to coax her into performing this humiliation. And if she refused, I would "insist" a bit more forcefully until she agreed. This was the awesome job that I was given.

Not a freaking chance, I told Suki. How could I instruct Catherine to go along with something so clearly misguided and cruel? I was basically told that I needed to make it happen and there was no wiggle room. The words were never spoken, but the implication was obvious: get in there and convince her to do it, or tell Haim why you're siding with an actor against the production, the company, Haim, and finally his children, who will surely starve as a result. I was completely screwed.

And then there was Shuki, doing the unthinkable to this sweet, angelic young woman he had plucked from Australia and relocated to the U.S. He was basically abandoning her now that Rangers was done with her. Were it not for the recent discovery of the famous howler memo, I would have thought it completely out of character for this wonderful man who had always been so kind to all of us. But I was no longer under the illusion that my dude was the kids biz version of Mahatma Gandhi. My world was spinning off its axis, ladies and gentlemen. I was getting one sign after the next that things were severely messed up, and I didn't know how to deal with it. I needed to figure it out though. In the meantime, I had to go down to the dressing rooms and have a conversation with Cat that I really did NOT want to have.

The brain is a powerful thing. It can keep things in the front of your mind so that you will never forget them as long as you live. And you don't have much control over this. You're basically at the mercy of this insanely complex computer that handles information the way it wants to, unless you are one of those people who have been able to train your brain to respond the way you would prefer it to when it comes to the data it receives on the daily. I am not one of those people. I can barely keep myself pointed in the right direction every day, trying to make sure I don't create a Karmic train wreck that I will spend the next several years cleaning up, or at the very least, paying for.

As such, I had completely put the issue with Catherine out of my head and literally had not thought about it for many years. This is not any sort of commentary on the importance or the significance of the scene that played out back then. It's more that I was in the middle of one of the most turbulent times in my life, and the idea that I was being forced to hurt someone I loved as a human being was almost more than I could bear. So whatever memory I have got of that terrible afternoon was compartmentalized and stuffed into a tiny area that would keep it away from my daily thoughts and allow me to bury it for as long as I could.

What sucks is that I should have dealt with that issue back when it happened and made things right with Cat and with Nakia at the time it was happening. What I REALLY should have done was tell them that Shuki was putting me in this position and whatever Cat wanted to do about the idiotic screen test with the woman replacing her best friend Nakia, she should do. I wasn't going to give her a hard time if she didn't, and what was Shuki going to do? He could hardly fire her. In fact, she could have told him to piss off and it would have been crickets in response. The whole ask was

MORPHERS, MONSTERS & MAYHEM   371

just ridiculous, and I should have said, "Sorry, no can do." But that's not what I did.

Trying to be the good employee, trying to be a leader and a boss, I actually attempted to convince Catherine that she really needed to do the test! I gave her all the reasons I thought it was a good idea, none of which I really bought, and I think we both knew that. It was a preposterous situation an actor should never be asked to go through. If I had it to do over, I would have told them I couldn't be a part of that. Cat had meant too much to the show and to treat her like that was just unfair. Looking back, it would have saved so much aggravation. In the end, Cat refused to do the test anyway, and it took us years to repair our relationship. And Shuki had basically set the entire thing up. How did I not see things going south? How?

The reappearance of Little BZ alone should have been a signal to me that things were changing. The same Little BZ who stood in my office with a somber look on his face, telling me that he was leaving so that he could spend his last days filling up his bucket list and that he didn't have time or energy for the grueling schedule of *Power Rangers*. Especially when Little BZ spent most of the day sitting in his air-conditioned office, running numbers on a spreadsheet for BZ. Not really the drain on one's life energy like some occupations had, such as directing a TV series.

When I recall that visit, it becomes painfully obvious that it was very weird for him to come see me and fill me in on his personal struggles like that. We just weren't that close. It was an over-share of epic proportions. I guess I must have felt like with things really being hard for him with his medical issues, he was feeling more comfortable being open and honest with me. I was so caught up in the moment at the time that I couldn't imagine there was anything more to it. And there still may not have been. Maybe it was just as innocent as it seemed at the time. Little BZ seemed sincere and really wanting to connect as human beings during the conversation. So, I was down with it and in no place to question.

A week later while all of this drama was still playing out, BZ appeared in my office doorway with a grave look of concern on his face. He was there to inform me that the footage from the shows Al Winchell was directing was starting to come in and were proving to be impossible to cut together in any logical fashion. In fact, I was told, the footage was nearly unusable. BZ was unsure if we could even keep any of it, and they were talking about reshoots.

First off, WTF was he talking about? I had seen the same footage and had quite the opposite reaction to Al's work, as did Ann and Jackie and even some of the crew who had wandered in and out of the office to watch what had arrived. What BZ was asking me to believe was that the work by a director who had nailed all his other assignments was suddenly doing such a horrendous job that was so poorly thought out and executed there was talk of actually reshooting it? And was I to believe that this information had been kept quiet by the head of post, my good friend who always warned me if there was trouble with something we'd shot? The first call I would have gotten that morning would have been from him. But there was no call. So, I decided I would pick up the phone and call to check on Al's work. Oddly, they had no idea what I was talking about. The work was fine. No. Wait. The work was actually pretty good, according to post. So, why was BZ poking his turtle head into my office and spewing out this complete and absolute fabrication, a lie that was so obvious it was almost embarrassing that he would try to tell it? What the crap was this guy up to? Not only that, but walking down the hall later, when Jabba met my eyes, she shook her giant Hutt head at me with a slight smile, like I was in some kind of trouble and she was enjoying it immensely.

I decided to brush this whole thing off as BZ just being BZ and wanting to get under my skin since I had brought Al into the fold and had vouched for him, even though everyone knew who he was and had watched the shows he had directed over at *Troopers*. Brushing it off would have been a great plan, had it not been for the fact that BZ seemed to have garnered some support for his insane opinions that made it impossible to ignore them.

My phone rang. Shuki. Thank the lord. I could finally get some clarity on this whole thing. Shuki knew what useable footage looked like, and he knew what unusable crap looked like, as we had seen our share of both on these shows. Surely, he would stand by me in defending Al's work.

Not exactly.

When I spoke to Shuki, he blasted the footage as well! At least as much as Shuki blasts anything when in a one-on-one conversation and not sending a howler. On this occasion, he hemmed and hawed about how it just wasn't his style and how Al wasn't right for the show. I remarked to Shuki that Al knew as much about directing the Saban footage shows as anyone. If Shuki had an issue with what Al was doing, at the very least he should pay a visit to Bob Hughes and get his take on the situation. Show Bob the footage and ask what he thought.

Unfortunately, Shuki never talked to Bob (of course) and seemed insulted that I would question his ability to evaluate the footage on his own. I feel like he was more annoyed that I made him defend the fabrication that was the lynchpin of this whole stupid lie he knew was BS but was playing a part for some reason. I would suggest that Shuki really didn't care whether it was the truth and probably forgot five minutes after our call that it had even taken place. Knowing Shuki, he didn't want to get too deep into the whole charade, and calling me was about as far as he was willing to take it. Now, I had to go deal with it with BZ. But not before I took one more phone call on the subject.

The last nail in the coffin, at least for Al, was the call to me from Haim. He too had mysteriously "not liked" Al's footage and wanted to tell me about it. The reason I say "mysteriously" is that we were four years into the show when all this went down. Haim was on the fast track to taking complete control of the kids TV business. His days were packed from morning till night with meetings, lunches, dinners, etc. Haim gave up watching anything but finished shows a long time ago. There was no reason to waste his time on footage that would be completely different once cut together with all the effects, ADR, music, color correction, etc.

QUICK SIDE NOTE: A TV episode goes through stages as it makes its way to becoming an episode ready for air. Here is a loose outline of that process, and I apologize to those of you who already are well acquainted with it. But this is the material that gets sent out to those on the list who need to see it and some who don't, like Haim with everything cut but #7. That's the only thing he ever watched out of everything that was delivered to his office.

1. Rough Cut—This is the first assembly of the show. Editors show this to the director so they can get a feel for where the show stands with the footage they have.
2. Directors Cut—This is the director-approved version that they worked on with the editor. This gets sent to the producers.
3. Producers Cut—On our show, this was where Ann Knapp would get in there and work her magic until the show actually became something that made sense and was what we had intended in the script. Ann was brilliant at this task. I always told her that if this producing thing didn't work out, she could crush it as an editor. Ann never failed to turn what looked like a mess into what was, at the very least, an enjoyable episode of the show and the best possible under the given circumstances. This cut was then sent off to Haim, Shuki, the toy company, Fox Kids, and anyone else on the list to receive the first look. This included Scott Page-Pagter and the ADR crew, a small group never shy to offer their opinions on an episode.
4. Locked Cut—This cut addressed any final concerns in terms of length, questionable broadcast standards, out of focus shots, etc.
5. ADR Cut—This was where all of the dialogue recorded at Scott's magical studio next door to *Power Rangers* was added.

6. Final Mix—This was where the show came alive with a vast palate of sound effects, music, and song. Normally, the showrunner would be at the mix giving the notes for fixes. But, since we had no showrunner, our post producer usually handled the job. This was actually a perfect fit. Paul Rosenthal was a musician with a great ear who could hear things mere mortals could not and would often save a moment by identifying an offending sound or musical note.
7. Color Corrected Final—This is where a team of well-trained experts manipulates the colors in every scene so that every shot matches with the palette of the entire show, giving it that final seamless feeling. This is the icing on the cake and was what the viewers would see on their screens.

It was a fact, that in all my years at Saban, I only received two calls from Haim about specific episodes. The first was the group of *Zeo* shows that he really liked and he called because he wanted to let me know how pleased he was. At the time, it was the greatest business call I had ever gotten. The worst I had ever gotten also came from Haim, and it was the famous "Fucking Monkeys" call where I was informed that the well-being of his children depended on the success or failure of two bargain-barrel chimps BZ hired to fill in for Bulk and Skull. But this was a special case in that it was his idea, or one that he shared with Shuki, and so he had a personal connection to these hairy bastards, and it had to be perfectly executed. The point I'm trying to make is that there were reasons Haim would call me and reasons he would not. The former far outweighed the latter, and some dailies from a director we had already used before fell into the "Why do I care about this?" category for Haim.

Finally, what really got my attention, was that the call was not your typical Haim scream-fest. It was almost halfhearted, lacking any real passion. It felt forced, like he had been asked to make the call but wasn't really buying it himself. This made sense when I later learned that he was, for some reason, doing it at the request of

Shuki, to back up BZ's premise that I had put forward a director that was unqualified and therefore I should stay out of that part of the production or worse.

Now, keep in mind I was in my mid-thirties at the time with little to no experience in the backroom maneuvering that went on at big companies, especially big companies that made movies and TV series. And beyond that, a big company that happened to be run by an incredibly cunning, single-minded, and highly competitive CEO. As I progressed further in my career, I learned what to look for, or more specifically WHO to look for when I arrived at a new job. There's always at least one person who will dislike you for whatever reason and, depending on how many allies they have at the company, will look for any excuse to bring you down. I found this to be the case at Disney, Nickelodeon, and DreamWorks. All of these huge studios had at least one BZ with an army of sycophantic minions who were there to assist in plotting against anyone who got in the way of their agenda. But at least, in the end, I knew how to spot them early and figure out how to stay out of their way. That was not the case at this point in my career.

> SIDE NOTE: I say this again, because I really want to drive the point home, Al Winchell got screwed in that whole deal. He did a great job, and it must have been confusing for him to hear the exact opposite from the Saban higher-ups. And especially to have been singled out by Haim himself. It was beyond unfair that BZ and the others dropped this on him to get to me. It was a cruel, nasty bit of business on their parts, but when BZ wanted something, he was going to get it, regardless of who it hurt. Al Winchell didn't deserve to be gaslit. He was a terrific director. I would have had him working all the time were it not for the dark overlord and his evil plot. To this day, I think that Al feels a sense of guilt, like he screwed up and made me look bad. But that is NOT the case. He did a great job, and I hope he will always remember that.

CHAPTER 62

I HELP THE BZ'S PUSH IT ACROSS THE GOAL LINE

While all of this was going on, BZ's new assistant, Jabba Jr., was growing bolder and more demonstrative in her distaste for me and my small department. Although she was smart enough to steer clear of Ann and Jackie, as neither had any interest in being baited into a conflict, she was more than happy to mix it up with me, sneering at me, arguing with me any chance she got, disparaging me to her office mates in regards to the scripts, my directing, me personally, and doing it openly, seemingly begging me to hear what was being said. It was getting to the point of insanity. And anyone who knew me back then was aware that I could take a lot of crap. But there came a point when I would lash out, and it was usually, and unfortunately, disproportionate to whatever was happening in the moment. I used to let all this crap build up in my head, like a pressure cooker, then when the lid came off, it was usually shocking to whoever was on the receiving end, as I just wasn't known for that. A dear friend once told me that I was a bit like a volcano in that way. I might stay dormant for years, but when the eruption comes, there are casualties.

Jabba Jr., multi-tasker that she was, while holding down the job of my personal tormentor had also apparently become the most important and busiest member of the crew, or at least that was the optic she was now selling. She trundled around the office at breakneck speed with the look of a stock exchange runner trying to beat the final bell, pushing past people as if her trip to the copy machine, or visit to the stationery closet had the same importance as selling 50,000 shares of Apple on the news that Steve Jobs had passed. At the same time, her jabs at me were becoming more and more brash, more disrespectful and were even noticeable to Jackie and Ann, who always try to see the best in everyone. But we all saw what she was up to and were trying to figure out a way we could pull her into Ann's office and talk to her about what was becoming an embarrassment. This was going to be a touchy move. She was BZ's personal assistant. It would be as if BZ did the same with Jackie behind my back. We knew that talking to BZ about the problem was pointless. He was probably rooting her on from the sidelines. As we considered our options, I stupidly made things very easy for team BZ. And although it was the best thing that could have happened to me in the long run, at the time, it was complete devastation.

On what was the darkest day in my professional career, it all came to a head and fell into what seems like perfect order for BZ and his pack of jackals. Here are the events as I recall them. Please keep in mind that I openly admit that I handled my part in this as poorly as one could have, and I regret the embarrassment I caused myself and my family to this day. I was young, I hadn't discovered the wonders of Zoloft, and I was writing and producing a show that was slipping through my fingers with every mandate that came from the higher ups. *Turbo* was a heaping pile of junk, and it seemed as though there was no way to correct the path of the series given the restrictions that the new story had placed upon us. And to top it all off, I had Jabba Jr., like a burr under my saddle, poking, prodding, and making life miserable.

The day started like any normal day. Jackie had brought her dog Asta to work, a little black Scottie who was very well behaved and mostly just sat under her desk. Anyone who has met me in the past 20 years knows that I am obsessed with dogs. They are such a calming force. Just their energy can diffuse a situation in a matter of moments. At the time of this incident, however, I was not the dog lover I am today. I was a bit obsessive when it came to germs. As a result, I felt like dogs were a walking, barking, crapping petri dish of bacteria that I didn't want any part of back then. I just didn't get it yet.

> SIDE NOTE: I have at various times in the past 20 years shared my bed with three Shelties and three Chihuahuas and have no clue why it took me so long to embrace the incredible unconditional love that a dog brings to a home. As of this writing, we are now down to one 15-year-old Chihuahua named Hoobiedoo. She is incredibly loving, nearly deaf, toothless, and has a kneecap that pops out from time to time, giving her the gait of an old sailor. We cherish every moment we spend with her and will be heartbroken when it comes to an end.

On that day, I went into my office to sit down and found a heaping pile of dog crap on the floor next to my chair, staring up at me, piled high, reaching out to test my gag reflex. I basically lost it, screaming out for whoever had let their dog crap in my office to please get in there and clean it up. The words had barely escaped my mouth when a familiar voice screamed back the following: "Would you shut your fucking mouth, I'm trying to have a conversation!" What came next was one of the few moments in my life where I became so angry I nearly blacked out. I have trouble remembering exactly what happened, but apparently, I ran from my office and unleashed a tirade of long built-up frustration on the person who had told me to STFU (the one and only Jabba Jr.) She was still on the phone as I ended the over-the-top, misguided, completely out of character rant with the one word you just don't use when speaking to a woman. I'll leave it to your imaginations, but it's simple to narrow down, and to you women out there reading this, I will carry that shame until the day I die. To my loving sisters and mother, I can never fully apologize for the embarrassment, as there are no words.

What a completely idiotic thing to let happen. From what I can remember, as the word left my mouth, everything fell silent. Although this assistant, who had been goading me into an altercation for weeks, had no business screaming profanity at me from her office area, I was the supervisor, and I should not have reacted the way I did. It was and is completely inappropriate, and if there is one thing I regret in my career, that moment is it. And the final irony of this whole thing, was that the dog crap in the office was fake, plastic, put there by our production coordinator Shawn Tarkington as a joke, hoping it would make for some good fun during the "dog days" of summer. Not so much.

Things changed drastically from that day forward for me and my happy little band of writers. I didn't see it at the time, but this was the opportunity that BZ had been waiting patiently for. This was me, at my absolute worst, in front of everyone, destroying any good will or respect that I had built up over the years at Saban. Jabba Jr. was told by BZ to take some days off to get over the trauma that I had inflicted upon her. In my shame and guilt, I called her at home and pleaded with her to come back to the office. I laid my soul bare and begged for her forgiveness. I was wrong and she shouldn't have to suffer for my transgression. Her response was an icy, "We'll see." That did not bode well.

The next few weeks were miserable. I had not only disgraced myself to the production team, but I had really let Ann and Jackie down. They believed in me and always had my back. There was no way they could stand behind this, however. It was just too much. We did what we could to slog through our work, but it was now a dark cloud hanging over my head. However, as neither Ann nor Jackie was particularly pleased with me, they still stuck by my side. Yes, I had done the unthinkable and there is no excuse. But they also made sure I knew that they knew how hard it had been to keep my mouth shut up until that point and that Jabba Jr. was, without question, a person who made it difficult to remain composed. Again, no excuse. But they understood how I had gotten to that place and were it not for that one terrible word, nothing would have come of it. But something did come of it.

On my way back from lunch several weeks later, I received a call in my car that I needed to get back to the stages immediately. It was Jabba Sr. and when asked if it needed to be right then and there, she chirped (suspiciously happy) that it did, as BZ was waiting for me. Little did I know that he wasn't the only one waiting for me. As I opened the door to his office, there sat two of the company attorneys, staring up at me blankly, holding thick legal folders in front of them. As I sat down, I noticed that BZ was doing everything in his power to hold back a smile. Whatever was about to happen was something he was very excited about, something he must have dreamt about.

In what was a short, ten-minute meeting, I was told to collect my belongings and that I my services were no longer required at *Power Rangers* due to the confrontation that I had with Jabba Jr. and, get this, my mistreatment of Catherine during the whole screen test debacle and that it wasn't my place to even get involved in such things. NO SHIT! I had been ordered to get involved and, in fact, drop the bomb on Cat's head by my direct boss against my better judgement, knowing it would end with hurt feelings and possibly endanger the relationship I had with Catherine, one that was incredibly precious to me. I was told that I was being fired for cause and that there would be no further compensation coming my way, although I had just signed a pay or play contract with Saban a few months earlier.

It was over. I was gone. BZ had pulled it off.

As I slunk back toward my office, I saw Jackie in tears. I can only imagine that Jabba couldn't wait to drop the news on her and had done it in the unkindest of ways. That was just Jabba being the big giant Hutt that she was.

When I entered what was now my former office, I noticed that my computer keyboard was gone. It had been removed by Shawn

Tarkington, the same person who had planted the fake dog crap. This was a true irony. Had I not been in shock, I would have appreciated it. I pleaded with him to just let me take my personal files off the computer. After a few moments, he relented and allowed me to. I guess there was a little twinge of guilt there for setting the whole thing in motion. But who's to say?

> SIDE NOTE: I went to work for the Disney Channel years later, and they were looking for a production executive. I instantly thought of Shawn. Although his timing with practical jokes was a bit suspect, he was a great worker and had a sharp mind for production. I suggested that they meet with him and that they would not regret hiring him if it came to that. In the end, they did hire Shawn and to this day, as far as I know, he is still working there. To be clear, Disney didn't hire Shawn because I told them he'd be great. They hired him because of his skills and his ease with people and his work ethic. All I did was open a door. But I was happy that I was able to give him any little leg up.

When I got in my car that afternoon, I set my pathetic little box of personal items down on the front seat and got out of the parking lot as quickly as possible. The last thing I wanted was for that stupid car, the symbol of my complete irresponsibility to break down and to have to wait for a tow truck while BZ and all the a-holes back inside watched. That would have been soul crushing. Once out of the lot and down the street, I decided that the first thing I should do was call Ann. She needed to be made aware that BZ had just grown in power, and it was going to be challenging for her in the coming months. I instantly reached her and was shocked to learn that Ann was let go as well. She was being fired in her downstairs office at the same moment I was in BZ's office. It made sense that they felt like they needed to axe both of us, as Ann would not have capitulated to BZ's demands and would have ruined his plan for creative domination.

So, there we were, unemployed. When asked if Shuki knew about this, the attorneys assured me that he did and supported it completely. Ouch. That bummed me out almost as much as losing the job. I didn't try to speak to Shuki, as I knew that he would have either dodged the call or taken it and been miserable trying to explain his side of the situation as he internally figured out how to get off the phone quickly. There was really no one I could turn to, except of course for Ann. It was at that moment that we decided to band together and find our next post as the sought-after team who had been part of the phenomenon that was *Power Rangers*. And someday, somehow, I would repay BZ for what he had done to me and to Ann, especially to Ann who was collateral damage in BZ's slimy power grab.

Since the day *Power Rangers* began, it seemed as though BZ was determined to be the boots on the ground creative voice on the show. For whatever reason, Haim and Shuki had not felt as though BZ was equipped to handle that role. Over the few years the show had been in production, there was a string of creatives who sat in the chair BZ wanted so desperately, from Tony Oliver to Winston Richards, to Ellen Levy Sarnoff and eventually to me and Ann. BZ had always been the logistics guy. And to be fair, he was quite competent at that. But like many line producers, he was desperate to get that pesky word "line" removed from his title and enter the creative fold. He wanted to be what Bob Hughes was on *VR Troopers*. The problem? BZ was not Bob Hughes. Bob was a genius at multi-tasking. He was also brilliant at delegating, which he happily did whenever appropriate. Bob also had a secret weapon: Danielle Weinstock. Bob allowed her a great deal of latitude in her job without lording over her like a kindergarten teacher supervising a finger-painting class.

This was BZ's problem. He wanted the responsibility but refused to see that he would have to loosen up the reigns and allow the crew to do their jobs without constant supervision. What he did realize was that he was spinning his wheels trying to get the job all to himself and that it probably was not going to happen. So, his plan had morphed (bad choice of verbiage) into the idea of installing Little BZ in the writer's chair and pulling his strings like he always had, thus making sure BZ's creative was THE creative while making it look like Little BZ was steering the ship. His plan was well hidden, as Little BZ had "retired" from *Power Rangers* to deal with his health issues. He had told me himself, right there in my office that he was leaving the show. I realize that this is all a bit confusing and in truth, I've spent years trying to piece it together based on what eventually happened. And again, this is the conclusion that I came to after looking at the facts and speaking to people who were there at the time. It's my view of things that seemed obvious upon reexamination. So, this is the sequence of events that took place leading up to our firing, at least as far as I can deduce.

1. BZ gets embarrassed in a meeting when I ask him to stick to the production-related issues and leave the creative to me, Ann, and Jackie. This was after BZ believed that now that I was there, and Ellen Levy Sarnoff was gone, he would be welcomed into the creative world of the show. This did not happen.
2. BZ decides he must find a way to get rid of me. He needs a way to hijack and take control of the creative without being in the actual driver's seat as that had failed in the past. He identifies Little BZ for the role.
3. Little BZ oddly comes into my office and bids me farewell, saying he's leaving the show due to an illness he was going to have to battle. I totally miss the possibility that there is more to this. Maybe there was. Maybe there wasn't. It was very weird, though.
4. BZ knows that Shuki is no longer my biggest fan, largely due to the notes I gave on the *Turbo* movie and the issues I still had with the villains in that storyline that I felt were going to bring down *Turbo* the series. Shuki is now much more likely to abide by a plan to oust me. Deborah was long gone, so that layer of protection was long gone as

well. Haim calls me and dresses me down mightily for taking the food out of his children's mouths with second-rate studio animals.

5. Shuki, out of the blue, instructs me to press Catherine to do the screen test with Tracy Cruz, a demand that he had to know would not be well received and could possibly have a negative effect on my relationship with all the actors. This may have been exactly what they were trying to do, knowing that the actors were mostly close to me, especially Jason. If I did something so heinous to Catherine, what kind of friend was I really? Of course, the meeting with Catherine goes as expected, with buckets of tears, anger and disbelief that I would turn on her like that. BZ builds this up to be way more than it was, insisting that I had bullied and emotionally manipulated Catherine.

6. BZ creates a firestorm over the dailies from Al Winchell's episodes, which were great, by the way. He then manages to gather the others and convince them that it's a travesty and we might have to reshoot. Shuki calls and tells me the Al Winchell dailies are no good. It's half-hearted and weird. Clearly, he had watched maybe the first two minutes and just decided to go along with BZ's request to rake me over the coals. Haim calls to chime in about the dailies and how awful they were. My immediate thoughts:
    a. When was the last time Haim watched dailies?
    b. When was the last time Haim even cared enough to make a phone call about dailies?
    c. His call, like Shuki's, was halfhearted and brief, as if he'd been asked to make it, which I believe he had.

7. I lose my mind over fake dog crap in my office and return fire to Jabba Jr. after she curses me out in front of the entire office staff. My fault. I should have been

smarter. I should have been kinder. I should have been silent.
8. BZ now has everything he needs to initiate my demise.
9. The Saban legal team sends Ann and I on our way, crying into the steering wheels of the cars we can no longer pay for.

INTERESTING SIDE NOTE: My father was in the business for many years, and because of that had quite a few contacts and acquaintances in various areas of the industry. His very best friend was a high-powered lawyer (name withheld) who was like a part of our family, joining us for dinner often and just kind of being around. Years later, this family friend reported to my father that he had recently had lunch with one of the attorneys who was at Saban at the time that Ann and I were pushed out. The attorney let our family friend know, off the record of course, that what Saban had done to us was a complete hit job. It was plotted and planned over months and months, and no one in Legal felt particularly good about it at the time, as they had just spent the last three months negotiating a new contract for me. As it turns out, BZ held more power than any of us could have imagined. He oversaw the money. He provided a fleet of relatively inexpensive rental vehicles to the show that saved hundreds of thousands over those years in Valencia. Haim and Ronnie Hadar would eventually bend to what BZ wanted. And as for Haim's question as to the firing of BZ? That was most likely Haim wanting to get a handle on the dynamics on the production and had I said yes, would never have come to fruition anyway.

As I drove home that day in the car I could no longer afford, to the apartment I could certainly no longer afford, I was panicking. I had never looked for a job before and was certainly going to have issues finding one that allowed me the creative freedom that *Power Rangers* had. In my mind, it was going to be back to working a crappy day job and trying to break back into the business. I didn't have a clue where to start. Not a freaking clue. At the end of the day, I was completely ill-prepared for the back-room chicanery and all-out attacks that Ann and I allowed ourselves to endure. I just thought I was there to write a show, help the actors through what was not an easy time for some, and come out of it with a nice first credit on my resume. Who knew I would be starting from square one?

Getting fired sucks. No two ways about it. It's happened to most of us, for any variety of reasons, at some time. It stirs up all sorts of emotional baggage you didn't even know was there. The one thing I wanted to do after being fired was email some of my friends on the show letting them know what happened and that I'd let them know the moment I landed somewhere.

One email I sent was to Cheryl Saban. We had worked together on many of her scripts, and I thought had a nice friendship and a mutual respect as I was a huge fan of her children's book writing. My note was a quick couple of lines letting her know how much I appreciated working with her and wishing her the best moving forward. A few moments after sending the email I received a notice that I had been blocked and that she would no longer be accepting messages from me. Man, that stung. I completely understood why they did it. I'm sure there were those in her camp who felt as though I would write to her pleading for my job back, asking her to talk to Haim. Of course that was the furthest thing from my mind. I still had some semblance of pride back then, at least I think I did. Who can say? The point is, this whole thing still bummed me out. I always really liked Cheryl, and Haim for that matter. Being blocked after getting the axe just felt yucky, especially since this was the very first time I had ever been blocked. It was 1996, so there weren't many of us who even knew how to block someone. I'm sure for the Sabans it was a skill they needed to have back then.

So, there I was, in the two-bedroom apartment I rented on Franklin Avenue in Hollywood, sitting in the spare room I had made into my office, that feeling in the pit of my stomach somewhere between a steady thud of my heartbeat and a knot the size of a slow pitch softball. For all the politics and the BS, I really had loved my job. I absolutely loved it. I loved the actors, the crew, the kids who would come to the set to meet their heroes. That was all gone now. What came next in that moment was something I couldn't have imagined in a million years. I laid my head down on my desk and just let the tears fall onto the glass top to form a glistening pool.

It had been a while, but I had experienced this exact same scenario once before. It was at the desk in my room in my fraternity house at college. I had laid my head down and just let the tears fall back in March of 1982 when I heard on the radio that my beloved guitar teacher, Randy Rhoads, had been killed in a plane crash in Leesburg, Florida. It was a death I've never gotten over. I knew I would get over the "death" of my career (overly dramatic, anyone?) but I suppose I found some comfort in laying my head on my desk, the same as I had 15 years earlier. Indeed, I would get over it, way over it and, in fact, wind up in a much better place. But there was a long journey and another trip through the *Power Rangers* galaxy to take first. So, take a breath, see what people are saying on the boards, and get ready. Part two is coming, and it's a freaking doozy.

> FINAL SIDE NOTE: Looking back on my journey, I have nothing but respect and appreciation for Shuki and Haim. They built an empire, created a cultural phenomenon, and allowed me to be a part of it. Their policy of hiring seemingly competent people, regardless of experience, and giving them the opportunity to learn and grow, it all changed my life. I will forever be grateful and do not hold a grudge that they allowed themselves to be influenced by what was clearly a well-planned and executed coup. (Not that either of them cares how I feel all these years later. I'm just going on the record here because this is the time and place to do that.)

I'm not even mad at BZ, Little BZ, Jabba, and Jabba Jr., the sinister clique that turned Shuki and Haim against Ann and me. It was a harsh lesson, but that evil foursome introduced me to what it means to swim with sharks. And in the end, they were good villains, and as I always say, every story needs a good villain.

SEE YOU DOWN UNDER!

ACKNOWLEDGMENTS

This book would not have been possible without the following amazing friends and family, who encouraged me to push forward and not hold back my truth:

Alix Sloan, Alan Sloan, Sally Sloan, Julia Marchand, Ginger Perkins, Dr. Gordon Plotkin, Paul Rosenthal, Jackie Marchand, Catherine Sutherland, Ann Austen, Art Brown, Adam Gaynor, David M. Barrett, Mike and Amy Mittleman, Howard and Sharon Bond, Carol A. Whittaker Hall, and finally, my unicorn, Mindy Lee Kowack, without whom I would be lost.

SPECIAL THANKS

A huge thank you to all of the Kickstarter backers for their enthusiasm and support helping get this project off the ground. What a ride!

Aaron Davies, Adam Condon, Adam Reed, Al Winchell, Alan Wilkinson (Cassius335), Alex J. Rosolowsky, Alex Leung, Alexis M Ortiz Perez, Amanda Bruce, Andrew Betts, Andrew Kibe, Andrew Lee, Andy Prudom, Ann Daly, Arline Kirkpatrick, Austin Allen Hamblin, Ben Hellman, Benjamin Bennett, Benjamin Read, Bennett, Bo Harper, Bradley Smith, Brandon D. Conklin, Brandon Helm, Bronson Buljan, BS&P: Bulk, Skull, & Power, Cameron Fletcher, Casey Gaul, Catherine Sutherand, Chad Bonin, Chad Mehkary, Chanzo T, Charles Sheets, Charlie Niemeyer, Christopher Garby, Christopher J. Barkasy, Christopher Luff, Cody Perry, Colonel Chrome, Craig Wilson, Cristina Sydnor, Damian S. Fowler, Dan Talbert, Daniel Evans, Daniel Howells, Daniel Sango, Dave Caplan, David "Vudoo" Vu, David Acosta, David William Coxwell Jr, David, Rylee & Regan Cochran, Davin Hun, DC Cathro, Devin Keith Mulligan, Devin Neuendorf, Doris Vincent, Drew Dietrick, Drew Fitzpatrick, ech0_nt, Edward Paz, Elias D. Mendoza, Eliazar

Medina, Elijah Hernandez, Eric "trekkieb47" Berry, Eric Bross, Eric D. Silver, Eric Immerman, Eric Trinh, Evan Meadow, Frank, Frank Kergil, Gabriel Rodriguez, Gary Baker, Gary Moir, Glenn Kimble Jr, Gordy Stillman, Greg Shelton, Gregory Holmes, Harry Portman, Hassan Ahmed, Heather K, Heidi Koch, I.A.W, Jack Brown, James Pappas, Jared M. Burnham, Jason R. Smith, Jason Stutzman, JD Lewis, Jeff Baxter, Jennifer Bode, Jeremey Pereira, Jeremy D. Simpson, Jesse Lee Herndon, Jessey Nettey, Jessica Hofflich, Jimmy Gaumond, Joe Molina (Lord Edd), John "GrnRngr" Green, John Leed, Johnny Dhaness, Jose C. Varela, Josh Coffey, Josh Heffers, Joshua Booth, Joshua M. Trope, Joshua Moore, author of "Morphenomenal," JP Caceres, Justin "McGruff405" Homan, Justin Saetia, Kal Forde, Katy Dibble, Kenneth W, Kevin Chevez, Kyle Bowalick, Kyle Wilkins, Lhii, Logan Holmes, Luke Westwood, Madhu Sharma, MarcFBR, Mathew Knowlton, Matt Sernaker, Michael Busuttil, Michael Holbrook, Michael Mittelman, Mighty Morphin Fan, Mike Chacinski, Mike Dahdouh, Mike Davis, Mike H, Mike Veich, Morphin' Legacy, Myles Griffin, Nathan Jahnke, Nathan Metcalfe, Nick, Nick Crum, Nick Helms, OARanger22, Patrick Ruth Jr, Patrick Whitfill, Paul Rosenthal, Paul Wilk, Power Rangers Academia, Rabbit Ranger, Rain Fletcher, Realm, Rizwan Merchant (AnimeSecrets.org), Rob Rood, Robert G. Butler, Robert Hedley, Russell Lum, Ryan Bravo, Ryan Clark, Ryan Hagan, Sam Fleming, Samuel A. R. Adams, Santana Collectibles, Sara Sikora, Sarah Gaertner, Scott "Action" Jackson, Scott Sandler, Sean McCormack, Sean Prince, Sebastian Maher, Secter0547, ShadowRay22, Shaun Springer, Søren Alfred Olsen, Stael Petit Blanc, Steve Marshall, Steven Godfryd, Steven Livingston, Steven Martinez "Random90sFan," Steven Vincent, thepowerscoop, Thomas Meckler, Tim Bates, Tim Caplinger, Tim Harrold, Travis Maley, Trevor Roberts, Troy Young, Tyler Brenman, Tyler Daniel Bozetski, Tyler Waldman, Umitencho, V I A, Vincent Blancas Nguyen, Wes Keefer, William Bruce West, Wilson Eduardo Ramirez, Yale Mael, Zachariah Casto, Zachary Bachert

ABOUT THE AUTHOR

Douglas J. Sloan is a multiple-time Emmy-nominated writer, producer, and director who spent 30 years in the ever-changing world of children's entertainment. Having been one of the key creatives on the *Power Rangers, Johnny Tsunami, Motocrossed, Princess Protection Program,* and 121 episodes of *DreamWorks Dragons,* he has witnessed some of the wildest, most unbelievable behind-the-scenes goings on imaginable.

Now, nearing that magic retirement age, he has decided to open the floodgates and tell the stories that no one has heard, proving once again that truth is WAY more bizarre than fiction.

You can find Douglas on Facebook and X.

facebook.com/DSloanwrites
x.com/vrdjs143

www.ingramcontent.com/pod-product-compliance
Lightning Source LLC
Chambersburg PA
CBHW060448030426
42337CB00015B/1524